10/17

D0516931

Web Design

FOR

DUMMIES®

3RD EDITION

Web Design

FOR

DUMMIES®

3RD EDITION

by Lisa Lopuck

WILEY

John Wiley & Sons, Inc.

Web Design For Dummies®, 3rd Edition

Published by
John Wiley & Sons, Inc.
111 River Street
Hoboken, NJ 07030-5774
www.wiley.com

WILEY

About the Author

Lisa Lopuck is an experienced digital creative executive with over 20 years building, inspiring, and leading creative teams; managing vendors; overseeing digital department and project budgets, brand identity, packaging, and point-of-sale design; and guiding innovation and best practices for web, mobile, social media, and e-commerce projects.

In 1988, Lisa got her first glimpse of multimedia while still at UCLA pursuing her degree in design. She saw a tiny, black-and-white, interactive HyperCard stack designed by The Voyager Company and immediately knew her career path. Her first job out of school was working at the Apple Multimedia Lab in San Francisco. She then moved on to Skywalker Ranch, working with George Lucas to design educational CD-ROMs. The rest has been interactive history — working with everyone from eBay to Disney, and speaking at conferences all over the world.

She most recently served as Vice President of Creative and Digital Media for Monster Energy, where she led the redesign and launch of their global website, e-commerce technology platform, and mobile applications. Under her leadership, Monster's Facebook brand page exploded from 500 thousand to over 12 million fans in just 1.5 years. Prior to Monster, she also designed several Disney e-commerce websites, including DisneyShopping.com (later folded into DisneyStore.com), and many of the Disney theme-park websites, including HongKongDisneyland.com and DisneyCruiseLine.com.

She currently is the co-founder of Front Row www.frontrow-studios.com, a digital marketing agency exclusively focused on the sports industry. She's an avid athlete herself (tournament tennis player) and resides in Southern California.

Dedication

For my husband, Matt, who is my chief evangelist, and for our daughter, Jasmine, who is turning out to be quite the talented writer and artist herself.

For my parents who always encouraged me to reach for the stars.

Author's Acknowledgments

I would like to give a big thanks to the many people who helped make this the best *Web Design For Dummies* edition yet in the series (funny how they are all men!): A huge thank-you to Aaron and his incredible team at Ekko Media Group, who know how to rise to any occasion and get things done — including providing great technical input for this book. Thank you, Paul, my editor, for keeping me on track. Special props to my crew at Monster Energy: LeRoy, Ryan, Chris, Eric, and Pete who do more amazing work with less than seems humanly possible for such a big ship to run. I know you guys will go far. And lastly, I'd like to acknowledge my current business partners in Front Row, Martin and Don, two of the most talented people I've had the pleasure of working with, for their support in the development of this excellent edition.

Publisher's Acknowledgments

We're proud of this book; please send us your comments at http://dummies.custhelp.com. For other comments, please contact our Customer Care Department within the U.S. at 877-762-2974, outside the U.S. at 317-572-3993, or fax 317-572-4002.

Some of the people who helped bring this book to market include the following:

Acquisitions, Editorial

Senior Project Editor: Paul Levesque

Executive Editor: Steven Hayes

Senior Copy Editor: Barry Childs-Helton

Technical Editor: Paul Maloney

Editorial Manager: Leah Michael

Editorial Assistant: Amanda Graham

Sr. Editorial Assistant: Cherie Case

Cover Photo: ©iStockphoto.com / Golkin Oleg

Cartoons: Rich Tennant (www.the5thwave.com)

Composition Services

Project Coordinator: Sheree Montgomery

Layout and Graphics: Claudia Bell

Proofreaders: John Greenough, Christine Sabooni

Indexer: Becky Hornyak

Publishing and Editorial for Technology Dummies

Richard Swadley, Vice President and Executive Group Publisher

Andy Cummings, Vice President and Publisher

Mary Bednarek, Executive Acquisitions Director

Mary C. Corder, Editorial Director

Publishing for Consumer Dummies

Kathleen Nebenhaus, Vice President and Executive Publisher

Composition Services

Debbie Stailey, Director of Composition Services

Contents at a Glance

Table of Contents

Introduction

*D*esigning professional websites is not just about making beautiful pages: it's about understanding your audience and crafting an information structure that not only meets their needs but fulfills business goals as well.

It's about working with a team of people, and understanding the interworkings of the production process from content development through to visual design, comp production, and technical integration.

Over the course of the next 300-or-so pages, I show you what it takes to understand the web-design process from start to finish, with an emphasis on creative design and development. At the end of this book, you'll have the understanding it takes to tackle a major, commercial website project. You'll still need lots of practice and experience to turn out the good stuff, but this book gives you the solid foundation that you need to succeed.

About This Book

This book is written for both the creative professional who's looking to get into the world of web design and the business professional who needs to understand the web creative and production process in order to manage it. I'm not talking about building personal sites with frilly fonts and loud background patterns. I'm talking about building enterprise-level websites for real-world clients — clients ranging from Fortune 100 companies to start-ups that need high-powered websites to function as an integral part of their global business.

Whether you're managing the process from an executive standpoint or are a contributing team member, you'll find that the processes, tips, and techniques covered in this book are essential to every project.

By the end of this book, you'll know how to

- Understand the team roles and responsibilities required to build a website
- Present web work to clients — even internal clients
- Turn an outline of your content and a list of requirements into an information-design strategy
- Create wireframe diagrams to plan each unique page layout and interaction design
- Craft visual-design strategies that enhance usability and create a unique brand statement

- Design graphics that download quickly and look great across platforms and browsers
- Design a user-friendly navigation system for a site
- Organize and conduct user tests
- Make technology choices

Conventions Used in This Book

Throughout this book, I use conventions in the text to make things easier to understand. For example, if I'm introducing a new term, I put it in *italics* and then define it. When I first use an industry-specific term such as *site map,* I make it italic and then give you the scoop on what it means. Usually these terms are also accompanied by a WebSpeak icon. (See the section "Icons Used in This Book," later in this Introduction.)

Code listings are set in a monospaced font like this: `<style type="text/css">`. If I want to call your attention to a particular line or section of the code, you'll see it set in bold like this: **`<body>`**.

Foolish Assumptions

This book is aimed at people who suddenly find themselves either in the business of designing professional websites or managing the production of major websites. Whether you are a project or account manager looking to understand the creative and production process, a businessperson in need of a website, or a programmer looking to widen your creative capabilities, this book is for you.

This book is also tremendously helpful for seasoned designers and artists in other fields, such as print design and architecture, who now want to apply their creative talents to web design. While this book is professional in focus, it is also helpful for those of you who have built personal sites and now want to take them to the next level.

You don't need to know HTML (the coding language of the Web) or high-tech programming languages in order to get the most out of these 18 chapters. In this book, you can find everything you need to know about the people, the planning processes, the design process for graphics and user interfaces, and the technologies needed to start your journey into designing and building professional websites. This book doesn't give you magical creative powers. It does, however, help you channel the creative juices you have into building better-looking, user-friendly, efficient websites.

What You Shouldn't Read

Whatever you do, don't let the techy stuff in this book lead you astray. Throughout this book, and especially in the later chapters, I include some technical examples and explain the basics of how they work. As a web designer or manager of a web project, you don't have to be a programmer; you just need to be familiar with the underlying technologies and their capabilities. The more you get into web design, the easier it is to understand the technical stuff, and it won't look as intimidating.

Whenever you see the Technical Stuff icon in the margin like this, you can choose to turn a blind eye and know that you won't miss out on too much for our purposes in this book. After all, this book is geared toward creative and marketing professionals looking to apply their skills to designing websites, not building laser-guided satellites.

How This Book Is Organized

This book is organized to follow the basic workflow of a major website design project. Part I starts out with an introduction to the team members involved, and the production process you'll follow. Part II begins the web production process by first gaining an understanding of the audience and then developing structural plans for your site. In Part III, you'll discover visual design strategies and how to prepare web-ready graphics. To round out production, Part IV covers the essential technobabble you need to understand, and finally, Part V sums everything up in a handy reference guide. Allow me to break it down . . . .

Part I: The Web Design Kick-Off

Professional website design involves a lot of interconnected tasks. To be a successful web designer or to manage a web-design project, you must understand the entire production process and the people you'll work with along the way. Chapter 1 introduces you to the roles and responsibilities of a typical web-development team, while Chapter 2 outlines the production process and how to manage it.

Part II: User-Friendly Design

Understanding your audience and then crafting a site structure that not only makes sense to them but also attains business goals is a tough balancing act. Chapters 3 and 4 help you to draft the blueprints for your website, and Chapter 5 helps you to design visuals that help people successfully navigate your site. Chapter 6 shows you how to test your designs with the end user to see how well a design works before you invest a lot of time in final production.

Part III: Designing Web Graphics

Designing the actual graphics for a website is the fun part. Chapters 7 through 12 discuss graphic design issues and techniques according to how they relate to the Web, along with all the technical stuff that you need to know. I also show you graphic production techniques and tips for preparing client presentations.

Part IV: Producing the Final Website

After you determine the graphic and user-interface design, the real work begins — assembling the designs into a working website. Here's where the scary technical stuff comes in. Don't worry — Chapters 13 and 14 give you a friendly tour of the inner workings of HTML, the basic language of the Web, as well as an introduction to Cascading Style Sheets, or *CSS*. Chapter 15 takes you a little further along the website-production road and illuminates the technologies that really turn websites into living, breathing business machines (which is scary in a *good* way).

Part V: The Part of Tens

True to the *For Dummies* style, Chapters 16 through 18 sum up the contents of the book into Top Ten lists that you can use as handy reference guides. Rip these chapters out and stick them under your desk at work where you can easily access them without anyone ever knowing. Your boss will be impressed with the fountains of knowledge that you suddenly possess. (Then, of course, you'll have to buy a second copy of *Web Design For Dummies* that's undamaged.)

Icons Used in This Book

To make this book user-friendly, I've tagged various sections with icons that point out cool ideas, things to look out for, and industry jargon. As you read, be on the lookout for these little guys:

In talking about web design, it's impossible to avoid the technobabble. That's why I like to give you a little advance warning with this icon so you can mentally prepare. The technical stuff is there to give you background, but you can choose to ignore it guilt-free. I won't blame you.

The web-design and development process is littered with land mines that can get you into trouble. Pay special attention to the stuff marked with the little bomb icon.

I love a tasty morsel of advice. I use this icon whenever I've got some inside information to share with you.

This icon is not exactly a bomb-threat warning, but it does mark things that you should keep in mind during the course of a website project.

Like any other industry, web design is fraught with insider terms. To make sure you get a high-class education here, I've pointed out all the good ones so you can carry on an informed conversation.

I'm Here if You Need Me!

Let me know what you think of the book (good or bad), if you have questions, or if you just have a good design story to share, find me online at `Facebook.com/WebDesignForDummies`.

You can also contact the publisher or authors of other *For Dummies* books by visiting the Dummies website at `www.dummies.com`. The snail-mail address is

John Wiley and Sons, Inc.
10475 Crosspoint Boulevard
Indianapolis, IN 46256

Occasionally, we have updates to our technology books. If this book does have technical updates, they will be posted at `www.dummies.com/go/webdesignfordummiesupdates`.

Part I
The Web Design Kick-Off

The 5th Wave   By Rich Tennant

J. MONK OPTOMETRIST

"Games are an important part of my Web site. They cause eye strain."

*P*rofessional website production involves a lot of complex, interdependent tasks and requires an experienced team of people to get everything done. As you embark on your adventures in web design and/or web management, a good first step is to understand this production process from start to finish — and the people involved — so you have a holistic picture of what to expect and know where you fit in along the way. In fact, even though many design firms tout their mastery of the web-production process as a selling point when they're trying to win bids, the truth is that most firms follow the same or similar process: Define, Design, Develop, Deploy. The client then gets to handle "Phase Five" — Maintenance!

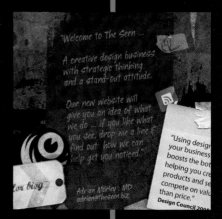

In Chapter 1, I introduce you to the different types of roles and responsibilities associated with the web-production process. In Chapter 2, I take you through the whole production process, showing how design agencies and in-house design teams manage Web projects from start to finish.

1

So You're Designing a Website

The digital industry has been exploding since its inception — from websites to mobile applications and social media, the opportunities are endless. This is great news for you if you're thinking about becoming a professional web designer. The industry is ever-changing and evolving — and exciting, rapid developments are around every corner.

Web design is not just about creating a series of pages that looks good. In this book, I show you how to design a cohesive site that links its parts together in a way that delivers on business goals and makes sense to the user. Modern websites can consist of hundreds of pages. As a professional web designer or manager, your job is to know how to integrate design and navigation using a myriad of technologies and techniques to build an effective site.

While building a professional-grade website may seem like a daunting task, if you understand the process from start to finish and the roles of the people involved, you'll be on better footing to get started.

In this chapter, I introduce you to the different players that you'll surround yourself with on your journey through professional web design.

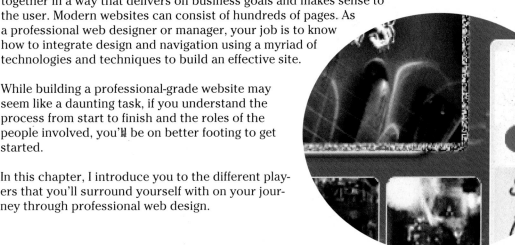

The People Involved

Designing websites is such a huge undertaking that to do it right, you really need a *team* of people — whether working with an internal team, with vendors, or independent consultants. Here is a sampling of the major players, their roles, and when you need them.

Business folks and clients

In the early days, you could get away with sticking a website up on the Internet and expect to get reasonable traffic without much further effort. In the crowded Internet highways of today, however, you really need a business strategy and a marketing plan. The business and marketing folks, whether internal or your client, must be involved with the website from the very beginning. They are in charge of the following responsibilities:

- **Setting the goals and requirements for the site.** You must always understand the business goals, in order of priority, of the site. For example, the number one goal may be to sell product. The business people not only provide the top three-or-so goals to set the site's direction but will also need to provide a list of site *requirements* — essentially a wish list of the site's capabilities — its "ability to do X."

- **Identifying the target customer.** The marketing team members are the ones that are closest to a business's end consumer. They should provide a profile picture of the ideal customer that the site must cater to. The "information architects" (discussed later in this chapter, these are people who design a site's underlying structure) on the team will use this data to develop a set of "personas" that will focus the creative team's efforts throughout the web development process.

- **Reeling in the visitors.** The marketing team also needs to figure out how to direct customers to the site. In the Internet business, *getting eyeballs* (attracting people to your site) is not as easy as it sounds; it involves search engine optimization (SEO), partnering with other companies, and developing an integrated online and offline strategy. For these reasons, the marketing folks need to get started on their plan right away.

Producers and project managers

Once clients and companies are committed to a new web project, invariably their eyes tend to get bigger than the budget. Often times, they will ask for the moon because they simply do not understand the complexities that go into web development. Among many other responsibilities, the main job of the *producer* or *project manager* is to set and manage client expectations so the project stays on track. (For simplicity's sake, from here on out, I'll simply refer to this role as the *producer*.) Using a variety of tools such as Microsoft Project, shown in Figure 1-1, the producer must keep the project, the team members, the client, and the budget on track from start to finish.

One of the most common problems a producer must address on a project is *scope creep*. Features and functions that you did not plan for have an uncanny ability to find their way into the design. Often you'll find that either the project team members are trying to prove themselves by "gold-plating" (overdoing) their contributions or clients are scrutinizing the site and suggesting way too many changes and enhancements. In either case, such constant noodling can add up to more time and money than you had planned. To limit scope creep, be sure to contingency-plan for a reasonable number of unforeseen changes, and watch for additions that crop up during the course of the project so you can manage or eliminate them.

> *Successful project management is keeping the members of the web development team "on the same page" throughout the project. Balancing the needs of the client, the goals of the site, and the reality of scope and budget are challenging tasks. Establishing clear communication means understanding the needs of the client and individual team members. Following a process and understanding the overall goals and objectives of the site from the onset is also critical to the success of a project. The goal is to maintain clear objectives through each phase of development, to manage scope creep (the tendency of projects to expand in size), and to predict the future.*

> – Kelly Goto, Company President, www.gotomedia.com

ⓘ	Task Name	Cost	Duration	Start	Finish
	⊟ **Design Conference Web Site**	**$447,554.55**	**75 days?**	**Mon 8/1/05**	**Fri 11/11/05**
	⊟ OVERHEAD	$274,859.10	75 days	Mon 8/1/05	Fri 11/11/05
📝	Project Team Oversight	$124,859.10	75 days	Mon 8/1/05	Fri 11/11/05
📝	Contingency	$40,000.00	0 days	Mon 8/1/05	Mon 8/1/05
	⊞ **External costs**	**$110,000.00**	0 days	Mon 8/1/05	Mon 8/1/05
	⊞ DISCOVERY PHASE	$0.00	27 days	Mon 8/1/05	Tue 9/6/05
	Discovery complete	**$0.00**	0 days	Mon 8/1/05	Mon 8/1/05
	⊟ PRELIMINARY DESIGN PHASE	$172,695.45	75 days	Mon 8/1/05	Fri 11/11/05
📝	Team resources	$172,695.45	75 days	Mon 8/1/05	Fri 11/11/05
	⊞ **Internal project kick off**	**$0.00**	**1 day**	**Mon 8/1/05**	**Mon 8/1/05**
📝	**Internal kick off meeting**	$0.00	1 day	Tue 8/2/05	Tue 8/2/05
	⊞ **Preliminary wireframing**	**$0.00**	**8 days**	**Wed 8/3/05**	**Fri 8/12/05**
	Preliminary wireframes complete	$0.00	0 days	Fri 8/12/05	Fri 8/12/05

Figure 1-1: Most web producers use project tracking software like Microsoft Project to manage schedules, resources, and milestones.

Information architects

This impressive-sounding title goes to the person whose job it is to sit down and figure out how the whole site fits together and how people will navigate from one page to the next. They also are the ones who develop *personas* — profiles of the target user — and will be the ones conducting "user testing" later in the development process.

Among the first tasks of an *information architect* is to design a *sitemap* diagram (like the one shown in Figure 1-2) that shows all the main sections of the site. The IA, as this person is often referred to, then dives into the page-level detail and creates a series of *wireframe* diagrams, like the example shown in Figure 1-3, that show the content and navigational elements that go on each major page of the site. The term *wireframe*, which crops up throughout this book, originates from an established technique in 3D modeling that uses onscreen lines that look like wire mesh to rough out basic shapes before rendering them further. The term was adopted early on by the web-design industry to refer to the diagram-like page sketches that precede the visual design stage. Between the sitemap and the wireframe diagrams drawn for each major page, the information architect, in effect, builds the blueprints for the entire site. This is a critical first step before you can dive into visual design exploration.

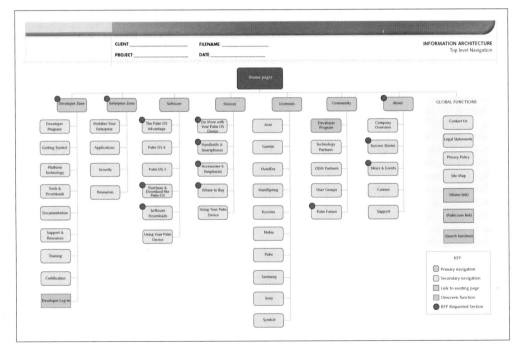

Figure 1-2: A sitemap is like a bird's-eye view of your website, showing all its sections.

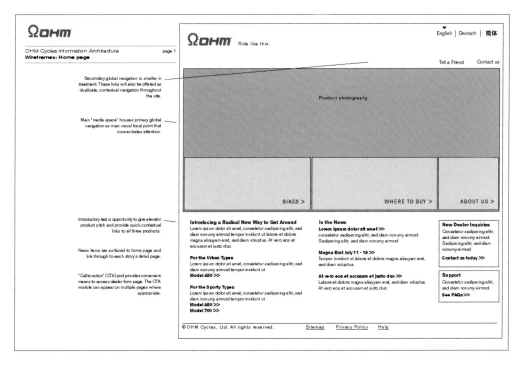

Figure 1-3: A wireframe shows the structural layout, interaction design, and content plan for a page.

Visual designers

Armed with the sitemap and wireframes that define the underlying site structure, it's the *visual designer's* job to extend a company's brand image and
character into a website look and feel. Visual design, however, is not just
about making a site look good; it can make or break a site's effectiveness
and even its usability. A good visual designer does not simply "color in" the
wireframes; they rearrange elements, adjust relative placement and sizing of
elements, and use good graphic-design principles of color, form, consistency,
and layout to accentuate navigation and important content, and indicate how
users should interact with each page.

I find that many web designers are print-design expatriates. If you're transi-
tioning from the print-design world, the hardest thing you need to learn is
how to maximize the technologies and navigation options at your fingertips
to design effective web interfaces.

Many print designers who are new to web design create graphically rich,
custom interfaces that certainly *look* cool but aren't very practical for the
web; you can see an example in Figure 1-4. These sites often download

slowly, are hard to automate or update, or are difficult to use because users can't easily distinguish clickable from non-clickable items. (I'm sure their beer is good, though!)

One alternative, of course, is having a website with nearly zero design sense. Figure 1-5 shows a website that deliberately illustrates as many bad design choices as possible — from blinding background patterns to annoying audio and animation.

Content developers

Websites, like any other medium, require more *copy* (a.k.a *text*) than people realize. In my experience, many companies and clients underestimate the need for having professional *web* copy developed, and instead rely on their go-to print-based writers. Developing copy for the Web is a unique art; not only does it require a different approach to disclosing information, but it also usually requires ongoing management (editing and updating to reflect current conditions) — typically through a CMS (*content management system*).

Figure 1-4: This design may look cool, but it's too busy; users have a hard time telling clickable from non-clickable items.

Figure 1-5: A deliberate display of as many bad choices as possible — to illustrate the need for good visual and information design.

For this reason, content development for a web project is often parceled out to two distinct individuals — or one individual wearing two distinct hats:

- **The content strategist:** The person who identifies the chunks of copy needed for each page — for example, headlines, bullet lists, and descriptions — and the rules for each, such as character limits and style of copy.

- **The copy writer:** The person who actually writes the text for each identified chunk.

Writing for the Web is a whole other animal. First, no one likes to read text-heavy web pages, so the content strategist and the copy writer have to convey the most impact in the least amount of space. Second, you need to lead off with the real meat of the message — put the conclusion first, and then follow with a few supporting details in case people get that far. Last, it's a good idea to use *action words* and phrases — such as "Learn more" or "Enroll now" instead of passive phrases like "More" or "Our enrollment plan" — next to the links and buttons you want your visitors to use.

Remember, the Web is a series of pages that one progressively navigates through. Therefore you have no need to put the entirety of a subject's information on a single page. It's a better practice to put teasers on your higher-level pages (such as the home page and top-level navigation pages) that lead your visitors into a variety of subjects. People can then quickly scan the teasers and drill down into lower-level pages to get more detail.

Media specialists

No modern website would be complete without a splash of video, audio, or even a Flash component. With so many specialized media formats and compression schemes, however, it's best to leave media development to separate professionals. This is especially true for Flash development. Flash is a software application that can create highly interactive applications and animation (look for Flash at www.adobe.com). The program is so powerful that Flash development and coding has become a highly sought-after profession in its own right.

Web developers

A *web developer* is the person who assembles the actual web pages in HTML (*H*yper*T*ext *M*arkup *L*anguage) and CSS (*C*ascading *S*tyle *S*heets). There is a real art to producing what is called the *front end* of a website (what you and I see when we visit a website) because there are so many browsers and computer configurations to account for.

Unfortunately, even despite the web standards introduced by the W3C (World Wide Web Consortium, www.w3.org), no two browsers interpret HTML and CSS the same. This fact is further complicated by these browsers running on different platforms — Mac, PC, smartphones, and various portable devices. Web developers must be sure to include redundant code that accounts for the way different browsers interpret it. For example, one browser may not recognize a line of code and so will ignore it, moving on to the next line. That next line might be a slightly different way of saying the same thing, but the browser now recognizes the code syntax. This redundancy helps ensure that the website displays correctly across many different devices and computers. It's a pretty tall order.

Programmers

Modern website projects would not be complete without a team of programmers. These folks can really give your website a turbo boost by making it a powerful business tool, whether it is an e-commerce site or a social networking site.

As I'm sure you've noticed from your own browsing, websites can literally consist of hundreds of pages. Look a bit under the surface, though, and you'll discover that websites like these are actually composed of a much smaller number of pages called templates. Anywhere from 5–20 templates can power an entire site. The trick is to link these few template pages to a database that houses all the content. For example, as shown in Figure 1-6, one Product Detail page template will display the appropriate image, price, and information for any number of products in a store's online catalog. In the industry, this is called a *dynamic* site, because the content of a single page template can reconfigure as needed to display unique content based on a user's action — such as viewing a particular product.

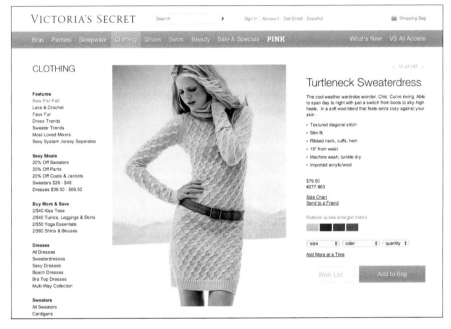

Figure 1-6: This product-page template gets imagery, pricing, and descriptions from a database and can create as many product pages as needed.

In addition to coding web-page templates with a scripting language such as PHP (*H*ypertext *P*reprocessor — go figure) or ASP (*A*ctive *S*erver *P*ages), programmers also create the online databases to house all the information the templates may need. Building databases can be so complex that many times you need a specialized database dude or dudette for that task alone.

Getting Started in Web Design

Now that you have a feel for the different types of professionals you'll be working with — or become yourself — it's time to start taking steps toward your own future in web or mobile design by educating yourself on the production process.

Understanding site goals

From small family businesses to companies the size of Disney, Step One is the same: Understand, in order of priority, the top three-or-so goals that the company is looking to achieve with the design (or redesign) of the site. These goals directly influence the site's concept, its structure, its visual design, and the layout and content choices you need to make for each page.

For example, when redesigning a micro site for a new product launch, the client wanted to appeal to the target customer — in this case, professional designers and photographers — and communicate the product's optimal use case scenarios, not just compare its great new features. The solution, as shown in Figure 2-1, was to profile the work of professional designers and photographers, so target customers could relate to the same needs. This two-part site for an Epson printer toggles between these professional stories and the product's features. Clearly the designers understood the client's goal: communicate ideal uses for their new product. What better way?

© Epson. www.espson.com

Figure 2-1: This microsite for an Epson printer uses real-life customer profiles and scenarios to illustrate the product's features. Smart.

Gathering business requirements

The next useful exercise is to sit down with the client (or internal stakeholders) and make a list of all the things the site needs to do. Here's a tip: Think in terms of finishing a bunch of these sentences: "The site should have the ability to X."

Here are some guidelines:

- **Keep it high-level.** Lay down the general ground rules up front with the client for this exercise. In my experience, clients can quickly dive into *how* things should be done instead of focusing on *what* needs to be done. The *how* is your job, the *what* is their job.

- **Make a list.** Capture a bunch of "ability to" phrases that focus on practical goals like these:

    - The ability to register users into a database

    - The ability to log users in, log them out, and manage their accounts

    - The ability to showcase a featured product each day

    - The ability to share customer testimonials for each product

- **Prioritize.** Group each of the "ability to" statements in order of priority, such as *1* is a must-have, *2* is a nice-to-have, and *3* is a could-have-in-the-future.

Developing an RFP

If you are on the client side, and will be engaging an outside agency to build out your website, you'll need to develop a detailed *RFP* (request for proposal). A good RFP will include an overview of the project, the business goals, and a list of the requirements. RFPs usually do not include a budget, as the expectation is for agencies to bid on the project, but they often include a target launch date.

Because RFPs go out to multiple agencies, they often spell out strict rules of response. For example, an RFP may state that agencies can only e-mail questions to a particular person at the company, or that agencies must e-mail an acknowledgment and an intent to bid — or decline — by a certain date. They typically outline a vendor selection timeline, including a due date for the response itself, and when a vendor may expect to come and present their proposal — on their dime — in person.

Building a project plan

After you have a good feel for the level of work involved in the new site, and its budget and timeline, you can assemble a project plan that lists all the steps — organized by these patented five phases — and figure out how much time, money, and people you need to accomplish each step.

An easy way to start a project plan is to work backwards from the launch date and sketch out some major milestones. Doing so can give you a better perspective of the project's *pacing*, as I like to call it. If you are developing a project plan in response to an RFP, then you are also backing into a proposed budget based on time and your estimation of the resources needed to accomplish the project's scope (padded for profit and contingency planning, of course).

Most web producers use Microsoft Project to map out all the steps, assign team members to tasks, and set up *dependencies* between tasks — the things that rely on other things happening first. Notice the stair-stepped Gantt view of the visual design steps in Figure 2-2; a *Gantt chart* shows a visual cascade of project steps indicating how some steps can happen in parallel while certain steps depend on the completion of other steps. The designer first creates a few design directions, the client then chooses one for refinement, and finally the look and feel is established. If the client takes longer than two days to choose a design or rejects the designs presented, the schedule slips, and the launch day is in jeopardy unless time can be made up elsewhere. Typically, producers pad in extra time for just such eventualities.

Look and feel development	$0.00	13 days	Wed 8/3/05	Fri 8/19/05	
Collaborate on preliminary wireframing	$0.00	6 days	Wed 8/3/05	Wed 8/10/05	
Develop design directions	$0.00	5 days	Thu 8/11/05	Wed 8/17/05	
Review with client	$0.00	1 day	Mon 8/15/05	Mon 8/15/05	
Refine design from client feedback	$0.00	3 days	Tue 8/16/05	Thu 8/18/05	
Client sign off on design direction	$0.00	1 day	Fri 8/19/05	Fri 8/19/05	
Look and feel complete	$0.00	0 days	Fri 8/19/05	Fri 8/19/05	8/19

Figure 2-2: A Gantt chart represents each project task as a bar. Notice how some tasks must be completed before others can begin.

Phase 2: Design

When you buy or receive toys labeled "some assembly required," you know you're in for a brain-twisting treat. If you're like me, you spend the first half-hour attempting the task without the aid of instructions. Not until you pull some hair out do you finally surrender to reading the manual. The design phase of a website is your chance to write the instruction manual for the team before anyone begins pushing pixels around.

Creating a sitemap

As with creating blueprints for a new office building, a primary task in the design phase for any website, large or small, is to create a *sitemap*, a diagram that shows all of a site's pages and how they interconnect. Without a sitemap like the one shown in Figure 2-3, you're headed for frustration. For one thing, the team won't have any unified direction. Secondly, without a plan, you can't possibly anticipate all the content, pages, and features that need to go into the site.

For example, imagine getting halfway through the design and then realizing that you forgot to include a critical feature such as user login and account management or online product support. Now you find yourself redoing an interface that could have been done right the first time — if you'd only had a plan. Check out Chapter 3 for more detail on building sitemaps.

Developing wireframes

While the sitemap shows the website from a bird's-eye view, it doesn't give you the detail you need to design and build each page. For that, you need a series of *wireframes*.

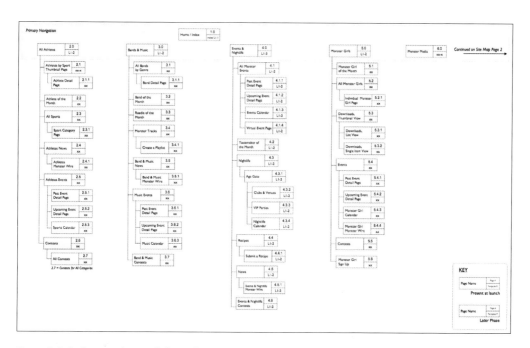

Figure 2-3: A sitemap shows all the major sections of a website and how they interconnect to lay the groundwork for your navigation scheme.

During the Design phase, the *information architect* (see Chapter 1) collects input from all team members and builds a diagram layout, called a *wireframe,* for each major page of the site. Like a sitemap, a wireframe is a diagram — but instead of displaying a zoomed-out view of all the site pages together, a wireframe shows a detailed view of a single web page. A wireframe like the one in Figure 2-4 shows the following elements:

- *Global navigation* scheme (the navigation that appears on each page of your site)
- Text and media chunks and their relative importance to one another
- Interaction design (how people use the elements on the page, which is documented — *annotated* — with callouts to label its parts)

See Chapter 3 for details on building wireframes.

User testing

Testing wireframes with users is an iterative process that you start in the Design phase and continue well into the Development phase. (By *iterative* I mean doing it over and over again, incorporating what each try tells you — in terms of testing, that's something you better get used to right off the bat.) Testing early in the Design phase helps you stay on track because you can quickly make small adjustments before going too far down the production path.

In Chapter 6, I show you techniques for testing important features of your website by building a series of *clickable* wireframes and sharing them with a group of users that represent a good cross section of your target audience.

Putting together a content plan

Hand in hand with wireframe development is figuring out a content plan. After all, how can you suggest content like a news area on a page without knowing where the news will come from, how extensive it will be, and how often the client will be able to update it?

If the site will be using a *content management system,* or CMS (a database system that houses all your text and feeds it to your pages), the *content strategist* defines a list of all the kinds of text components that go on each page and establishes names and rules for each. For example, an "item title" may have a certain character limit and must use initial caps.

Lastly, during the Design phase, the content team thinks about the writing tone that would be best suited for the site, given the company's brand personality and business goals established during the Definition phase. For example, should the site's text read as warm and inviting, be irreverent street language, or written as just-the-facts? The writers need this input to guide their writing style during the Development phase.

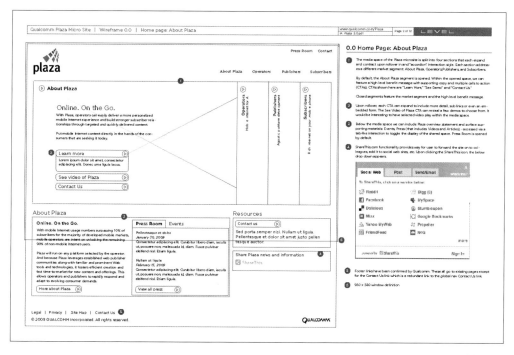

Figure 2-4: A wireframe is a diagram-like plan for a web page.

Establishing "look and feel"

After you finalize the sitemap with the client and develop the wireframes to the point where content and interactive elements contained on each page are more or less decided, the visual designers can explore different design directions for the site. Designers use the wireframes as the underlying skeleton to understand what content and interaction design they need to account for. They don't simply "color in" the wireframes; they use them as a guide to understand the relative importance of items while they're creating their layouts.

The general practice is to create a design treatment for the home page and a *subpage* (anything but the home page). This forces the designers to figure out a design that can tie the whole site together and account for the site's navigation scheme. I like to have at least three different design directions — developed by three different designers. This strategy gives you enough variety to give the client some options. Figure 2-5 shows two designs made by two different designers from the same wireframe. Notice how each design conveys a very different feel.

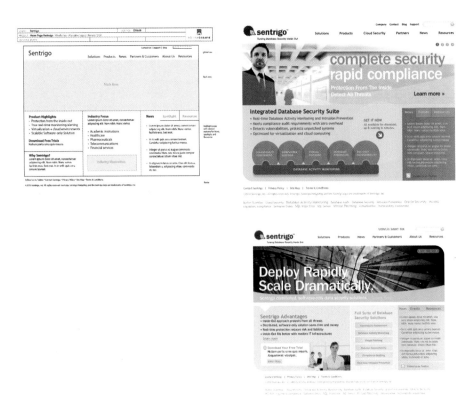

Figure 2-5: These designs developed by Solhaug Grafik derive two very different approaches from the same wireframe.

Getting input from a focus group

Most often the client chooses the final design direction after one or two rounds of noodling or "frankensteining" (patching elements from different designs together). For high-profile websites, however, it's a good idea to get input from a focus group to see which design resonates most clearly with them before you present the design to the client. That way, you have customer-feedback ammo when you present, and can help steer the client more objectively in the right direction. (For more on focus groups, see Chapter 6.)

Phase 3: Development

The time has come to commit pixels to the screen and move on to the Development phase. In this phase, all video, audio, Flash animation, and graphics are prepared for the Web: They're compressed to speed up their travel across the Web, saved in a web-friendly format, named, and uploaded to the server. All programming and HTML work is done, and the site comes together, ready to be tested.

Producing comps

After the client chooses a design direction for the site, the production work can really begin. The graphics team will produce a series of *comps* — graphical mockups that show how the page could look — that account for the design and layout of each unique page template. Comps are usually produced in Photoshop, although you can find some designers who use Fireworks. Generally, you commit to no more than 20–25 comps, even for the largest websites.

These comps serve as the visual benchmark for the technical *build-out* (putting the site together). The HTML and CSS developers will use these comps to derive the necessary graphics, backgrounds, toolbars, buttons, and styles for text and other objects, and will try to match the visual design and layout of the comps as closely as they can.

The comps can also contain templates for producing the multitude of site graphics needed, such as product shots or so-called *hero images* — large marketing images designed to convey the primary focus of the page. The templates are already sized to the correct size and may include a special effect on the image. A production artist simply needs to compose the unique images within the template and export each one.

Content development

During the Development phase, the content team is busy writing all the copy (text) components for the site. How do they know what to write? That's in the Design phase: The content strategist (defined in Chapter 1) maps out all types of copy needed for the site, how many blocks of each type of copy are needed, and on which pages they live. As shown in Figure 2-6, this is all neatly organized into a spreadsheet called a *content matrix*. Content strategists, along with the writers, also decide what the tone of the site should be.

Armed with a checklist of copy to write (the aforementioned content matrix) and the tone to convey, the writers can begin their task.

Media development

Most sites have some sort of *rich media* (also known as *multimedia*) — whether it's Flash animations and applications, audio, or video. In fact, some sites — like the one shown in Figure 2-7 — are entirely built in Flash except for the one HTML page that the site sits on.

Page ID	SITE SECTION	SITE SUB-SECTION	AUDIENCE	Persistence	NOTES and/or SUGGESTED COPY	TEMPLATE ASSIGNED
					Content Identification Information	
	SubHero Rotation 2 Infograph	Title	Primary - Customers, Prospects	Homepage only	Inspirational title	Homepage
		Subtitle			Descriptive copy.	
		Image			Graphic image to support the copy.	
		CTA			CTA: Action-based CTA to drive user to a key section of the site.	
	SubHero Rotation 3 Infograph	Title	Primary - Customers, Prospects	Homepage only	Inspirational title	Homepage
		Subtitle			Descriptive copy.	
		Image			Graphic image to support the copy.	
		CTA			CTA: Action-based CTA to drive user to a key section of the BV site.	
	SubHero Rotation 4 Infograph	Title	Primary - Customers, Prospects	Homepage only	Inspirational title	Homepage
		Subtitle			Descriptive copy.	
		Image			Graphic image to support the copy.	
		CTA			CTA: Action-based CTA to drive user to a key section of the site.	
	SubHero Rotation 5 Infograph	Title	Primary - Customers, Prospects	Homepage only	Inspirational title	Homepage
		Subtitle			Descriptive copy.	
		Image			Graphic image to support the copy.	
		CTA			CTA: Action-based CTA to drive user to a key section of the BV site.	
	SubHero Rotation 6 Infograph	Title	Primary - Customers, Prospects	Homepage only	Inspirational title	Homepage
		Subtitle			Descriptive copy.	
		Image			Graphic image to support the copy.	
		CTA			CTA: Action-based CTA to drive user to a key section of the site.	
1.3	Video	Video	CMOs, Customers, Prospects	Homepage only	Bazaarvoice Sizzle Reel	Homepage
		Title				
		Subtitle				
		By Line				

Figure 2-6: A content matrix is a spreadsheet that accounts for all the copy components needed for a website.

Flash development can be so complex that it has become a process and a profession unto itself. Not only do Flash designers need to create their own version of a site map and wireframes to make their plan of attack, but they also need to be one part designer and one part programmer in order to build an effective Flash component.

As for audio and video production, both involve acquiring source material to work with. This means that either you need to license existing material or — you guessed it — you have to go out and produce it yourself. While today's smartphones and easy-to-use desktop tools from iMovie to Final Cut Pro make video production much simpler, professional-quality video is still a significant production effort. You need locations, casting, talent wrangling, permissions, release forms, wardrobe, a good script, and multiple takes before you even make it to the editing and post-production floor. You then need to compress the files and save them in a web-ready format. As you can imagine, depending on the project, media can range from simple and inexpensive to a hefty part of your budget and timeline.

Building the presentation layer with HTML and CSS

It's like that joke that says, "Duct tape holds the world together" — HTML is certainly the glue that holds the World Wide Web together. *HTML* (*HyperText Markup Language*) is a simple coding language that tells your web browser how to string formatted text, graphics, and media elements together on the page. *CSS* (Cascading Style Sheets) is a set of rules that you can define that govern the appearance, size, position, color, and shape of your elements. Together, HTML and CSS create what the user sees: the *presentation layer* of a website. The web-design industry customarily thinks of a website as organized in layers. As you can see throughout this book, a website comprises many layers.

Every page of every website is built with HTML — even if the HTML is simply organizing some other component such as the Flash elements (refer to Figure 2-7). You can write HTML code in any simple text editor (such as Notepad in Windows) or use a more full-featured editor such as Adobe Dreamweaver. After you finish, you can load the web page into a browser right there from your desktop and see instant results.

HTML is pretty limited in what it can do, and CSS just focuses on the looks and the layout, so you can't build a complete online shopping system (for example) using just CSS and HTML alone. For something like an e-commerce system, you need to bring out the big guns — special programming, databases, and applications, all of which I discuss more closely in Chapter 15.

Figure 2-7: All the interaction for The Seen's website is contained inside a Flash movie on a single HTML page.

Developing the backend

If you're designing a website that's going to do anything beyond a simple show of nice text and graphics, you have to enlist programmers to build a website layer generally referred to as the *backend*. The backend is all the stuff that happens behind the scenes to enable site features such as search, customer feedback, buying products with a credit card, or registering for special events. All of these actions require specialized programming. You can't build this sort of functionality with HTML alone.

Programming languages such as PHP (*H*ypertext *P*reprocessor) or ASP (Microsoft's *A*ctive *S*erver *P*ages) are integrated right into the HTML code for the page — making your page a funky hybrid of coding languages. The HTML and CSS portion controls the page appearance and layout, whereas the programming code does all the cool stuff such as linking to an online database to automatically display a product of the day. If you take a peek at Figure 2-8, you'll see a new redesign in progress for Steelcraft by Ekko Media Group — all nicely laid out with the help of HTML and CSS. Figure 2-9 gives you a behind-the-scenes look at the PHP code for this page that connects to an online database, where it can grab a product's price, name, image, and so on.

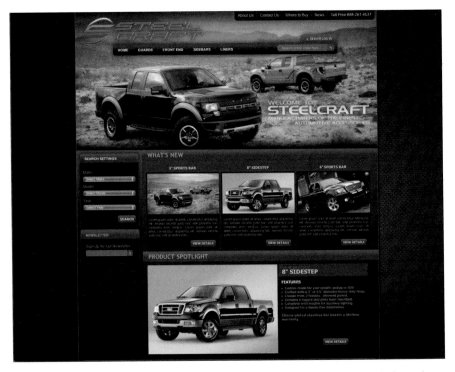

© Steelcraft Group. www.steelcraftautomotive.com

Figure 2-8: The features and functions on this page, developed by Ekko Media Group, are too complex to do with just HTML.

To build complex pages with login capabilities, e-commerce, and more, you can either roll up your sleeves and type PHP code using editors such as PhpStorm or Eclipse or you can use tools like Adobe Dreamweaver as shown in Figure 2-10.

So now that your head is spinning from the technical fly-over, it's time to start working on the home stretch — Deployment.

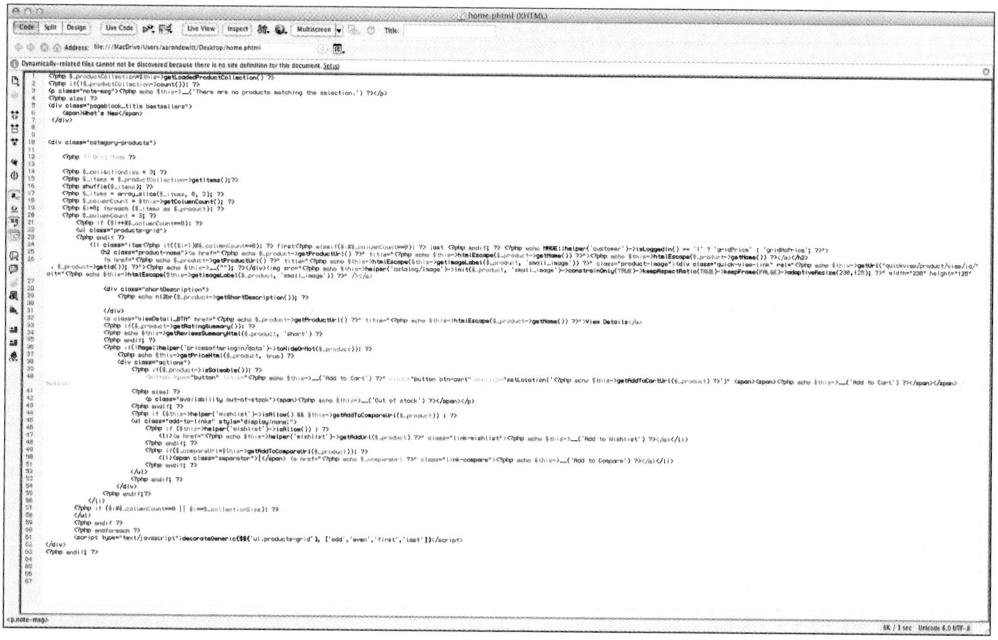

© Steelcraft Group. www.steelcraftautomotive.com

Figure 2-9: Looking behind the scenes at PHP code.

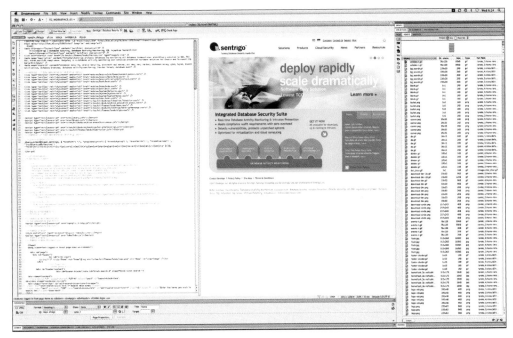

Figure 2-10: Dreamweaver has a visual interface that makes it easier to code websites.

Phase 4: Deployment

Just because the Web is a flexible publishing medium, don't be tempted to throw the site online and just fix any problems after it's live to the public. Users *notice* misspellings, broken links, and whatever other gaffes are left over from publishing in haste; they'll be left with a negative impression of your business. Before you go live with a site, make sure you subject it to a rigorous cycle of testing and *debugging* (correcting errors).

Quality assurance

So many details go into building a website that you're bound to make mistakes along the way — and remember, no site ever looks the same on different browsers, computers, and devices. Plan ample time at the end of a project for a formal *QA* (quality assurance) period. For large Fortune 100 projects, I've used every bit of four weeks to identify and correct problems — and often that's not enough time, and we have to keep a list of non-show-stopper things to fix after launch.

In addition to checking for misspellings, missing images, bad links, and so on, check your site on different platforms (Mac and Windows, smartphones, and other handheld devices) and different browsers (Firefox, Safari, and the multiple versions of Internet Explorer) to make sure that everything works and looks the way you expect it to.

The other thing to check is how fast various pages load. Rich media such as Flash animations, video, and audio — or (for that matter) improperly compressed images — can really make your pages limp along, even on fast connections. Notice how giving up a slight amount of image quality, as illustrated in Figures 2-11 and 2-12, gains tremendous savings in file size, resulting in a faster load time — a better "user experience" as they say in web-design circles.

In Chapter 15, I delve a little deeper into ways to speed up your website's performance.

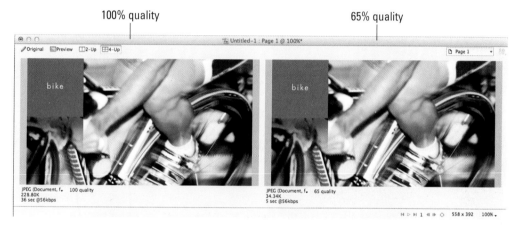

Figure 2-11: Over a slow connection, using 65% quality JPEG compression reduces load time from 36 seconds to 5 seconds; the image looks pretty much the same.

Figure 2-12: Only when you zoom in to the image do you see some pixelization around the text and in the image.

Launch day

During development and testing, you don't want the outside world taking a sneak peek at your site. So you can hide sites in many ways leading up to launch day — putting them on different servers, enabling *IP blockers* (software that allows only certain computers to access the server), or developing sites on a staging server that mirrors the target live environment. Ergo, on launch day, you need to take steps to undo all this hiding to make the site available for all to see at your prescribed moment.

For larger sites, you need to create a plan that chronicles the steps you and your team will take leading up to launch time. Tasks such as getting your new DNS (your web address, such as `www.companyname.com`, as it's associated with an IP address) to propagate throughout the Internet can take up to a couple of days — and should be part of your launch plan. Removing IP blockers and setting up *redirects* (sending people to different, specified URLs when they type a URL) are tasks and double-checks that you need to include in the launch plan.

Once a site is working in the real world on the servers it was designed for, a whole new set of technical problems can arise. I like to watch a site closely for the first couple weeks after it launches to make sure it settles nicely into its new home on the Internet and can handle the incoming traffic.

A word of advice: Don't launch on a Friday, and keep the engineers close at hand in the hours after launch just in case!

Phase 5: Maintenance

The minute after a site launches marks the beginning of the often-overlooked — yet all-important and ongoing — Maintenance phase. I have found that agencies are notorious for not setting up their clients well on this front.

To be relevant, a site needs to be kept fresh. New products, new prices, new images, updated news, and such are all things that can change daily if not hourly. Typically, sites manage all this change through a CMS, a *content management system*, which is built (or is customized from off-the-shelf software) in parallel to the main site. A good CMS will have a web-based, easy-to-use interface that allows you or your client to log in and handle simple content updates as often as needed.

At this point, you also may want to fix any bugs left over from the QA period, and can consider adding features that were initially left out for time or budget reasons. Larger upgrades or additions are miniature web projects in themselves, in which case you get to repeat these five phases all over again.

Part II
User-Friendly Design

The 5th Wave   By Rich Tennant

"Look into my Web site, Ms. Carruthers. Look deep into its rotating spiral, spinning, spinning, pulling you deeper into its vortex, deeper...deeper..."

Who Is the Audience?

Before you can design a site, you must first understand the target audience who will be using it. If (for example) you're designing a website for a cruise line and you're not familiar with the cruise industry, you could assume — mistakenly — that the audience for the site would be families.

Unless you sit down with your client and ask a lot of questions, you'll never know that the real audience for the client's particular business is (in this case) empty-nesters looking for a unique travel experience, or the young singles crowd looking for a party vacation and the chance to meet new people. This changes everything about your concept for the website — from the graphical appearance and photography choices to the content features and site organization.

Having structured conversations with your clients and asking them many questions about their industry, competition, and intended audience is a critical step in the design process.

Question checklist for clients

The best way to extract customer profile information from your clients is to have a chat with them and run through a list of prepared questions. What sorts of questions should you ask? Table 3-1 is a generic list to get you started. You should ultimately create your own list and modify it for each new project.

Table 3-1	Customer Questionnaire
Question	*Reason for Asking*
How many different types of customers do you have?	Some businesses have a segmented customer base. For instance, they may have *current customers*, *prospective customers*, *business customers*, and *consumer customers*. Your web interface may need to cater to different customer segments.
How would you describe each customer type?	Have the client describe each customer type in detail. Are the customers primarily male or female? Are they professionals? What is their income bracket? Are they web-savvy? What's their level of education? What is each customer segment trying to accomplish online?

Question	Reason for Asking
What are the barriers for each customer?	Customers always have at least one thing that will make them hesitant to engage in your client's offerings. For example, is the product perceived as too expensive? If so, your content has to really push the value and/or financing options.
What's the biggest value this new website will provide to customers?	You need to know what the website will offer that solves a customer's need. For example, will the new site offer exclusive site discounts or help each customer zero in on the right product for him or her and compare product features side by side?

Personas

The client checklist can give you a good idea of the customers you're after, but sometimes going a step further and developing a one-sheet profile for each customer type is helpful. In the web industry, these one-sheets that profile a unique customer segment are called *personas*.

Each persona has a name (fake, of course) and even a picture along with a short bio, age, income, and other detail. (See the collection of three different customer segments in Figure 3-1.) The idea is to make the customer come alive in the minds of the web team.

While clients usually have a good idea of the characteristics, wants, and needs of their customers, for projects that can afford it, it's a good idea to schedule workshops with actual customers to get a better view into their heads. These workshops make each persona you create that much more accurate.

User scenarios

Scenarios are plausible situations involving each persona. For example, a scenario for "Helen" might run as follows. Helen is moving cross-country to accept a new job in Los Angeles. She has accumulated enough stuff throughout her first couple of years out of college that her car just won't do. She needs to find an affordable moving solution for her small amount of stuff that's not a semi.

From this example, you can see that an online moving company targeting this customer needs to quickly convey multiple affordable options from small vans she can rent to full-service, small-scale moving services.

Figure 3-1: A persona gives a name and a face to each type of customer.

By thinking through a couple of different real-life scenarios, you have a better context from which to design the site's architecture, suggest rich media — such as interactive Flash elements and videos — that serve a real purpose (and don't just look cool), and plan a content strategy that anticipates and meets the customer's needs.

Building an Outline for Your Site

At this point, you must balance everything you learned about the target customers and their needs alongside the list of your client's business requirements and start sketching an outline for the site. From this outline, you can build a *sitemap* (a flowchart-like diagram) that shows how you can organize all the content in the site.

Balancing business requirements with user needs

As stated in Chapter 2, gathering business requirements is really an exercise of a client building a wish list for their new site. If you recall, you create a list of business requirements by completing a bunch of "the site must have the ability to do X" statements. The client then rates these "ability to" statements from most to least important to determine priorities for the business.

Not all features and content described in the business requirements will make it into the first phase of the site — or ever at all. Not only do time and budget affect what makes the cut, but also the user's needs now come into play as an additional filter. After thinking through various user scenarios, and the customer segments that the site must accommodate, go through your list of business requirements again and rate each idea according to where it fits in the user's priorities. You may also find you need to add features and content to your list that customers expect to see.

Categorizing and prioritizing information

After you have a prioritized list of user and business-driven content and features, translate them into an old-fashioned outline. This outline, like the sample shown in Figure 3-2, ultimately helps you build a sitemap.

The key to producing a successful outline is your ability to group similar items and features together. As you become more familiar with the list of content and features, a pattern begins to emerge. Some items go together quite easily, whereas other ideas don't fit in at all.

Here are the steps for converting your prioritized requirements list into a workable outline:

1. **Group ideas together.**

   Find features and content that seem similar and place them next to each other. For example, investor information and partner information fit nicely together. Set these aside and give them a temporary group title, such as About the Company. This group title can ultimately become a main-level navigation choice, and the stuff inside the group might all be accessed via a drop-down menu.

   Think of each entry within a group as one web page of content.

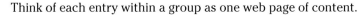

2. **Limit the number of groups to 5–7.**

   For usability reasons, identify no more than 5–7 main groups. If you find that difficult to do (as it may be with larger websites), you may identify up to three sets of groups, prioritized as primary, secondary, and tertiary sets.

3. **Limit the depth of each group to just two levels.**

   Within each group, you will have a list of items. In some cases, you'll have subcategories of a particular item. For usability reasons, limit yourself to just one additional level of subcategorization. If you get any deeper than this, and have subcategories *of* subcategories, you run into navigation design challenges. Here is an example of two levels of depth within the About the Company group. Notice the numbering scheme:

1. About the Company

    1.1 Contact Us

    1.2 Partners

        1.2.1 Clothing partners

        1.2.2 Footwear partners

    1.3 Press

    1.4 Our History

    1.5 Executive Team

4. Group global features into their own set.

If the list of requirements contains tools like a member login or a search function, or mandated pages like privacy policy or terms of use, set them aside into a "Globals" group. Do not count this Globals group in the limited number of 5–7 content groups. Tools and links to pages such as these will ultimately find a happy home either in the header or footer of your website.

Establishing navigation sets based on priority

The end goal of all this grouping and categorizing of information is to arrive at a navigation system for your entire website. These groups and categories are the main choices that appear on every page of your website. Since there can be so many choices for a user, the key is to group navigation sets and give them high, medium, and low visual treatments to help users digest the page and become oriented in your site.

If you just have one set of 5–7 groups, this is your "primary navigation" and your design life is a lot easier. If you have multiple sets of groups, however, you will need to determine which set will be your primary navigation. The other sets will be your secondary and tertiary navigation sets; each of those will get a different — and lesser — visual treatment as well as a different location on the interface.

Take a look at Figure 3-3. In this example, the primary navigation set has seven groups. You access the items within these groups via drop-down menus. Secondary and tertiary navigation sets are also on each page of the website, but are smaller, visually different, and in the header and footer of the page.

For usability reasons, be careful not to have more than seven groups within your primary, secondary, and tertiary collections. Studies have shown that users have difficulty getting their brains around a site when they are bombarded with more than seven items to choose from in each navigation set.

0.0 Mountain Outfitters Home Page

1.0 Shop Our Catalog
    1.1 Clothing
        1.1.1 Children's
        1.1.2 Women's
        1.1.3 Men's
    1.2 Gear
        1.2.1 Tents
        1.2.2 Sleeping bags
        1.2.3 Backpacks
        1.2.4 Accessories
    1.3 Brands
        1.3.1 Brand A
        1.3.2 Brand B
        1.3.3 Brand C

2.0 About the Company
    2.1 Our Story
    2.2 Contact Us

3.0 Global tools
    3.1 Search
    3.2 Log in
    3.3 Store Locator
    3.4 Manage My Account
        3.4.1 Profile
        3.4.2 Order History
    3.5 Shopping Cart

Figure 3-2: An outline of content ideas shows a number of content elements within each group.

Also, as illustrated in Figure 3-3, when you get to the Design phase, it's good practice to locate all the primary navigation elements together and give them the same visual treatment. This helps users differentiate each navigation set and understand their relative importance.

A primary navigation set

A tertiary navigation set

A secondary navigation set

Figure 3-3: This page shows a visual design treatment for the primary, secondary, and tertiary navigation sets.

Creating a Sitemap

The outline you create for your website directly translates into your *sitemap*. The sitemap helps you visualize the structure of a website — its *information architecture* — before you build it. To create a sitemap, you translate each main idea and subcategory from your outline into a diagram of boxes connected by lines and arrows to show how the pages interconnect.

A sitemap is critical to the construction of your website, and you'll refer to it often throughout the development process.

To transform your outline into a sitemap, follow these simple steps:

1. **Start with a huge piece of paper.**

   I like to start on paper because you can quickly sketch out ideas and you have plenty of available design space. Find a large piece of paper and work in landscape orientation. (You'll find that you need a lot of horizontal space.) After you work out the map's details on paper, you can re-create it on the computer to make a nice, clean copy that you can distribute to both the client and the team.

   When you're ready to transcribe your paper sitemap into a digital copy, try using a program like Inspiration (www.inspiration.com) or Microsoft Visio. These tools allow you to build flowchart diagrams quickly. For you designers out there, you can also use Adobe Illustrator or InDesign (my personal choice). As shown in Figure 3-4, using one of these tools allows an agency like LEVEL Studios to present a polished, branded sitemap to clients.

2. **Draw a box for each web page.**

   Starting with the home page, draw a box to represent each web page of the site. Put the home page box at the top of the paper. Then, as shown in Figure 3-4, start a new row below and draw a box for each of your primary, secondary, and tertiary navigation group titles.

3. **Draw the subcategories.**

   Begin a third row and draw a series of boxes for each page within the main sections. For space concerns, you may want to stack these pages vertically beneath their respective main idea boxes.

4. **Number the sections and subsections.**

   An important step is to number each section so that you can refer to it more easily in the future and match it up with the official page index you create (as detailed later in this chapter). As shown in Figure 3-4, assign 0.0 to the home page and 1.0, 2.0, 3.0, and so on to all the navigation sections. Within each navigation section, label the subpages as 2.1, 2.2, 2.3, and so on. For your second level of navigation (pages under your sub-pages), use 2.1.1, 2.1.2, 2.1.3, and so on.

A good sitemap foreshadows usability problems before your site goes into production. If your map has too many primary navigation categories that are each a little thin on content, you end up with a site that overwhelms the user with choices and clutters the screen without providing a lot of depth of content. Conversely, if your sitemap has just a few primary categories that each have a ton of stuff, you end up with a site that takes forever to navigate — making people click too many times as they drill down to the info they need.

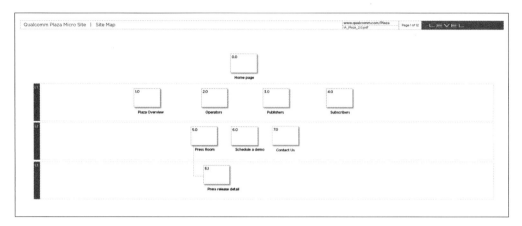

Figure 3-4: Simple sitemap for a "micro site," created in Adobe InDesign so that LEVEL Studios can create a polished, branded presentation to show clients.

The best balance to have is five to seven choices within your primary, secondary, and tertiary navigation sets, and content should be no more than two levels deep within each category.

Reading between the lines and boxes

To show how the pages on your diagram link together, you must draw a series of lines. This is literally a game of connect the dots or, in your case, boxes. The following list includes some design conventions that many designers often use on sitemaps to show navigation, technical, and content plans for each page:

- **Direct links.** The most basic way to show how two pages link together is to draw a line that connects them. Generally, all lines sprout forth from the home page's box and connect to each of the main section boxes. Considering how many boxes you probably have on your diagram, this can get messy quickly. To keep the map clean, draw one line coming from the home page and have it branch into individual lines that connect to each subpage, as shown in Figure 3-5.

- **Linking to a global navigation pages.** Pages like Search Results, Contact Us, Terms of Use, and Privacy Policy that are part of your secondary and tertiary navigation sets — and therefore accessible throughout the website — are best represented on your sitemap as cordoned-off set. Just as Alaska and Hawaii are traditionally shown pulled out on a U.S. map, you can create a special areas on your sitemap, as illustrated in Figure 3-6, for these particular navigation sets.

- **Restricted pages.** If you have a password-protected page or section, draw a smaller box representing the login *gate* that precedes the area.

- **Automatic flow from one page to the next.** Sometimes clients want a web page to display for a few seconds, or a Flash movie to play, and then automatically flow to another page without requiring the user to click. (I'm not a fan of this tactic. If you do have an intro sequence, however, make it short and provide users with a link or button for them to skip it.) For example, websites like the Hansens.com site shown in Figure 3-7 have an animated intro sequence that plays before you get to the home page. To accommodate situations like this on the sitemap, I draw two boxes on top of one another and connect them with a squiggly line, as illustrated in Figure 3-8.

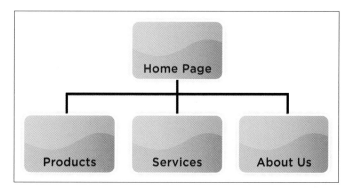

Figure 3-5: Clean up the connecting lines by using a branching approach.

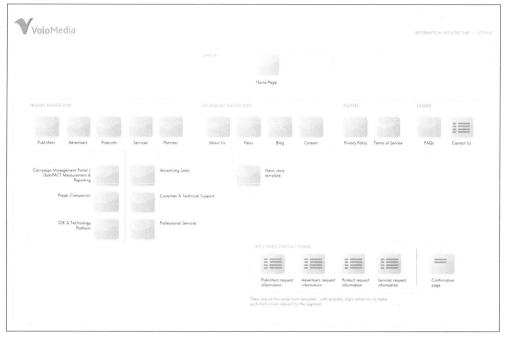

© VoloMedia. www.volomedia.com

Figure 3-6: This sitemap shows groupings of global navigation sets.

Figure 3-7: This animated intro sequence plays before you get to the home page of the Hansens.com website.

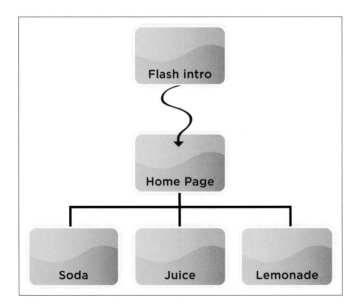

Figure 3-8: To show automatic page flow, draw the pages stacked and connected with a squiggly line.

Developing your own set of symbols

As you blossom into a seasoned web designer, you develop your own lexicon of symbols, lines, and shapes to represent various elements and interactions of a website on your sitemap. When creating your own symbols, the only rule is consistency. Regardless of the symbols or line art you decide to use on your sitemaps, just be sure to use them consistently and to clarify their meaning in a legend.

Here are a few miscellaneous elements that you may encounter and some ideas for representing them on your sitemap:

✔ **Databases.** To represent a database on a sitemap, most agencies use a cylindrical container symbol that looks like a can of soup. The database "soup can" can go anywhere on your sitemap, but most often I see it placed in the center or on the bottom — wherever it's most convenient to link multiple pages to. Pages that access the database have either a dotted line connecting to it, as shown in Figure 3-9, or simply include a small icon on the page's box next to its name and number.

✔ **Flash movies.** Flash is a software application that creates highly interactive animated movies and game-like applications that you can place on a web page. Because Flash movies can be fairly complex and require their own concentrated development, you should have a dedicated symbol to represent them on the pages where they occur on your sitemap (people usually use the little "f" symbol that Macromedia uses to denote Flash movies).

✔ **Template pages.** Websites are often created out of a handful of template pages. A database *populates* or fills the template with data. For example, an online store may have hundreds of products that all use the same "product detail" template for each product. To indicate a template page on your sitemap, draw it as a stack of pages — like the one shown in Figure 3-10 — and remember to draw either a little database symbol or draw a dotted line to the database "soup can."

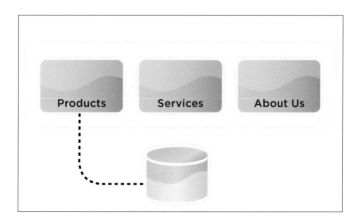

Figure 3-9: To connect a page to the database, draw a dotted line to it.

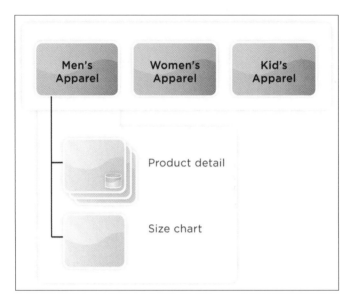

Figure 3-10: Indicate template pages on your sitemap by drawing a stack of pages. For large sites, specify a database and draw it as a symbol.

Everyone's singing from the same song sheet

Establishing clear communication between you, the team, and your clients is a high priority throughout the web design process. Sharing the sitemap with the clients is an excellent way to make sure that you're on the right track and that the clients know exactly what they're buying.

Many web-design firms have clients sign off on the accepted sitemap in order to confirm and manage their expectations for the scope of the site. This way, the client can't come back to you in the future asking about a missing "Founder's Bio page" or "Investor Relations page" not in the approved design. Armed with the client-approved sitemap, you can simply remind the client that the page in question was never part of the deal.

Although this sounds harsh, remember that the sign-off works both ways! If the sitemap *included* a Founder's Bio page, the client has every right to wonder where the page is in the developing design. In addition, an agreed-upon sitemap helps the design and HTML production teams anticipate and plan for all the pages of the site so nothing gets left out. Make sure that each production-team member working on the site has a copy of the sitemap to refer to throughout the project. Ultimately, a sitemap is a great tool to keep both sides singing from the same song sheet, so to speak.

The official page index

Another function of the sitemap is to help establish an official list of each page, a.k.a. the *page index*. I like to make a spreadsheet that has a few columns of information, such as the page's common name (About Us), its technical name (`aboutus.htm`), and even its URL path (`http://www.company.com/products/detail.php`). That way the development team can know the directory structure of the entire site before building it.

For large database-driven sites, the page index is extremely important because you can't possibly show all possible pages in the sitemap. As you can see in Figure 3-10, the sitemap shows the individual product pages as a generalized stack-o-pages based on a template. The page index, however, in Figure 3-11, lists all 100+ products in a spreadsheet format. Also notice how the page index uses the numbering scheme from the sitemap so you can match up pages between the two documents.

Why is it important to know that you have 100+ products? Three reasons come to mind:

- To understand the scope of a project, accurately and truly

- To ensure that the information architects can come up with the best way to navigate to all the products

- To ensure that the writers and media folks have a checklist from which to develop the content matrix of needed copy and images

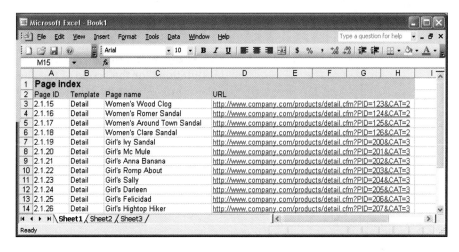

Figure 3-11: The page index shows all pages planned for the site. Notice how it references the numbering scheme of the sitemap.

Building a Map for a Site Redesign

Many people assume that web design is always about creating a new website from scratch. Well, almost every organization of any size already has a website. The primary need, therefore, is to keep the existing website fresh and evolving with the latest technologies and the changing needs of the company. Therefore, more often than not, clients approach you to *redesign* their website.

Sitemaps come in handy not only in the design process, but also in the redesign process. By developing a sitemap of the current site, you can see the site in its totality and how the pages relate to each other. You can also see where usability problems lie, and you can get ideas for a better design.

Deconstructing a website

So how do you create a sitemap for an existing website? You build it by picking the site apart to see how it's made. Here are four easy steps to get you started:

1. **Start with the home page.**

   Go to the home page of the website and look closely at all the navigation sets on the page. On a large piece of paper, draw a box at the top for the home page, and below that, draw large containers for each navigation set you see. Within each container, draw all the navigation links for that set. For example, within a "Footer" container, list all the footer links. This list helps you stay oriented in the site as you pick it apart.

2. **Identify the main categories and subcategories.**

   Click all the navigation links and see where they take you. Do they have subcategories? If so, draw them as extensions of their main entry. You may be surprised to discover that some important content is hidden, while other content is duplicated and found under multiple navigation entries.

3. **Look for database interactions.**

   Keep an eye out for pages that rely on a database. These are easy to spot — look for pages that collect data. The data is obviously going somewhere when the user submits it. Also look for pages that have a funky URL. If the URL has a long string of weird characters like $ and ?, it's a sure sign of a template page filling itself with content from a database.

   Also, ask the client how many databases the website uses and for what purpose. The client may have a CMS (content *m*anagement *s*ystem) for all images and text, have a database for products and prices, and a separate database for customers. Most likely, you need to incorporate these existing databases into your redesign. If not, you need to know how your client plans to upgrade those systems.

Finishing the sitemap

Completing the sitemap for a redesign involves the same process as creating a sitemap for a brand-new site — use your set of symbols and line art to fill in the detail of what's happening in the site. In a redesign process, you don't have to get too detailed in your deconstructed sitemap — save your energy for the redesigned sitemap. The purpose of making a sitemap for the old site is to give you a better idea of the site's current information architecture. It serves as a good point of discussion with the client so you can ask a lot of questions and formulate ideas for the redesign.

Here's a sample list of questions to ask the client:

- **What do you like least about the site now?** Find the root of the current site's problem by probing to see if the information architecture of the site or the content needs revising. Maybe both are fine, and the client just wants a new look to the site or to add new features.

- **Should any new content be added, or old content removed?** If you're adding or removing a great deal of content, the site's information architecture may need a substantial redesign.

- **Has the site's purpose changed?** Many times a company has an existing website that was originally designed to act as a marketing piece, but now must act as a revenue-producing business machine. If so, you are faced with a substantial redesign of both content and architecture.

- **Has the company changed its focus or market positioning?** In such a case, the site's content and navigation, as well as its look and feel, may change drastically. When you design sites like these, you are almost starting over from scratch.

Developing a Marketing Plan

After you thoroughly define your target audience for the website, it's a good idea to get started on the marketing plan for the site. This planning can begin to happen in parallel to the site's development.

Do not underestimate the importance of marketing websites. The Internet simply has too many websites for anyone to find — or care about — your site unless you bring it to their attention.

Therefore you or a dedicated marketing person on your team must sit down with the client and brainstorm a plan. Although some clients may not know the best way to market their website, they do know a lot about reaching their customers. Together, your team and the client should develop a list of ideas, a set of action items, and a budget.

Offline marketing

The most effective way to market a website is to combine *online* and *offline* marketing campaigns. *Offline marketing* refers to all media that's not on the Web — radio, magazines, in-store point of sale, product packaging, TV, event sponsorships, trade shows, and so on. Wherever a client currently advertises its product or service should always include the company's web and social media addresses. Since my area of expertise is online, we'll do a deeper dive into online marketing methods.

Online marketing

Online marketing refers to a web-based campaign (for example, buying those banners at the top of web pages or ads that get inserted inside YouTube videos). What is significant and superior about online advertising is that the measuring tools are so good that you can really "keep score" of how well your campaign is doing and see in real time who is responding to your message. Also unique to online advertising is the trend toward *content-based advertising* — where the ad itself is entertaining and informative, and not purely a sales pitch. Content-based advertising goes beyond simply stating a product or service exists, but offers engaging content in and of itself, and thereby indirectly influences a person's connection with the brand. Here are some common outlets for your creative online marketing campaign:

- **Facebook marketing.** Buying a Facebook "sponsored story" ad is highly effective because when someone — say "Linda" — "likes" your page, her network of friends will see your ad appear as "Linda likes Lopuck Watercolors." Facebook "page ads" are less personal but have a wider reach because you determine the demographic and geographic that should see your ad. All in, Facebook ads cost about $1.00 per new fan you acquire. Facebook also allows you to create *custom tabs*. These are embedded applications that you can run special promotions and contests through, or offer special content to your fans. Miramax developed a custom tab, shown in Figure 3-12, which allows their fans to rent and watch movies right from the Facebook website, using Facebook Credits to purchase.

- **YouTube marketing.** YouTube also offers many ways advertisers can reach a targeted demographic. You can either purchase an in-video ad that plays before a video starts or as a little pop-up during the video, or you can pay to promote your own video by purchasing *keywords* (words that people might enter into a search field to find your company, product, or service). When someone searches for videos with those keywords, a thumbnail of your video will appear alongside the search results. YouTube only charges you if that user clicks to watch your video. If you really want to make a splash, YouTube even allows you to "take over" their home page with a custom design.

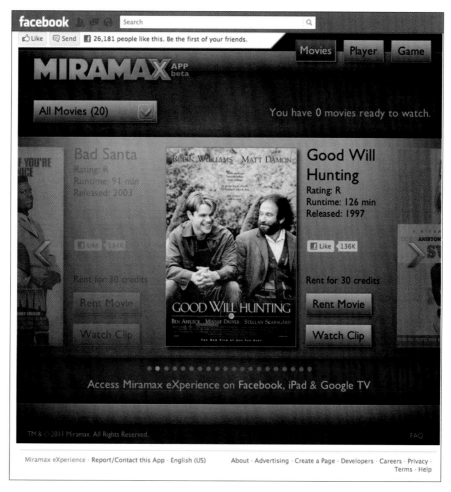

Figure 3-12: Miramax created a "custom tab" in Facebook that allows their fans to rent and watch movies right on Facebook.

✓ **Twitter advertising.** On Twitter, you can purchase a Promoted Tweet, a Promoted Trend, or a Promoted Account to target users based on their geographical location, interests, or keyword searches. Promoted Trends are a little different in that they are topics of conversation. Topics occur organically, but you can purchase a topic and have it appear in the list to hopefully start a conversation around your brand. A free alternative is to incorporate existing tweet trends into your own tweets. For example, if #MeAndYouCantDate is a hot trend, if you include this hash tag in your tweet, your message will appear to those following that topic. The key to using this free tactic successfully is to keep your tweets *relevant* and not just piggyback on the trend's popularity.

✔ **Mobile and device marketing.** With iAd, Apple offers advertisers a way to target iPhone and iPad users, based on demographics, geographical location, and their interests. These unique ads can be highly interactive mini applications that allow users to do things like get instant coupons or even configure an outfit and have it set aside at the nearest store for pick up. Another popular marketing tactic is the use of QR (quick response) codes. These are the funny symbols, as shown in Figure 3-13, which you can print in your offline marketing materials. Users scan these codes with their phones, which brings them to whatever web page you desire — a content entry form, a video, or even an instant discount coupon.

© PhotoARTZ. www.photoartz.com

Figure 3-13: Users can scan QR codes with their phones to quickly access a website. QR codes are becoming increasingly creative, as this example for PhotoARTZ illustrates.

✔ **Search engine marketing.** Most people find new websites by using a search engine such as Google. When you type a term in the Search field of one of these sites, up comes a listing of sites that match your key words and phrases. If you do nothing other than publish your website, a search engine will find you simply by looking in your page's meta tags, alt tags, page title, and actual page content for keywords. This is what's called *natural search* (or SEO — search engine optimization, which I discuss further in Chapter 14). You can also purchase keywords at search engines to help ensure that your site appears in the results list when people search. This paid search tactic is called SEM, or *search engine marketing.*

✔ **E-mail marketing.** Depending on your customer demographic, e-mail marketing may or may not be an effective tool. When you register at a website and give them your e-mail address, unless you specifically uncheck all the hidden boxes, expect to be bombarded with daily or weekly e-mails. There are all kinds of studies that say what days, and even what times, are best to send out marketing e-mails and why. It makes a difference if you are targeting a consumer or a business customer. If you are trying to reach teens, a lot of them don't even have e-mail addresses; they are on social sites instead. If you do decide on an e-mail campaign, your e-mails must contain a link that the customer can use to unsubscribe.

✔ **Link exchanges.** In the past, exchanging links with partner sites was a key way to navigate the Internet. Today, with modern search engines, link exchanges are primarily important for SEO purposes. Chapter 14 delves deeper into how links can help make your site rate higher in a user's search query (meaning it would display more toward the top in the search results list). The short explanation is that search engines see "inbound" links (as they are called) to your site as a boost to credibility. For example, if Coca-cola.com had a link to your site, search engines would assume that you are an important or popular player and give you a better ranking. It counts as a "vote" for your page.

Be sure to limit your inbound links to the genuine article — and that you have a reasonable number of them. If a site uses too many link exchanges, search engines see that as _link farming_ — in effect, spamming with links — and penalize such sites with lower ranking.

Wireframing

After a pre-wireframing exercise, you can fill in the details of each page. (A pre-wireframing round is an optional step recommended for large, complex sites. Most sites just go right to wireframes from the sitemap.)

Wireframes serve as a sort of laundry list of what goes on each page from a content and media perspective, and also map out the *interaction design* (how users use tools on the page or navigate content). Here are some examples of what your wireframe might show:

- ✔ What copy — and how much of it — goes on the page
- ✔ Which CMS objects go on the page (if you're using a content management system)
- ✔ What kind of images and media (such as Flash and video files) go on the page
- ✔ Your technical and interaction plan for the page — links, widgets such as drop-down menus, expanding content areas, check boxes, and buttons

I create wireframes at-size, meaning they are the same widths and heights of my final web page. (As of this writing, 800 x 600 is still the lowest common denominator size for a web page — which accounts for laptop and device viewing.) That way, I can get a real sense for how much content comfortably fits on each page before a user has to scroll. Otherwise, you may have trouble at the Design stage trying to squeeze all the stuff required by the wireframe onto the page. Conversely, the page can look sparse if the content doesn't actually take up as much room as the wireframe suggested.

Wireframing is an important step that you should not leave out of any interactive project — whether it's for a mobile app, a Flash presentation at a trade show, or (of course) a website. Like a good architectural blueprint, the wireframe is your opportunity to work out all the content and interaction design issues on paper with not only the client but also the technical team who builds the site.

You don't need to build a wireframe for every page of the site. You need only to make a wireframe for each unique layout. For example, if you have 100 product detail pages in your page index, you can build just one wireframe that shows how the product detail page works. If one or two product pages have a slightly different layout or content twist to them, however, it's a good idea to make a special product-detail wireframe just for them.

It's important that your wireframes look as boring and diagrammatic as possible. They're usually in grayscale, with lines, boxes, gray boxes, and dummy text. This is to make sure clients understand clearly that they are looking at a skeleton and not a proposed visual design. All too often, I see designers try to create beautiful wireframes, only to have it backfire: The client focuses on the design instead of the function.

Presenting Content on the Page

When building your wireframes, remember that you are not limited to a static presentation of text and graphics. Many technologies — from Flash animation to DHTML — help you maximize your page space and present content in more interesting and interactive ways. In this section, I discuss insights for presenting differ-ent kinds of content and how to "annotate" such features and functionality in the margins of each wireframe.

Indicating text on a wireframe

Because you're sharing wireframes with clients and team members alike, I indicate all navigational elements and headlines for major content sections with readable text to orient them. All other copy components can be indicated with so-called *greek* text (which is actually Latin gibberish) that reflects their allocated character count (the number of letters, punctuation, and spaces) so you get a sense of actual text-block size. Figure 4-3 shows an example of integrated readable and greek text.

You can search the Web for **lorem ipsum generator** to find sites that generate paragraphs of greek text — and even specific character counts — that you can copy and paste right into your wireframes.

Be clear with clients and team members alike that the readable text is for communication purposes only and that final copy comes from the writers in due time. I've found placeholder text, and even greek text, on high-profile websites upon launch because the developers simply copied what they saw on the wireframes and no one caught it!

Working with a content management system

A *content management system* is a user-friendly website or application that offers site administrators secure access into the database that populates their website. By logging in to a CMS, a website's manager can easily add, remove, and update content stored in the database. The benefit of using a CMS to store text and graphics is that once you define a bunch of content types such as "short description," "product name," and "product thumbnail image," you create instances of these objects, fill them with actual copy or images, and then assign them to one or more web pages. That way, if you update the instance in the CMS, the content automatically updates wherever it's used on the site. This strategy separates the content from the web page presentation to give you more flexibility for future design and content changes, making the site easier to maintain.

If your site uses a content management system, a Content Strategist works closely with the Information Architect (on smaller teams, this can be one and the same person) to first identify all the different content types a site has and then determine which content types go on each page. To keep track of all the content types, their instances, and which pages they reside on, you can create a content inventory spreadsheet.

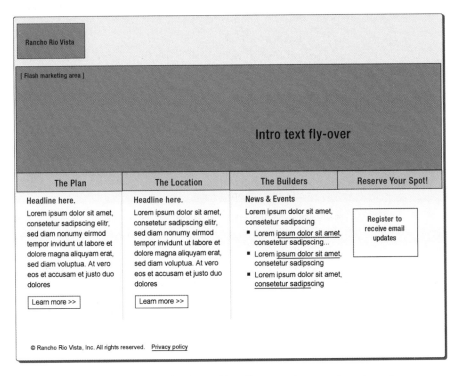

Figure 4-3: Use legible text for navigation and headlines to orient people and greek (unreadable) text for everything else on your wireframe.

Maximizing your space

Most people have small computer monitors, and many people are browsing websites through smart phones and devices. If you hold up an 8½ x 11-inch piece of paper horizontally, you're looking at the size of most people's windows on the World Wide Web. After you factor in the browser's interface with all its buttons across the top, favorites tabs, and scroll controls, the viewing space devoted to the Web is whittled down to a postcard size, or about 800 x 600 for many users. This scrawny window is your web-design canvas.

Here are some organizational and interactive strategies to help you better present your content on this wee little space:

✔ **Scroll to see less important content.** You simply can't shove everything into the viewable area — the first 800 x 600 pixels of the browser window. So, place the high-priority items within that initial window and lower priority items below the fold (described in the earlier section "Mapping out content zones"). During the zoning exercise in the pre-wireframing stage, you decide which elements are above and below the fold.

Give visual clues to let users know more stuff is below the fold by purposefully showing headlines or the tops of images that lead to more stuff below. Users don't mind scrolling, just as long as the page doesn't go on forever. A good rule is to target the total page height to twice the initial viewable height (so 1200 pixels for an 800-wide-by-600-tall page).

✔ **Use horizontal space too.** You can use technologies like Flash or HTML 5 to present horizontally scrolling content or a "carousel" of rotating content. Take a look at Figure 4-4: On this page, there are three horizontally scrolling areas (*carousels*): the top *hero space*, the middle *brand finder*, and the bottom *product finder*.

This interface has enough visual clues — also called *affordances* in highfalutin circles — to let users know they can explore a horizontally rotating array of content.

✔ **Layer your content.** Another way to maximize the viewing space is to reveal layers of content on top of the web page as the user rolls over or clicks something. You can hide and show content layers through technologies like JavaScript, DHTML (Dynamic HTML), and Flash. Typical uses of this strategy are expanded content views upon rollover (shown in Figure 4-5) and enhanced drop-down menus like the one shown in Figure 4-6.

✔ **Design a revolving door of content.** Because web page space is at a premium, another dimension that you need to consider is time. If you can't fit everything that you want inside the viewable area, you may want to think about animating the area. This way, you can cycle a lot of clickable links in and out over time in a relatively small space rather than crowding them all on the page at once. Take a look at Figure 4-4 again. The *hero area* (large central image and message) at the top automatically rotates through a number of promotions, each one a link to a detail page.

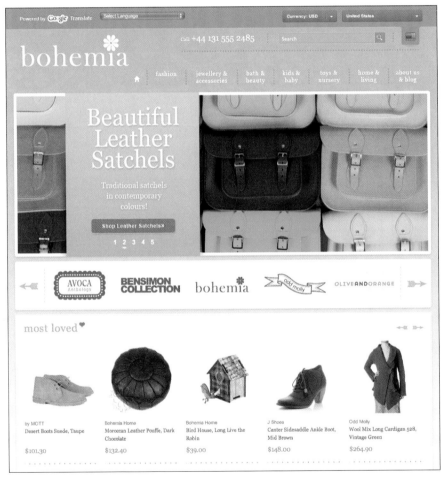

© Bohemia Design Ltd. www.bohemiadesign.co.uk

Figure 4-4: Three scrolling carousels with the featured item at the top, brand finder in the middle, and product finder at the bottom.

Figure 4-5: A user rollover expands this content module on a Disney website to reveal more information.

Figure 4-6: DHTML can produce an "enhanced" drop-down menu that offers organized options when a user rolls over a navigational item.

Annotating your wireframes

Sometimes web pages contain highly interactive components that must be explained in the wireframes via annotations. *Annotations* are simply margin notes that describe how elements on the page work, what triggers the interaction, and what content displays in different scenarios. By numbering areas of the wireframe, and numbering your notes, you can efficiently describe the interaction detail. Often, as shown in Figure 4-7, you'll also need to include an inset diagram that shows a different state that appears upon a user action such as a rollover or click.

TIP

If the web page has a robust interactive Flash component on it, your web page wireframe can't possibly capture all of its interaction design too. Therefore, simply indicate a Flash element by drawing a box representing its relative size and shape. In your annotations, indicate that the box is a Flash element, and reference any external wireframe or storyboard documents — such as the example shown in Figure 4-8 — that it may have just for itself. Take a look at the accompanying sidebar for some ideas of how you can utilize Flash as part of your user interface.

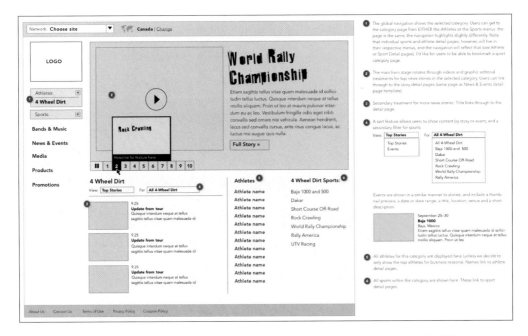

Figure 4-7: This annotated wireframe with numbered callouts also has insets that show the different states of content as users interact with it.

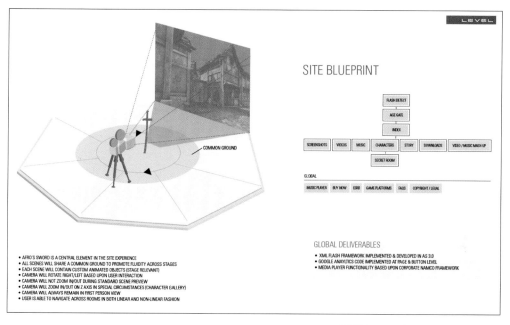

SITE BLUEPRINT

- AFRO'S SWORD IS A CENTRAL ELEMENT IN THE SITE EXPERIENCE
- ALL SCENES WILL SHARE A COMMON GROUND TO PROMOTE FLUIDITY ACROSS STAGES
- EACH SCENE WILL CONTAIN CUSTOM ANIMATED OBJECTS (STAGE RELEVANT)
- CAMERA WILL ROTATE RIGHT/LEFT BASED UPON USER INTERACTION
- CAMERA WILL NOT ZOOM IN/OUT DURING STANDARD SCENE PREVIEW
- CAMERA WILL ZOOM IN/OUT ON Z AXIS IN SPECIAL CIRCUMSTANCES (CHARACTER GALLERY)
- CAMERA WILL ALWAYS REMAIN IN FIRST PERSON VIEW
- USER IS ABLE TO NAVIGATE ACROSS ROOMS IN BOTH LINEAR AND NON-LINEAR FASHION

GLOBAL DELIVERABLES

- XML FLASH FRAMEWORK IMPLEMENTED & DEVELOPED IN AS 3.0
- GOOGLE ANALYTICS CODE IMPLEMENTED AT PAGE & BUTTON LEVEL
- MEDIA PLAYER FUNCTIONALITY BASED UPON CORPORATE NAMCO FRAMEWORK

© LEVEL | A Rosetta Company. www.level-studios.com

Figure 4-8: Flash wireframe storyboards show dynamic interaction models such as this interactive 360-degree panoramic space.

Creating flexible interfaces with animation

One entertainment client wanted its website to showcase a variety of movies on the home page. Each month this client wanted to show a different collection of movies — some months, only four movies; during other months, as many as ten. This simple requirement, however, would result in an interface that looked sparse one month and overcrowded the next, which presented a big challenge for my design team.

The solution was a modular, animated media space on the home page that rotated through all the choices. The interface showed no more than three to four choices on the screen at any one time. In addition, the modular approach made updating easy. Each month, the client simply built icons for the new movies and put them into rotation.

Getting Around in Style

Other than the visual design, determining how a user will navigate the site is one of the more challenging creative tasks that you face. The main goal is to make people feel in control of the site and capable of getting around quickly and efficiently. Nothing is worse than a user feeling lost in your site.

To help people get around and stay oriented, your navigation scheme must be a road map of the entire site, complete with "you are here" signs. In this section, I discuss a number of tips and standard design conventions to keep in mind when designing your interface.

Global navigation

Remember the famous line from the 1970s TV commercial: "How many licks does it take to get to the center of a Tootsie Pop?" With candy, the more licks, the better. On the Web, however, the opposite is true: Users won't find anything tasty about navigating through gobs of pages. Your goal is to get users as quickly as you can to their desired content.

The best way to reduce the number of clicks is to provide your primary, secondary, and tertiary navigation sets on each page of the site. This strategy, called *global navigation,* enables people to quickly navigate from one main section to the next without needing to retrace any steps. Additionally, it's important that these navigation sets are always located in the same place and do not change what they offer (swapping navigation options in and out). This consistency provides a mental anchor for the user.

A global navigation system also gives people a sense of the website's size. For example, Apple is well known for their high usability standards. Figure 4-9 clearly shows which section you are in by highlighting it in the navigation, and how many other options there are to explore.

Section navigation

After users select a category from the primary, secondary, or tertiary navigation group (see Chapter 3 for more on navigation groups), they're transported into a section. Assuming that the section has a few levels of content within it, you need a way to navigate through it. A typical practice is to reveal a set of *section navigation* choices on the page. These choices are unique to their section, but the region you select to display them is the same region used to display section navigation for other areas of the site.

Figures 4-10 through 4-12 illustrate a few common ways you can represent section navigation. In Figure 4-10, the user clicks the Products link and sees the first level of section navigation displayed on the left. As shown in Figure 4-11, if the user clicks the Shoes link, the user goes to the Shoes page, and the section navigation expands to reveal a second level of navigation within Shoes.

Alternatively, as shown in Figure 4-12, you can display the section navigation fully opened. The advantage is that users can quickly see all the first- and second-level content with a section. The disadvantage is that the navigation can take up a lot of room and may look cluttered and overwhelming to the user.

© Apple, Inc. www.apple.com

Figure 4-9: Apple's global navigation system allows users to stay oriented and to quickly traverse from one section to the next.

Figure 4-10: This section navigation design reveals the first level of pages in the Products area of the website.

Figure 4-11: This section navigation design reveals first- and second-level pages in the Products area.

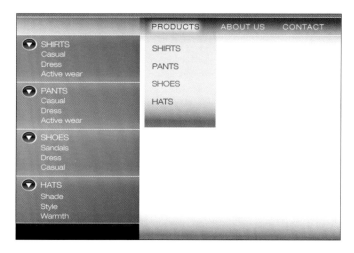

Figure 4-12: Section navigation is often shown as a drop-down menu as well as on the page itself.

Figure 4-12 also shows how section navigation is often included as a drop-down menu that displays when the user rolls over a main navigation choice. Typically, just the first level of pages is shown, but *flyout* menus can provide quick access to second-level pages. It is okay to have redundant section navigation — showing it both on the page and including it as a drop-down menu in the global navigation system.

Leaving a trail of bread crumbs

If Hansel and Gretel can use a trail of bread crumbs to find their way back through the forest, just think of what a digital version of bread crumbs can do for visitors to your website. *Bread crumbs,* as they're actually called in the web-design industry, are text links you leave in a trail that marks your steps as you go deep into a section, as shown in Figure 4-13.

Bread crumbs are helpful to navigate sites that have navigation that goes more than two levels deep within a section. For example, if you use the section navigation to go down to a page that has even more links on it, you are now diving into a third or fourth level of the section's hierarchy. It's just not practical to display third- and fourth-level navigation on the page. So the bread crumbs can simply record your steps and get longer and longer as you dive deeper (hopefully no more than four levels or you're getting into the catacombs of the site!).

Bread crumb trail

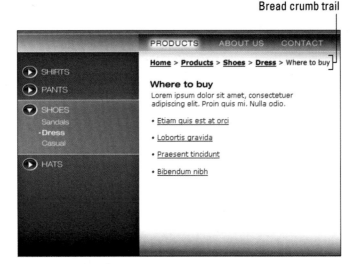

Figure 4-13: This bread-crumb trail provides a convenient way to retrace your steps in a site.

Each bread-crumb link provides a quick way to retrace your steps back up the hierarchy. You don't have to follow the links in sequence; you can click any link in the trail to jump quickly back to a different level in the hierarchy. The trail also gives you a good idea of where you are in the site. Unlike with a global navigation scheme, however, you cannot jump across to *another* section; you can only jump back to a level *within* a section. Think of a bread-crumb system as the browser's Back button on steroids.

Graphically, the design convention for a bread-crumb interface is to show each previous step as an active text link followed by a character (arrow, colon, or pipe), all in a simple row. The last entry at the end of the trail represents the current page you're on, so it should *not* be a link — and it should look different. If it were a link, it would simply reload the page — not the ideal user experience.

Combining navigation techniques

When you combine the power of a global navigation system with a bread-crumb-style navigation trail, you have a flexible interface that's pretty close to foolproof, and one that's robust enough to handle large-scale sites with multiple levels of content within each section.

Stay in control of your metaphors

A client once asked me to fix a project that was long overdue and way over budget. The project used a 3D office interface to organize all the navigation choices — choices that had nothing to do with an office, by the way.

The 3D artwork looked cool, but it took up the entire screen, leaving no room for the actual content except to appear in a layer on top — covering up the navigation. The interface looked like an actual office — with desks, file cabinets, phone, computer, and so on. All the content choices were mapped on the various objects in the room, and there were no labels to tell you

what was what. Not only did the "office look" have nothing to do with the content choices, but the 3D interface was also expensive to design, produce, and update.

User test after user test revealed that no one could correctly associate the navigation choices with the room objects. Even though the client was totally infatuated with the 3D interface, it just wasn't working for the site. In less than 30 days, we chucked the 3D interface and designed an elegant, straightforward solution that salvaged the project.

Here's how to use these navigation devices together: Use the global navigation system (your primary navigation set plus your secondary and tertiary navigation sets if your site is large) to provide access on every page to all your main sections. This lets people bounce around quickly to find the areas they're looking for. If your primary sections have a lot of subpages, use a drop-down menu to reveal subsection navigation. As people drill down into a deep section, provide a bread-crumb navigation trail to help them stay oriented and able to back out of the section. The idea here is functional simplicity; the accompanying sidebar provides an example of what happens when style overcomes substance and metaphors run amuck.

Use graphical themes, not metaphors

As Freud once said, "sometimes a cigar is just a cigar." Designers are commonly tempted to use real-world metaphors as a creative way to organize and navigate web content — or other interactive content, for that matter. In my experience, these kinds of metaphors can get quickly out of control. They constrain your content and navigation options because you're forced to find things that make sense for the metaphor *and not the content.*

For example, take a look at Figure 4-14. In this case, the website for an ice cream company has been designed to emulate a pantry shelf. There are no labels visible at first, and you must invest in rolling over each item to see what it is and where it might take you.

Interaction Design

Interaction design is different from information design. This is often a major point of confusion for people new to web design. While information design deals with the overall structure of a website and the best way to organize content, *interaction design* is the actual flow that users follow to complete tasks such as signing up for a site's newsletter, navigating from one page to the next, or buying a number of products and going through the checkout process.

As a designer, you must think through all the possible steps your users have to take to complete a task. You must anticipate their questions and concerns each step of the way, and think of how you can facilitate successful completion. If the steps are too complex or the interface is unclear, the users will get frustrated and abandon the task. In addition to deciding on the appropriate use of widgets like check boxes, menus, links, icons, and buttons, the visual design and physical placement of the interface elements can either enhance or detract from the user's ability to navigate successfully through a task. For example, if you place the Submit button on the top-left of a form, you're putting it in an uncommon spot. Users are accustomed to completing a form first and *then* clicking a Submit button found at the bottom. Or, if your Submit button is just a simple text design, the users may not recognize it — it's a good bet they're looking for something that *looks* like a button.

Creating user flow diagrams

In order to work out the most logical path users should take to complete a task, interaction designers often create *user flow diagrams* like the one shown in Figure 5-1. These diagrams anticipate all the possible paths that users could take to make their way through a task. As you can see, each decision junction can go in a couple of directions, often looping back to a prior step in the task.

After you account for all the possible outcomes, you can figure out how best to design the interaction. For example, you might decide to do the following with your design:

✔ Present the initial set of options in a menu that dynamically updates the page with the appropriate content.

✔ Include a Forgot Password link, and ability to create a new account, on the first page of the login sequence.

✔ Include a Register Me check box at the close of an online sales process to encourage registrations because you've already captured more than half the data you need anyway.

✔ Provide users with feedback, letting them know they're on (say) Step 2 of 5.

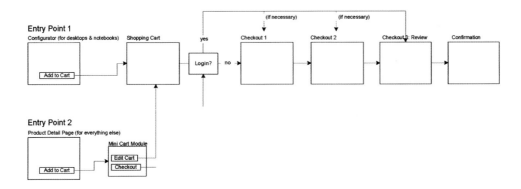

Figure 5-1: A user flow diagram maps all the possible routes a user can take toward completing a task.

Going with the flow

Most tasks are unique to your website, requiring you to create site-specific user flows and figure out the best interface design to get someone through a particular task. However, your website includes a number of common tasks such as logging in, getting back to the home page, and searching. For these everyday tasks, you can use standard interaction models that have emerged as the Web has matured over the last few years.

Here are a few common conventions to keep intact, or at least understand fully before you tweak them into new variations:

✔ **Search function.** If you're providing a search function on your site, keep in mind that most search functions are located on the top right of the web page. People look for search functions in this general location so if you place it elsewhere, your visual design really needs to call it out, as shown in Figure 5-2.

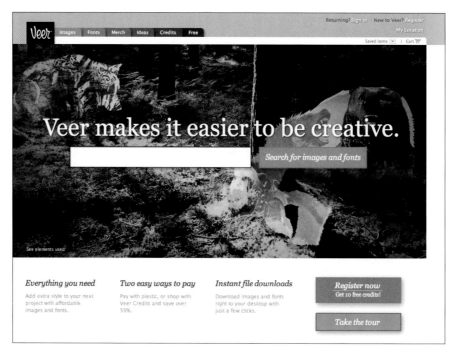

Figure 5-2: Veer.com is a media resource for designers, so search is an important feature of the site. Here you can see the search function featured prominently.

Additionally, as Figure 5-3 illustrates, search functions commonly have a 1-2-3-punch formula: The word *search,* followed by an input field (sometimes followed by a modifier drop-down menu such as All Categories, as in this example), and a button to execute the search. If you use a word other than *search* (such as *find*), or provide a text link instead of a button to execute the search, people might second-guess the functionality because it's not the formula they're accustomed to seeing.

✔ **Link to the home page.** For some reason, it has evolved that the company logo on a Web page (usually located at the upper-left) is typically the official link to the home page — especially for Western cultures. To accommodate a more global audience, however, most sites also provide an explicit Home link as part of the overall navigation scheme.

✔ **Login link.** Unlike the search function, most websites do not provide text-input fields on every page for the login function. Instead, they provide a single Login text link, somewhere at the top of the page, which doubles as the registration link (even though nothing explicitly says "registration" on the link, although often I see sites that show a combined Login/Register link). The link takes people to a login page where they can either log in with a user name and passwords or sign up to be a new user (with that function falling below the login area).

This login page often has other features like a Remember Me link, which sets a *cookie* (a wee bit of data stored on your computer) so that users don't need to log in or re-enter their credentials the next time they visit the site. There should also be a Forgot Password link for people like me who continually forget their passwords.

© *Target Brands, Inc. www.target.com*

Figure 5-3: Place the search function at the top-right on the web page, where users generally look for this feature.

Visual Design's Role in Usability

Working out the interaction design for a task is one part common sense and one part logic when it comes to figuring out the widgets to use and the flow to arrange them in. The rest is all visual design. The very placement, grouping, relative arrangement, and design of your interactive components can go a long way toward making a task flow nicely or stop in its tracks.

Compare the two examples in Figures 5-4 and 5-5. Figure 5-4 shows all the same interactive components as Figure 5-5. Figure 5-5, however, is better organized from a visual perspective, with added helper text, headlines, and examples of how to fill out the form. The example in Figure 5-5 is clearly easier to use than the example in Figure 5-4. You can use a number of design organizational and visual strategies to aid in the usability of your interaction design. The following section offers some ideas to think about.

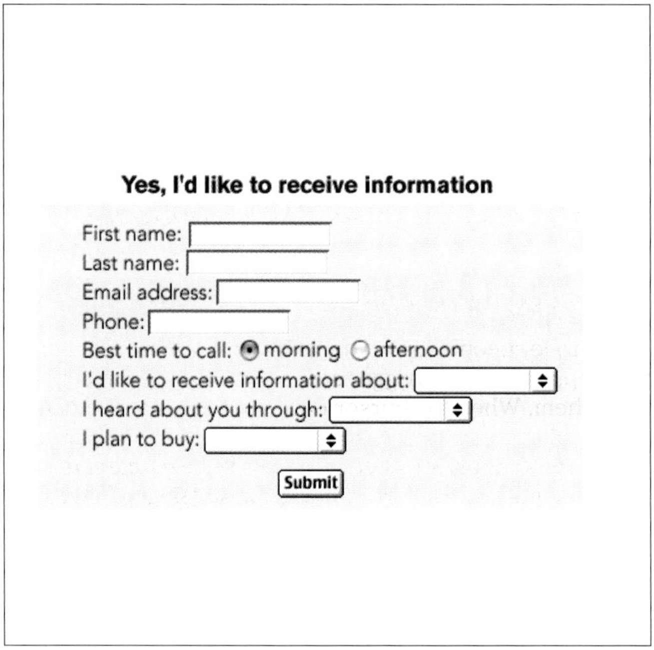

Yes, I'd like to receive information

First name:
Last name:
Email address:
Phone:
Best time to call: ● morning ○ afternoon
I'd like to receive information about:
I heard about you through:
I plan to buy:

Submit

Figure 5-4: This form example lacks visual design and organization, which makes it harder to follow.

Yes, I'd like to receive information

PERSONAL INFORMATION
* required

*First name:

*Last name:

Email address: (i.e. name@company.com)

*Phone: (with area code)

*Best time to call: ⦿ Morning
                       ○ Afternoon

ADDITIONAL INFORMATION

I'd like to receive
information about:

I heard about
you through:

I plan to buy:

Submit

Figure 5-5: This example has a better design organization, slightly better visual design, and helper text that make this form much easier to use.

Giving rollover feedback

One sure way to let people know that things are interactive is to make them change their appearance or trigger some action when the cursor comes into contact with them. When the cursor comes into contact with something onscreen, it's called a *rollover*. A number of things can occur when the mouse pointer rolls over an interactive component. If the element has a link, the cursor itself changes from an arrow to a pointing finger. That's a simple, built-in way to provide visual feedback so you can let people know that an element is interactive. However, you can provide additional feedback upon rollover — feedback that can even coach someone in how to use the navigation. Here are some ways to do that:

✔ **Change the appearance of the graphic.** You can change its appearance when the user rolls over or clicks it. For example, a normal state for a button might be a certain color, the rollover state might be orange, and the clicked state might be a dark red. Take a look at Figure 5-6. Here you can see the normal, rollover, and clicked state of a single button.

Often designers don't bother with providing a clicked state. Remember, each state is a unique graphic that you have to produce — and that the browser has to load.

✔ **Expand or animate the element.** One way to provide interactive feedback is to make the element expand or move when the mouse rolls over it. An expansion can even give users a preview of what information they'll get if they click. That allows users to see quickly which element is the one they're looking for.

Figure 5-6: A rollover changes appearance when a user rolls over or clicks it.

Designing buttons that look clickable

If you simply rely on rollover feedback (say, the cursor changing into a hand-with-pointing-finger upon rollover), you're making the user scrub the cursor all over the screen looking for interactive stuff. Therefore it's important to make interactive elements *look* clickable to begin with.

In general, you can make graphical interface elements look more clickable in one of three ways:

✔ **Label buttons with action phrases.** Uncommon-looking buttons without a text label are often disregarded. Without a label, either the button can look like a page graphic or users have no idea where it will lead them when clicked — in either case, they ignore it. Therefore it's a design best practice to put short, to-the-point labels on buttons and lead the user with no-nonsense action verbs such as *Print* or *View map.* Passive labels like *Virtual tour* or nebulous marketing-speak labels like *Magical journey* are less effective.

✔ **Add dimension.** Make button elements physically stand out on the page by giving them a three-dimensional quality.

Taking clues from everyday life

The visual design and texture of your interactive components help people know how to interact with them. Objects that you interact with on a daily basis, such as buttons, drawers, and dials, are great inspirations for the design of interactive elements on your web page. People are already well trained to use these everyday objects — everybody knows how to push buttons, pull drawer handles, and turn dials.

WEB SPEAK

For example, if you design an interactive element that looks like a nubby handle, the implication is that the user is to click and drag on that spot. In user interface-design circles, such visual clues are called *affordances*. Therefore, if your interface graphics have affordances that look like everyday objects, users have a good idea how to use them.

Take a look at both the dial interface and the drawer scheme on Apple's QuickTime player in Figure 5-7. Figuring out how to use these little widgets to control the volume and access a menu of options is easy. For the volume, you click and drag the dial to turn the audio up or down. For the drawer of options, you grab the handle-like area and drag downward.

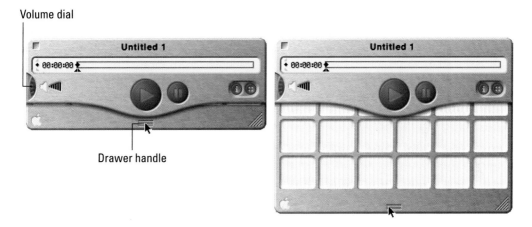

Figure 5-7: The controls on Apple's QuickTime player need no explanation on how to use them.

Grouping and nesting elements

The relative location and clustering of interactive components is as strong a clue to their interactive nature as any other visual treatment. For example, just grouping a series of similar-looking interface elements together in one graphical unit can give them a clickable appearance — even if the individual graphics themselves don't look clickable.

For example, as shown in Figure 5-8, if you group and contain a series of plain text elements that have the same font treatment, you create a strong graphical element that stands out from the other things on the page and imply interactivity. Seeing like-designed elements together in a group accomplishes two things:

- ✓ **A group implies interactivity.** A set of text or graphical elements grouped together creates one visual unit that draws people's attention. Even if the elements are not contained within a box per say, as long as they are located together and have the same visual treatment they will read as a group of interactive elements.

- ✓ **A group implies a similar function.** By visually associating a set of links, you imply that they all perform similar functions and have the same relative priority in the site. For example, all of the primary navigation buttons should look like each other. The secondary navigation set should have its own visual treatment and placement on the page to differentiate it from the primary set.

You can also imply a relationship within grouped items by *nesting* certain elements under others. For example, take a look at Figure 5-9: Because Services and Products are indented, you know that they are subsections of Offerings and not other (wholly unrelated) sections; users are unlikely to mistake the clickable elements for non-clickable elements such as headlines.

Figure 5-8: Put simple text links inside a container to set it apart from the page design and imply interactivity.

Figure 5-9: By nesting elements under others, you can imply a hierarchical relationship between them.

Providing "You are here" feedback

When users browse through sites, they like to have a sense of where they are in the scheme of things and, if they are working through tasks, how long before they will be done. To help answer these questions, your interface can provide "you are here" feedback as follows:

- **Highlight selected navigation options.** When a user clicks a navigation item, even if they selected something within a drop-down menu, it's best to keep that section highlighted to let them know which section they are in. The website shown in Figure 5-10 makes it clear which of the sections you are in.

- **Show progress.** If someone is working through a multistep task, it's a good idea to show a progress meter letting them know where they are and how much more they need to do. Figure 5-11 is a good example of a graphic that spells out all the steps and highlights the current step.

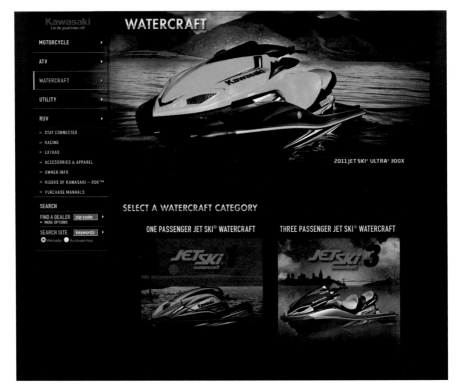

Figure 5-10: This website places its global navigation vertically down the left side, but it's still clear to see which section you're in.

Color-coding is overrated

I only mention color-coding because so many people put credence in it. I am not one of them. *Color-coding* is the practice of using a different color scheme for each section of your website. The only place color-coding works is when you have only a few sections and you want to brand each one (say, a conference with three different tracks). With only three sections, users can better associate each color with its respective area, and the color becomes meaningful. Conversely, if the site has a lot of sections, color-coding falls apart — the site gets crazy-busy, and people ignore it. Excluded in this debate are sites that use color for branding purposes and are not expecting to get a usability boost out of it.

In addition, while you can find a few colors that work well together, finding a lot of colors that work well together is difficult. Consider this: When selecting colors for the purposes of branding a number of sections, you need to select colors that all have the same *value*. Value is the relative lightness and darkness of a color. Check out Figure 5-12, where I've selected three colors that all have the same value and one that is way darker. When I go to use these colors in a site, the fourth color is going to require special handling that isn't consistent with the other colors. For example, I plan to use dark text on top of the first three colors. The fourth color requires that I use light-colored text.

Differentiating between clickable and non-clickable things

Have you ever clicked a button or icon on one page, but when you got to the next page the same button or icon was a non-clickable decoration? In Figure 5-13, the same graphic that is a button on one page changes to a static element as part of the headline on the next page. This is a big no-no. Remember the old skit on *Saturday Night Live* that featured Chevy Chase hawking a magical product: "It's a dessert topping *and* a floor wax!" In this case, the button is sometimes a "dessert topping" and at other times a "floor wax."

© Evite. www.evite.com

Figure 5-11: Numbered steps help the user keep track of where they are in a process.

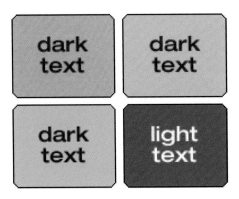

Figure 5-12: The first three colors work well together;
the fourth color requires me to treat it differently.

Reusing graphics from page to page to save on download time is smart, but not when it affects usability. The key to a good interface is to visually differentiate the interactive stuff from the content stuff.

 When you're designing a site, come up with a consistent visual strategy, or *style guide,* for the various types of clickable things from buttons, to links, to primary, secondary, and tertiary navigation elements. This way, users always know what's clickable and what's not across your entire site.

Figure 5-13: Using the same icon for different
purposes confuses form and function.

Consistency Is Everything

When users first come to your site, they look around to get oriented. Hopefully, they quickly absorb your visual and navigation strategy and get on to finding what they came for. After people initially invest in figuring out the interface, they don't want it to change on them — the interface should become *transparent* to them.

The best way to make an interface familiar and transparent to the user is to be consistent. Once you establish your visual language for clickable and non-clickable things and decide on the location for your interactive elements, follow it to the letter everywhere in the site — from the home page to the deepest subpage.

As Figure 5-14 and Figure 5-15 illustrate, changing your visual approach and/or placement strategy for interactive elements within the site not only can confuse people but also can make them think button functions have changed — even if they retain the same name. Although not recommended, the only situation in which this can work is a change from the home page to all other subpages, as in this example. Where it is unadvisable altogether is changing navigation from one section of a website to the next.

© Zinc Bistro. www.zincbistroaz.com

Figure 5-14: The home page of this website introduces the main navigation as an unconventional cluster at the bottom center.

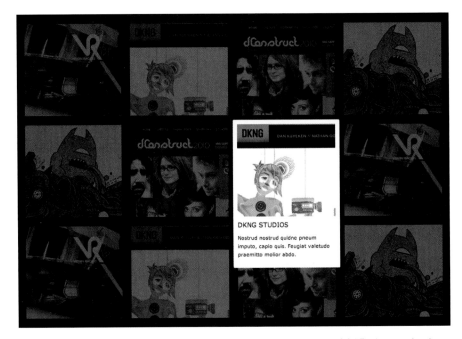

Figure 5-18: Upon rollover, this image enlarges and provides more information.

✓ **Enhanced drop-down menus.** Most people think of a drop-down menu as only a text list that expands underneath a main navigation component. This limitation doesn't have to apply to your drop-down menus. Instead of a simple text list, you can design an "enhanced drop-down menu" that reveals a neatly organized list — even with images and daily promotions.

6

User Testing: Lab Coats Not Required

In This Chapter

▶ Creating clickable wireframes to test

▶ Testing your visual designs with focus groups

▶ Prototyping key task flows

▶ Recruiting users for a test

▶ Conducting user tests

▶ Evaluating test results

*A*t some point in the design process, you have to put your work in front of a group of strangers for the ultimate litmus test: Can they figure out how to use it? And do they like how it looks?

Ideally, you should test your work as early in the design process as possible, in order to stave off any unforeseen usability problems *before* you're knee-deep in production (which is too late). By putting together a workable prototype early in the design phase, you can organize a user test, complete with a list of questions to ask and a plan for recording and evaluating the feedback.

Although a user test sounds academic and may conjure up visions of white lab coats, it's actually a fun and truly enlightening experience. You'll be surprised at the things a user test reveals about your design, both from a visual standpoint and from a usability standpoint. In this chapter, I discuss how to make prototypes that you can put in front of users and offer pointers on how to get the most out of your testing efforts. In the end, you'll be glad you took these extra steps. You'll end up with a website that is not only beautiful, but works for your audience too!

Developing Testable Prototypes

Before you can gather any useful feedback, you have to assemble a prototype that you can test. Working with a sketch on paper isn't good enough; people need to see and touch the real deal — web pages working in a browser.

I have found it useful to create two sets of testable prototypes during the design phase — *clickable wireframes* to test your information design and *HTML click-throughs* to test the usability of your visual designs. You should share both prototypes not only with end users but also with your clients so they can get a feel for — and can approve — the end product before it's built.

Creating clickable wireframes

Early in the process, clients need to understand how the site is organized. As discussed in Chapter 4, wireframes (detailed black-and-white drawings of each major web page) show what goes on the page, how the navigation and interaction work, and the general page layout. In my experience, for large or complex sites, just looking at blueprint-like wireframes on paper is not enough for the clients to visualize the interaction and organization of a site. So, after you work out the sitemap and begin wireframing, set aside some time to assemble a quick-working wireframe *prototype* of the site in HTML in which many of the clickable items are functioning. That way, clients can physically click the sketch versions of the navigation and buttons to see where they go. (***Note:*** For small sites that don't have a lot of complex interaction or many sections, walking clients through a PDF of your wireframes is plenty.) For more on sitemaps, see Chapter 3.

Most designers and information architects use Microsoft Visio or illustration programs such as Adobe Illustrator and Adobe InDesign to create wireframes. All three of these programs can export wireframes as GIFs and JPEGs. Then you can use an HTML tool such as Adobe Dreamweaver to import those GIFs and JPGs and overlay links on top of the clickable areas.

I recommend exporting wireframes as GIF files. Because wireframes are (should be) grayscale and text, you get better quality and compression when you save them as GIFs.

In Dreamweaver, insert the whole GIF wireframe into the page, just as you would insert an image. As shown in Figure 6-1, you can then draw *hotspots* (clickable regions that you define) on top of your navigation and link them up to go to your various pages. Voilà — a quick, clickable wireframe prototype that's ready to share with your clients.

If you are handy in HTML, you can take your prototype one step further by building both a working navigation system as well as any dynamic features you plan to include, such as drop-down menus or accordion spaces.

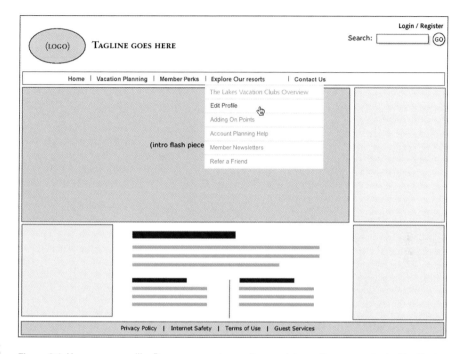

Figure 6-1: Use a program like Dreamweaver to create a prototype site you can test with clients.

Present your clickable wireframe edition to the clients as a way to help them visualize how the site is organized and how users would navigate through key tasks such as ordering a product. You can also present the clickable wireframes to end users to see if the site makes sense from their perspective. Later in this chapter, I discuss ways to conduct tests with users. At this stage, it's important to work out all the kinks in the site and get client approval before moving forward with visual design and HTML coding.

Testing your visual design

While the wireframe details are being worked out, the visual design team can create a few different "look and feel" options and test them with users. Aptly named "look and feel," these designs look real enough to pass for a home page and an interior or subpage of your site — check out Figure 6-2 — but they are not 100 percent accurate in terms of final navigation, photography, or text. However, keep in mind that users and clients are very literal. Selecting headline copy and photography that are fairly accurate to get a good read on your audience is important. All non-major text should be *greek* (gibberish Latin text, actually), but navigation choices and key headlines should be a close approximation.

For high-profile consumer websites, it's a good idea to conduct a focus group before committing to a design direction. Otherwise, the design is chosen based on the personal tastes of a few client executives — which is okay if the site is for a small-to-mid-size company. I like to get focus group feedback before showing the design options to the client. That way, you can rule out designs that just don't work at all, and come prepared with user feedback when you go into the client creative presentation to help guide the decision-making process.

To test your visual designs, follow these steps to put together a focus group:

1. **Recruit seven to ten people who represent your intended audience.**

   You can recruit them online through CraigsList.org.

2. **Print each of the design options.**

Figure 6-2: This design direction was one of three shown to the client and was ultimately selected. Notice the "greek" text.

I like to present at least three different design sets of a home page and a subpage.

3. **Mount all the designs on boards so that your focus group can get a good look at each one, refer to them, and compare them side by side.**

4. **Prepare JPEG versions of your designs (saved at 100% quality for the purposes of demonstration) and place them in HTML pages using Dreamweaver.**

   This enables you to show the focus group how each design looks on a computer screen in a browser window.

5. **Gauge people's emotional reactions to the designs.**

   See which design resonates most with the audience, given the type of business your site reflects. There's nothing fancy or scientific required here, only your keen observations of people's reactions. Sometimes there are clear winners and losers. If all rate about the same, then truthfully any of the designs can probably fare just fine in the real world.

Building an HTML click-through to test for usability

Not only do users respond to the mood created by a site's visual look and feel but, as Chapter 5 discusses, the visual design also has a big impact on how users identify interactive elements and understand how to navigate through a site. So, it's a good idea to mock up a few pages in the chosen look and feel to illustrate a user's path through a key task such as purchasing a birthday gift.

Assemble these few key pages into an HTML *click-through*. As shown in Figures 6-3 and 6-4, the click-through looks real and contains all the pages that users would see if they were to step through a task successfully. Each of the pages can be a mock-up saved as a single JPEG and placed in an HTML page. You can expand upon your initial design directions to make your first testing prototype.

For testing purposes, don't mock up only half the page and leave the rest blank. During the test, users will ask about these neglected areas. Even if you give them an explanation, they are forced to use their imagination to fill in the gaps. This can skew their reading of the page. Users need to see the page in its full context to give you the most accurate feedback.

For testing purposes, the HTML coding for each click-through page should be just enough to place the mock-up image in the page and apply a few hotspots to interactive areas that link to the next page in the task sequence. At this point, you just want to see whether the visual and interaction design work as you intended.

Now, if I were designing the page in Figure 6-4, I'd add a couple of features to give users more reasons to buy:

 ✔ A sort feature to rate selections by price and other user-selected criteria

 ✔ A drop-down menu next to "for her" so users can browse gifts in any of the "6 ways" the home page mentions

TIP

On testing day, you may consider having a few design options on hand for the users. As you begin to ask questions, you may present alternative ways of visualizing the same page — with different button treatments or layouts, for example — and ask users to compare which way they prefer.

During the testing phase, users may offer suggestions on how the interface can be better or different. After all, the whole point of user testing is to open up the design process to new ideas that better serve the end user. If you've already invested a lot of design time to make the site work a certain way, you may be reluctant to change it without a good reason. User tests may provide one.

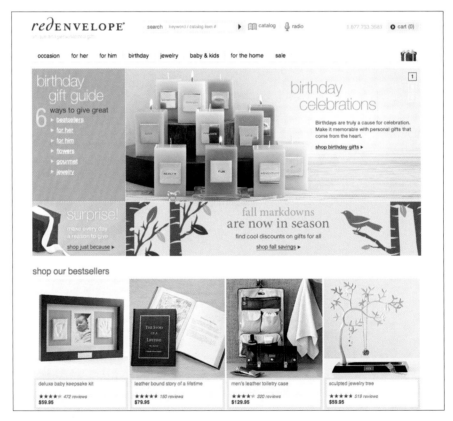

© Provide Commerce, Inc. www.redenvelope.com

Figure 6-3: This home page shows where to click to get ideas for a birthday gift, and offers "6 ways" to find one.

Cruise-line case study

For a major vacation cruise-line company (with ships bigger than the *Titanic!*), we created each wireframe in Dreamweaver. Because each wireframe was already in HTML, the prototype site virtually built itself as we created each new wireframe page. While the IAs (information architects) took some time to get comfortable building wireframes in Dreamweaver (as opposed to Visio), the time was well made up during the client approval stages. Each week we'd walk the client through a different section of the site — the online booking process and the reservation retrieval process for example. The client sessions were highly productive because, for such a large and complex site, we could ensure the site accounted for all the technical details (there were a lot of behind-the-scenes databases and processes that the site tapped into), and the client could navigate through the site to provide accurate feedback and faster approvals.

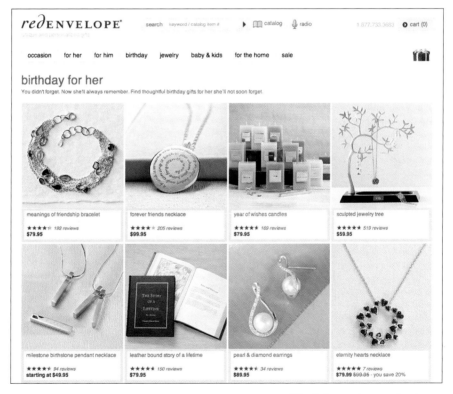

© Provide Commerce, Inc. www.redenvelope.com

Figure 6-4: Browsing a scrolling page of gift ideas "for her" is a good start but I think the site can take the design further.

Prepping for the User Test

The most efficient way to conduct a user test is to send people on a kind of scavenger hunt to perform certain tasks. Prepare a list of two to five tasks that you want to test and then create a series of click-throughs that contain all the pages needed to move through each task. Keep in mind that the click-throughs are *your* ideas about how the tasks should be done. In a user test, it's always interesting to see which path a user wants to take to get through the task. Your click-throughs, if possible, may need to support a couple of ways to get through the same task.

Along with your list of tasks, you should start thinking about what you want to find out from testing each task. Make a separate list of your own questions. This helps you to standardize a testing methodology that you can use on multiple people.

The more people you test, the more accurate the feedback you get. For example, if only one person out of five doesn't like the button design, you can probably chalk it up to the minority's subjective taste. But if that one person was the only person you tested, you could end up redesigning something that was fine in the first place.

Preparing to-do lists for users

In preparing a list of tasks for the user test, keep in mind the main goals of the website. For example, if the main objectives of the site are to get people to buy products and to become registered users, these goals should drive the list of tasks to test.

Create a task list you want each user to have (say, like the one shown in Figure 6-5) but be sure to make a separate edition for yourself that includes your own questions for users about each task. In the following example, I assume that the goals of the site are "First, get users to buy products. Second, sign up to be a registered user." Given these objectives, here's how to make a task list:

1. **Create a scenario that places the user in a particular role.**

   For example, tell them, "You're a customer looking to buy a book and sign up to be a registered user because you've heard you'll save 10 percent on your purchase." As you can see, this scenario exactly mirrors the top two goals of the site, but is a little more focused on a specific task.

   Place this scenario statement at the top of the document that you give to users. With the proper mindset, users' comments become more focused and relevant. For example, they may say, "Well, if I hear that I can get 10 percent off by registering, I'd want to register first." This is a great nugget of information! Because you want them to buy first, not register first, perhaps your designs should include a "Save 10% on your purchase by registering during checkout" message prominently throughout the store. This way, users see how to get the discount and can focus on shopping.

2. **Create three to four mini-tasks that you want the user to try.**

List these tasks below the scenario statement. The tasks can either be in the form of questions, such as "How would you buy a book called *Web Design For Dummies*?" or action requests, such as "Tell me how you would sign up to receive e-mail coupons from the company." The questions should be targeted toward a specific action — such as "How would you buy a book?" — and not too broad.

3. **Make your own cheat sheet.**

Create a separate document for yourself that lists each scenario and task set just as it does on the user's copy. At the top of your cheat sheet, however, list the main objectives of the site. Within each set of tasks, be sure to write your own questions so you can remember to ask the same things of each user. The example in Figure 6-6 shows you what I mean.

User scenario:
You're a customer looking to buy a book and register because you've heard you'll save 10% on your purchase.

Task 1:
In looking at this interface, where would you start to buy Web Design For Dummies?

Task 2:
How would you add a second product to your order, say a music CD?

Task 3:
How would you get to the check out area?

Task 4:
How would you sign up to be a registered user?

Any additional comments or suggestions?

Figure 6-5: A sample user testing sheet.

Goal:
Sell products and generate sales leads (via registration).

User scenario:
You're a customer looking to buy a book and register because you've heard you'll save 10% on your purchase.

Task 1:
In looking at this interface, where would you start to buy Web Design For Dummies?
• Can the user find the books section of the store?
• Can the user find and use the search function?
• Is the navigation clear?
• Does the user understand how to add the book to an order?

Task 2:
How would you add a second product to your order, say a music CD?
• After the user adds the book to the shopping cart, can he or she find the other product sections?
• Does the user think their initial book order will be lost if they continue shopping?

Task 3:
How would you get to the checkout area?
• Does the user find the checkout area?
• Does the user know how to continue shopping even while in the checkout process?
• Is the ordering process clear?
• What sort of order confirmation sequence does the user expect?

Task 4:
How would you sign up to be a registered user?
• Does the user see how to register?
• After registered, can the user see where to log in upon returning to the site?
• Does the user understand or care about the benefits of registering?

Any additional comments or suggestions?

Figure 6-6: Create your own "cheat sheet" version of the testing sheet.

Developing a testing methodology

After you create a list of tasks for the user and your own cheat sheet (as described in the preceding section), the next step is to come up with a testing methodology. By standardizing on one testing methodology, you have a more accurate means of evaluating the test results. In addition, you can delegate the testing to a few people on the team.

Here's a checklist to help you build your own testing methodology:

⯈ **Target audience.** Before you recruit a bunch of people to be your test subjects, you must know what kind of people to go after. Recruit people who fit the Persona profile you developed for the site (as Chapter 3 discusses). For example, a shopping site with books, music, and videos may target Internet-savvy 30- to 45-year-old professionals.

⯈ **Number of users.** The more users you test, the better your results. Testing more than a few people is critical because you can minimize the effects of each individual's bias.

For example, if five out of the six people have the same complaint, you know you have a genuine problem. A good number of people to shoot for is seven to ten people. Make sure to cast a good sampling of your target demographic.

⯈ **Testing style.** Because you can test in more than one way, you should decide which style of testing you want to use. The serious, lab-coat style of testing involves setting people up in a room by themselves behind a one-way mirror (I kid you not) and videotaping their actions as they work through the task list. I've found that this method is expensive (you'll likely need to rent a user-test lab) and it's way too intimidating for users — they don't want to look stupid on camera, so they hold back.

The other, more casual way is to sit down with them one on one, asking questions and taking notes as they respond. This method is more empowering, and I've found users are generally pretty honest with you. You can still videotape the session. Videotaping enables you to see where the mouse pointer goes on the screen as a user works through the tasks, and record any feedback in case you can't keep up with notes.

Carrying Out the User Test

The whole point of user testing is to catch the usability problems of your design before you go into production. Therefore, you must be mentally prepared for the feedback that comes out — it may not be pretty. In some cases, you may be faced with a substantial redesign if users aren't responding well to your designs and getting through key tasks.

Give yourself a good two weeks before testing day to line up enough people to make the test worthwhile. Recruiting people to drive across town and spend an hour with you can take some doing. You'll probably need to pay them, or offer some sort of perk if your client or company has something of value to offer. To help recruit them, tell them exactly how long the test takes — hopefully no more than one hour — and let them know what sort of compensation you will offer.

After you get people in the door, make sure you honor the time commitment that you promised and stick to your testing plan. Other than that, just sit back and take notes!

Finding willing guinea pigs

The real trick in user testing is to actually find and convince a bunch of people to be willing guinea pigs for your test. If your target audience is 25-to-40-year-old busy professionals, you may have a harder time recruiting people away from their jobs and families than if your target audience doesn't work in the 9-to-5 world or has flexible work hours.

If your client has an established clientele, coming up with a list of people to call on is fairly easy. Simply cull its customer database for people in your local area (unless you are conducting tests in a few cities). The best approach is to call these people directly. I've found that in this impersonal online world, people respond warmly to a personal phone call — especially when they are made to feel that their opinions count. For new websites that have no clientele yet, try finding users online through sites like CraigsList.org or recruiting on Facebook.

Friends and family may be more lenient in their feedback because they don't want to hurt your feelings. If you are using this group, remind them that the only way they can help is to be honest and forthcoming with their feedback.

After you identify a list of testers, you have to sell them on the idea of taking time out of their day to come test, or alternatively, you can bring the test to them. Here is a handy, consolidated list of a few tactics that I've found to be successful:

- ✔ **Set a time limit.** Put a time limit on the user test so people know what they're committing to, and schedule a time that's convenient for them. For example, tell a potential tester that the test portion only takes one hour, plus an extra half hour for setup and conclusion. If they come in at 1:30 in the afternoon, they can be out by 3:00 p.m.

   Make sure you follow through with the promised schedule. If you don't finish all the tasks in one hour, it's your loss. Conclude the test and thank them for their time. If you're almost finished, however, the user usually offers to stay.

- ✔ **Give out swag.** In appreciation of their participation, offer small gifts at the end of the test. Most companies have products or services that may be valuable as gift items, like event passes, software, or apparel. Or they have marketing items like nice computer totes they can offer.

✔ **Pay people.** Depending on your client's "awesomeness" factor (a car-part manufacturer may be less fun for test participants than a high-profile entertainment company), you most likely will also need to pay people in addition to giving out swag. Depending on your market, pay them a reasonable hourly rate. Provide appetizers and drinks, and they are more than happy.

✔ **Send out thank-you cards.** After the test, send users a thank-you card in the mail. Although this isn't a sales tactic to sway people to come in, it's a great way to build good faith for the future. You may be able to call on these people again, or use them as references to find other testers later.

Another testing method to consider is online testing, whereby your users can log in to a website and test from the convenience of their location. Online resources such as UEgroup, at `www.uegroup.com`, offer such services.

Conducting the test

Before you sit down with users in front of a computer, you need to get them to sign a release form and let them know you're videotaping the session. If you are testing with minors, you need to check state laws on videotaping them.

Before you start the test, prepare your users by reviewing the scenario and the task list and describing how you plan to conduct the test. Tell them (for example) that

✔ You'll be asking a few questions about each task, and taking notes.

✔ They should vocalize their stream of thoughts and reactions as they work through a task.

✔ They can criticize the design or express doubts such as "I'm not sure what that button does or where it will take me."

✔ If they can't do something, it's probably the design's fault and the reason they are here today. So they shouldn't feel stupid about not completing any of the tasks or voicing their honest reactions.

✔ They're looking at a semi-functional prototype, and not all the functionality is hooked up yet. Ask them to tell you where they would click before clicking, and to tell you what they expect will happen when they click.

Start on the first page of your HTML click-through and ask the user to complete the first task. Then, sit back and start taking notes as they talk out loud about what they're thinking. Observe where their eyes and the mouse go on the screen. You should hear them say things like "I'm looking for a Search field. I should be able to just type what I want to find and click a button." Give them some time to think through the problem before you ask any questions about the task.

Avoid asking leading questions that give clues, such as "Do you think that this Search button looks clickable?" Not only are you pointing out a button that users should find on their own, but you're also expressing doubt about the button's design — thus skewing their perception of it.

Because your click-through storyboard is limited in its functionality and only illustrates a couple of paths through each task, you must moderate each click. As soon as users tell you where they would click, ask them what kind of page they expect to see next. If they choose a button that you've enabled for the prototype, let them click and then gauge their reaction as they view the next page.

If they choose a path that's not illustrated in your click-through, they may have just given you a great alternative way of navigating to consider. On the other hand, maybe your interface isn't clear. After they guessed "wrong," show them the path that you're proposing and ask them what they think. They may yield and tell you "Oh, that makes more sense, I just didn't see the button," or they may say, "That makes no sense at all." If their response is the former, you need to redesign the button or put it in a different place. If they say the design makes no sense at all, ask them (in a spirit of polite curiosity) if they can think of a better way to perform the task.

After the user completes a task, or you notice that the user is stuck, ask the bulk of your remaining questions and then ask for opinions on the best ways to do the task. After you wrap up the task and your questions, move on to the next task. Each task should take about 15 minutes to complete.

"Houston, We Have a Problem . . .": Evaluating Results

After a day of spending an hour or so with several people — running each one through the same set of tasks and questions — you should have many pages of notes to evaluate. The best way to sift through and make sense of all this data is to transcribe your notes into some sort of visual graph.

Consolidate all the feedback for each task into one table, as shown in Figure 6-7. This table shows how you can organize the feedback from testing the click-through in Figure 6-3. A table is a great way to compare all the notes for each task so you can better see where the problems lie. Make a grid that lists each user down one axis and each of your questions along the other axis. Also, leave one column for the users' suggestions and comments. At the top of the document, include the site's goals, the user scenario, and the testing methodology you used, so that you and the client have a better basis from which to analyze the feedback.

Site Goals:

Sell products and generate sales leads via registrations.

User Scenario:

You're a customer looking to buy a book and sign up to be a registered user because you've heard you'll save 10% on your purchase.

Testing Method:

3 subjects aged 25–40, all professionals with incomes over 60K per year.
One-on-one testing, 1 hour video taped session
On-screen click through shown Web browser

Task 1: How would you buy a book called Web Design For Dummies?

	Can the user find the books section of the store?	Are the navigation buttons clear?	Can the user find and use the search function?	Does the user understand how to add the book to an order?	Additional Comments and Suggestions?
User 1: Male aged 32	Yes, store sections are clearly marked.	Yes, likes consistent mini tab for all buttons.	Yes, though not sure why it's different color or upside down.	Yes, once I found the book, it was easy to use the mini tab button to add the book to my order.	Thinks the search function should always be present on the page.
User 2: Female aged 25	Yes, likes button treatment	All the buttons except for the subnav buttons under main tabs. Not clear that you are in the Featured Products section.	Did not realize that it was clickable. It looks different than the rest of the buttons.	Yes, very clear.	Make the subnav buttons look like the other tabs or like mini buttons. Try a different highlighting system.
User 3: Female aged 36	Yes, easy to find	Not sure about the subnav treatment under the main tabs. Didn't realize that they were in the Featured Products section.	Found it ok, just does not like it's treatment. When you click the other tabs, you go to a page. When you click the Search tab, a mini search window appears. Thinks everything should be consistent.	Yes, likes the way that all the mini buttons look the same.	Feels strongly that the Search button should not be an upside down tab– maybe have the mini search function always visible on the page. Also, try a different way of highlighting the subnav – make it look more like the main tabs?

Figure 6-7: User test results arranged in a table help you see what worked and what didn't.

With this sort of visual arrangement, you can easily see where the problems lie and evaluate what things need fixing. By using a spreadsheet, you'll notice that the comment column often fills up with the same suggestions for fixing the big problems. This makes your redesign process that much easier.

Armed with this data, you can *iterate* your designs — try new, improved versions — and share the updates with your client. You can now move forward into production with more peace of mind that you are on the right track.

Part III
Designing Web Graphics

The 5th Wave   By Rich Tennant

"Why don't you try blurring the brimstone and then putting a nice glow effect around the hellfire."

looks to be a credible site. These are two big responsibilities for a humble graphic interface. As I discuss in Chapter 5, the way you design buttons — even text links — and where you place them can make or break the usefulness of a website or mobile application.

If visitors can't find your site navigation elements because (a) nothing on the page looks clickable, or (b) elements take forever to download, or (c) are placed "below the fold," people will get confused and your site will not be very successful. Notice the difference between the two buttons shown in Figure 7-1. The image on the top just looks like a graphic, but the image on the bottom looks like a 3D clickable button. What could make this button better? A better label. "Holiday Sale" is too passive. Leading with a verb like "Shop" or "Visit" works best.

Figure 7-1: Although both images are buttons, only the 3D lozenge one looks clickable.

Aside from designing the interactive components to look interactive, you also need to be mindful of where you place them in the layout. If you change the relative location of a button from one page to the next, it makes it that much more difficult for the user to find. For example, imagine a "Shop Sales Items" button sometimes placed at the top-right of a list of store items and sometimes at the lower-left. I'm sure the user would find the button — especially if it had the same visual treatment — but it just makes them have to look for it all over again. The rule of consistent location and visual treatment is especially rigid when it comes to site navigation graphics.

Developing page templates

To aid in the quest for design consistency, ease of use, and to make engineering more practical, most modern websites are built with just a handful of different design layouts called *templates*.

These templates are designed to handle all the different kinds of content, messaging, and tasks that the website will require. To give you an example, the Monster Energy website (shown in Figure 7-2) uses only about 12–14 different layout templates to make up the whole website. I know because I designed the site. Some of those templates include Home, All Sports Landing, Sports Landing, Athlete Detail, and News Item Detail. All athletes use the same Athlete Detail page template. The template is populated dynamically from a database with the athlete's unique images and information.

The other thing to note about templates is that while they each allow for a variety of layout arrangements (of internal page content), the navigation is held in the same location throughout the site. In Figure 7-2, the primary navigation is located vertically on the left, while the secondary "header" navigation goes across the top, and the footer navigation brings up the bottom.

© Monster Beverage Company. www.monsterenergy.com

Figure 7-2: The Monster Energy website uses just 12–14 templates to power the whole site.

Incidentally, this site has a good example of a *super footer*. As shown in Figure 7-3, a super footer is a footer-on-steroids that lives at the bottom of the page. It contains a number of redundant text links to all portions of the site, but notice that it is very *keyword-rich* by design. Super footers not only provide a quick means of navigating the whole site but are also an opportunity for SEO (*search engine optimization*): By injecting your site with more searchable words and phrases, you enhance your site's natural search ranking when people search for those terms.

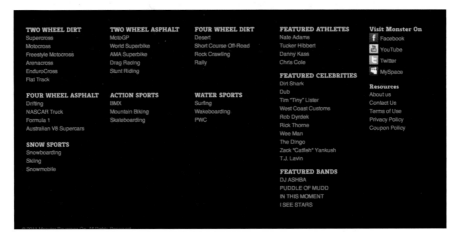

Figure 7-3: Super footers are an SEO opportunity, boosting your site's natural search ranking, giving users an alternative way to navigate.

The information and wireframing process will ultimately determine the number and types of templates that you'll need to design for a site. Once the different templates are identified, you can begin to design visual "comps" for each template.

Creating comps

Comps, as they're called in web-design circles, are visual mock-ups of the proposed design. They are the designer's chance to establish what the site will ultimately look like — from the page's background colors and textures, font choices, colors, and sizes to navigation and button design. The key to designing comps is to focus on designing the templates discussed in the last section. There is usually a comp developed for each template (often with multiple Photoshop layers and layer sets that show different states of interactive components). Therefore, when designing a comp, you must think of each template's pillars. What is the grid that this page uses? How and where will different types of text elements display? Are there expandable and collapsible sections for which you need to show both views? Is there a special treatment or border for images or forms? What do the navigation and buttons look like?

When developing comps, I like to pick a sample page that uses one of the templates. I will use actual headlines, button copy, and photos (or close to what will be the actual copy and photos) in order to capture the right mood and tone of the proposed site. For photos, try searching `http://www.istock photo.com`. For all other support text, body copy, and such, just used "greek" text (actually Latin gibberish). You can generate paragraphs of "greek" text to copy and paste into your comps from `http://www.lipsum.com`.

Often times, a comp will require you to include browser system elements like scroll bars, radio buttons, and check boxes. There is no need to chop up screenshots or (worse) create custom widgets from scratch (unless that's what you are going for). There are online sites such as Designers Toolbox (shown in Figure 7-4) that allow you to download Photoshop files that have these elements on transparent layers, making it easy to incorporate them into your designs.

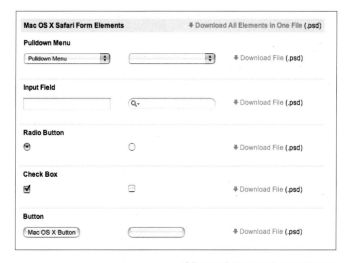

© Designers Toolbox. www.designerstoolbox.com

Figure 7-4: Online design resource sites like Designers Toolbox provide common interface graphics that you can download and incorporate into your comps.

Blending color, type, and graphics

To create an effective web page, you have to follow basic design principles for blending color, type, and graphics. You must also use your page space efficiently to achieve a layout that's not too crowded, is feasible and practical from an engineering standpoint, is flexible enough to display a variety of media, and keeps all the important elements "above the fold" — within the initial viewable space. Whew! That's a lot.

Here are some guidelines for color, type, and graphics to consider for applying tried and true design principals in the context of designing digital sites.

Choose a brand-appropriate color palette

Most businesses creating sites already have an established brand color palette and guidelines that give you a head start for these types of projects. For new products or initiatives, events, and so on, however, there may not be an established look. In these scenarios, it's helpful to ask your client for a list of adjectives that describe the mood of the site they are looking for. Or ask them if they have a palette preference or aversion. From there, you can establish a color palette and a set of styles that will work for the entire site. Here are some thoughts:

- **Lights and darks.** Your site will always need a range of color values in order to create contrast. I like to pick four sets of colors like the color palette shown in Figure 7-5: the primary brand colors, the accent colors, the lights, and the darks. I like to pick lights and darks that are not too strongly colored so that they support the primary and accent colors and allow them to "pop" visually. Additionally, I ensure that all of the colors I select work well together when placed side by side. By establishing a standard color palette to draw from, you can help ensure a consistent and harmonious feel across the site.

- **Background color.** There are really just two choices for the background that goes behind *content*: a light or a dark background. A mid-range color background will not provide enough contrast to make text and other content legible. For information-rich and utilitarian sites, it's best to choose a light background for content unless the brand requires otherwise. A lot of light-colored text on a dark background is simply hard to read. This does not mean that your web page must be all dark or all light. See Figure 7-6 for a nice blend of light and dark backgrounds, and light and dark content on top of them.

- **Text color.** For me, the color choices of website body copy and headlines say a lot of the site's professionalism. Unless the design otherwise calls for it, I like to avoid using pure black or pure white for body copy, or colors that have too much saturation. These colors are very strong and can "buzz" on the page while the user tries to read a paragraph of text. Instead, I'll use a deep gray, perhaps hinted toward a warmer or cooler tone. Otherwise I'll use a similarly hinted off-white. This strategy allows you to choose stronger or brighter colors for headlines, bullets, and subheads.

You have to be careful with fonts because they can project a lot of personality. Depending on the font you choose, your website can express edginess, professionalism, and everything in between. Just as you choose an appropriate color scheme, you must also choose appropriate fonts for your website.

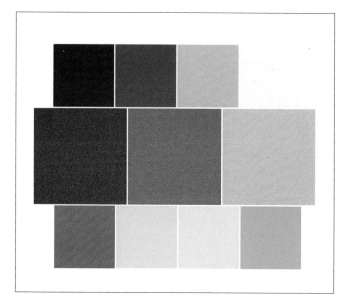

Figure 7-5: A sample palette: Muted light and dark colors are on the top row. Brand colors are in the middle row. Accent colors are on the bottom row.

Use fonts to set the mood

Generally, *serif* fonts (fonts that have little ledges on the tips of each letter, as shown in the primary navigation of Figure 7-6) convey feelings of stability, professionalism, and class. The body text of this book, for example, uses a serif font. *Sans-serif* fonts (no ledges on the tips, as shown in the body copy of Figure 7-6) convey feelings of modernism and cleanliness. On the Web, sans-serif fonts are often used for blocks of body text and subheads, as they tend to read better on the screen. Serif fonts, on the other hand, are often used for short phrases and headlines, because they are typically shown in larger font sizes, and so are legible on the screen. (Of course, this is just a baseline. Many sites use serif and san-serif fonts in the opposite way.)

Mix fonts wisely

You aren't limited to using just one typeface for your entire website. In fact, using a combination of a few fonts for different situations is best: one for headings, another for captions and pullquotes, and yet another for the body text. More than three or four fonts, however, can be excessive. Choose a few different fonts and stick with them for the entire site. Define a particular font style for each type of element and use it consistently. For example, always use the same font, color, and point size for all headlines, and use another point size and/or color for subheads.

© Peachy Green. www.peachygreen.com

Figure 7-6: This cleanly designed site uses a nice mix of darks and lights to present content.

Many designers use a mix of both serif and sans-serif fonts for a website. You can create a nice look by using one style for a heading and the other style for the body text, as illustrated in Figure 7-6.

Use graphic elements efficiently

In print design, you can use graphic elements rather freely, but in web design, large photographs or complex graphics that take up the whole page can be like lumbering elephants. Big photos mean big file sizes that download slowly. When designing web pages, use large graphics sparingly, and try to reuse graphic elements (such as button styles and background tiles) wherever possible. That way, you can define a standard set of graphic styles that the developers can turn into CSS styles that can be applied throughout the site. Additionally, as shown in Figure 7-7, you can simply use CSS code to assign color and shape to HTML elements, removing the need to use graphics at all, and making it a simple process to update an entire site just by changing a few lines of code. Such a combined use of CSS styles and images can create a visually rich site that is efficient to build and maintain, and that loads fast.

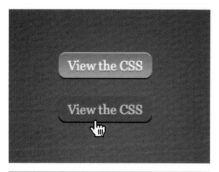

© CSS-Tricks / Chris Coyier. http://css-tricks.com/examples/
ButtonMaker

Figure 7-7: This button is not a bitmap. It is made entirely with a clever use of CSS code to define the color gradient, the corner radius, and the text.

Using a grid system

To help you lay out your web page, set up a grid that you can use to align graphics, text, and HTML elements. A grid can be anything you like — a three-column layout, two horizontal sections, or a page broken into multiple sections, as shown in Figure 7-8.

As of the writing of this book, print design can still do some tricks that HTML and CSS can't do as efficiently. For instance, an angled grid like the one in Figure 7-9 is easily possible with print design — but if you use HTML and CSS, their very nature limits your web-page grid to horizontal and vertical lines.

Also, while it's possible to rotate website elements using CSS (covered in Chapter 13), not all browsers will reliably render such effects.

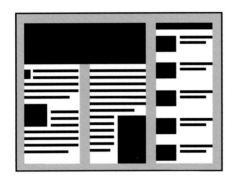 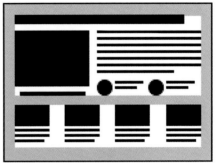

Figure 7-8: These two web layouts use a grid to divide the page into a few areas.

Figure 7-9: Angled grids, as in this print layout, are rare in web design and are accomplished with programs such as Flash.

One way to get around the horizontal and vertical alignment is to place a Flash movie on the web page that has an angled layout. Unlike HTML, Flash gives you a lot more design flexibility in your layouts. The Flash movie is simply embedded in the HTML page just like a graphic — and like a graphic, it's ultimately aligned by your grid system.

The grid is unavoidable, and that's a good thing. Grid systems are intended to impose a logical order on your web-page layout. Rather than randomly carving out a spot for everything that is to go on the page, aligning the elements with each other makes the page easier to read, easier to build, and more professional in appearance. Compare the two web-page layout sketches shown in

Figure 7-10. In the example on the left, the elements look thrown on the page. In the example on the right, the same number of elements is neatly presented.

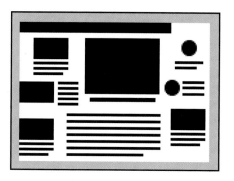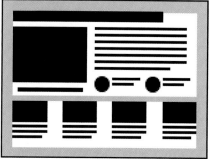

Figure 7-10: A grid system organizes the page and makes it more legible.

Establishing Visual Priority

Clients are often so close to the subject matter that they have a hard time deciding which things are the most important on the page. Their inclination is to make everything big and include as much detail about each item as possible. As the designer, you have to help them create a descending order of importance. If you make everything the same size, everything competes for the user's attention — and nothing stands out.

Compare the two illustrations in Figure 7-11. In the top illustration, it's impossible to determine which section is the main point of the page. Because everything is the same size, no visual priority is established. No one particular element looks more important than another element, and so your eye naturally starts at the top left and works its way down — regardless of whether the designer intended you to consume the page elements in that order. In addition, the viewer doesn't get any white space (sometimes referred to as *breathing space*) to take a mental break from all the information on the page. The bottom illustration, by contrast, has a clear visual hierarchy.

The key to achieving a balanced, well-prioritized layout is to focus on one thing at a time. Decide which elements are the most important and give them a larger share of the screen space. Also make sure that the important things are within the initial viewable portion of the screen: Don't make viewers scroll to reach the most important content. The next few sections offer a few design tips to help you make the most of your screen space without overwhelming your visitor.

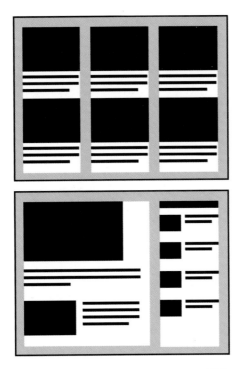

Figure 7-11: Which of these sketches establishes a clear visual priority for the content?

Implementing the "big, medium, small" strategy

When designing a web page, consider it divided into three sections — a big section for the most important stuff, a medium-sized area for the next most important stuff, and the rest of the page for the less important stuff. By thinking of the page in terms of areas that have "big," "medium," and "small" visual importance, you automatically limit the amount of detail you can include for the less-important things on the page. For example, if the Founder's Story area is one of the least-important items on the page, you may leave out a picture and just use a short heading and lead-in sentence that leads to another page with more detail.

Take a look at the home page shown in Figure 7-12. In this example, the "big" area has large photos, also known as *hero* shots, that romance the product (in this case white-water river vacations). The "medium" area is the Expeditions module — not necessarily because of its relative size but because of its clear visual strength so that your eye goes to it next. Everything else on the page collectively makes up the "small" area of the page — in terms of its visual priority.

© Holiday River Expeditions. www.bikeraft.com

Figure 7-12: This home page is an excellent example of the "big, medium, small" strategy.

Using a "big, medium, small" strategy prevents you from giving the same visual priority to everything on the page. This not only allows you to guide a user's eye around the page in a prescribed manner, it also helps make the page easier for the user to read and navigate. It's a win-win.

Breaking up the page into manageable areas

Sometimes you can't avoid the fact that your web page has a lot of stuff going on. For a news-oriented website, for example, breaking the page into a few different areas that you can design separately helps to organize your layout. By using color fields and rule lines to break up the page, you create the illusion of more space because each section operates independently for the eye to digest.

For example, the Red Bull website, shown in Figure 7-13, conveys a lot of information, but they have it divided into three sections and make the most of each of them. Notice also how the "big, medium, small" strategy works for graphic images. Your eye goes to the large graphic at the top first. The smaller graphics in the right column make up the "medium" area. The content area below is the collective "small" area in terms of visual priority. Notice how that content area uses a tabbed system of "latest" and "popular" to get the most out of that space.

Figure 7-13: The Red Bull site conveys a lot of information effectively by using three main sections and rule lines to break up the space into visually digestible chunks.

Designing around the fold line

If you are a print designer, you're probably familiar with the term *fold line*. The term refers to the spot where a brochure or newspaper or other kind of printed item folds in half. Anything above the fold line is immediately visible;

everything below it is hidden until the viewer unfolds the paper, or performs a similar action. On the Web, the immediately visible portion is pretty small because of the screen size. The point where your web page gets cut off from view — requiring people to scroll — is called the *fold line*.

Another way that the Web differs from the print world is that the fold line is never quite the same from one computer to the next. Some people have large monitors; some are viewing the Web through mobile and tablet devices; and some people purposefully make their default font size settings bigger or smaller. This means you have to design for the worst-case scenario or decide that your site will only cater to certain-sized monitors. The worst-case scenario is a viewing area of about 800 x 600 pixels. Accordingly, to accommodate most users, you must place the important stuff within the first 800 x 600 pixels. Otherwise you run the risk of viewers not being able to see them, as illustrated in Figure 7-14.

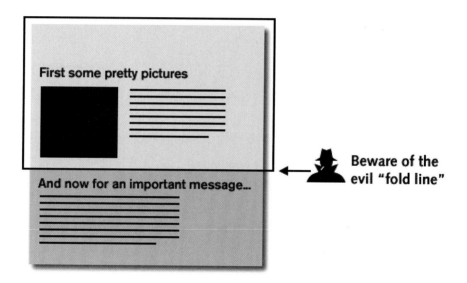

Figure 7-14: Be sure to place important stuff above the *fold line*. Otherwise viewers may never know it's there.

Adding Breathing Space

Web pages that have tons of stuff packed into every nook and cranny make the page difficult to read and don't give the eye a chance to rest. When building a web-page layout, always plan for some open space around your design elements. The open spaces not only create a more inviting atmosphere that doesn't feel cramped but also allow the eye to identify all areas of the page quickly — making it more legible.

Here are a few design techniques to open up your layout and create more breathing room for the viewer:

- **Use white space wisely.** *White space* refers to the collective of open clear area around your design elements (not necessarily using the color white). The physiological effect is an open-air, comfortable feeling. A good tip is to leave larger chunks of white space around the most important area of the page, making it stand out like an island. Apple's website at `www.apple.com` is famous for its extensive use of white space.

  Of course, the same principles apply when designing websites on a black or dark-colored background, but the feeling that a dark background conveys is somewhat different. A lot of space around objects on a dark background creates a sense of drama and excitement. Figure 7-15 is a good example of using dark space around graphics to create drama.

- **Let some elements float.** Web page layouts are, by nature, fairly geometric and boxy. Although it's normally a good idea to align all your elements to a grid, your page can look too rigid if you follow this rule to the letter. To add visual interest, have some fun with one of the more important elements on the page. Allow an important element to break the rules a little by falling outside of the grid. This also helps it stand out from the rest. See how the "Expeditions" module back in Figure 7-12 disrupts the flow and grabs attention by overlapping the main image area.

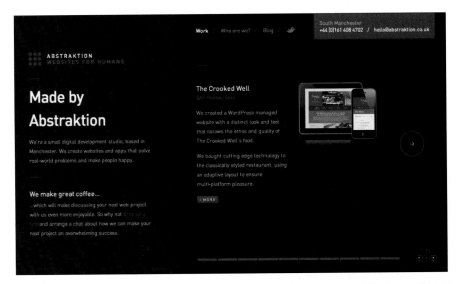

© Abstraktion. http://abstraktion.co.uk

Figure 7-15: This web page creates impact by leaving a lot of dark space around the text and graphics.

✔ **Remember that less is more.** Of course, the less you have going on in the page, the easier it is to include white space and floating elements that break out of the rigid grid structure. Limit the amount of detail you include about the less important things on the page — save the detail for another page that focuses on that element.

Establishing a Design Style Guideline

At the beginning of this chapter, I stress the importance of creating design templates — comps — for each unique page layout of the website. Before you invest time in creating all those comps, however, you would likely start out building just one to two pages that get *approved first by the client* (or internal stakeholders). After the design is approved, it's a good idea to establish a visual style guide that governs the color palette, font usage, and graphical treatments. Developing a style guide first — or starting one and refining it as you go — will help you stay consistent throughout the development of your comps. In addition, the graphical and text styles you define now will ultimately be translated into CSS (Cascading Style Sheets) styles by the developers during the build-out phase.

Graphic style guides

There are so many elements that you can visually define just with simple CSS code alone as you saw in Figure 7-7 earlier in this chapter. Visual elements such as borders, fill colors, rollover colors, link colors, background colors, and rule lines should all be defined by the designer. Questions such as these should be documented: How thick are rule lines? When you roll over a content area, does its background color change, and if so, to what color?

For other common elements on the page — such as custom textured backgrounds, fancy buttons, and border treatments that do need graphic support — you can create a library of such items. This library, created in a program such as Adobe Fireworks or Adobe Photoshop, would be in addition to the page comps you have already created. All production files and comps should be saved as layered files in the software's native format (PNG and PSD, respectively). The layers and layer sets should be clearly organized and named so any designer can pick up where you left off.

Button styles

One thing I often see overlooked in web-design planning is a hierarchy of styles for buttons and links. As Figure 7-16 shows, you should have a plan for different grades of buttons and links: an important button, a less-important button; an important text link and a less-important text link (or a link found in line with other body copy). Often a page's links and buttons are placed on backgrounds of different colors. If the same style doesn't work on both backgrounds, have a separate style for each background.

Notice how in Figure 7-16, the two top-tier buttons work well on both a light- and a dark-colored background. The green and the orange accent colors for the Tier 3 and Tier 4 links, however, do not work well on both backgrounds. In this case, both the green and the orange were "cheated" to be lighter and brighter for use on dark background and darker to work on light backgrounds.

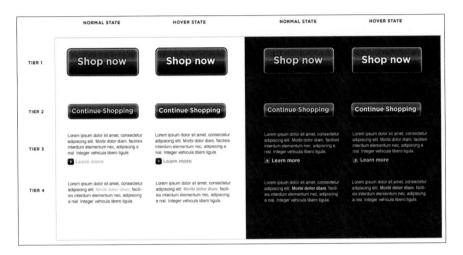

Figure 7-16: Part of your graphic style guide should include rules for button and link treatments in different background color scenarios.

Type styles

Nowadays it's rare to utilize *graphical text* — text that is simply a graphical image — in web and mobile sites. There are several reasons for avoiding the use of graphical text. First, graphical text is hard to maintain: It's much easier to retype or translate words in HTML or in a database and have CSS apply the appropriate styling than to redo an image. Second, graphical text is not searchable unless you apply `alt` tags with keywords.

In the past, designers used graphical text because fonts were an issue on the Web: Only a limited number of (rather boring) fonts were available on every user's system. Now it's possible to *embed* fonts — have your website link to font files — through various services and technologies. (Chapter 8 provides more detail on extending your font choices through font embedding.)

As with buttons, you have to define design styles for all types of fonts and the situations in which you use them — from body copy to headlines, subheads, and captions. These font styles will ultimately become a series of CSS styles applied to dynamic text. As a designer, you don't need to write the CSS classes; you can simply create a style sheet that shows all your font styles in Photoshop. The developers can glean what they need from the layered Photoshop file. CSS is surprisingly accommodating — you can get a lot of cool effects, even the drop shadows you see in Figure 7-17. Chapter 8 dives deeper into the CSS font-handling capabilities.

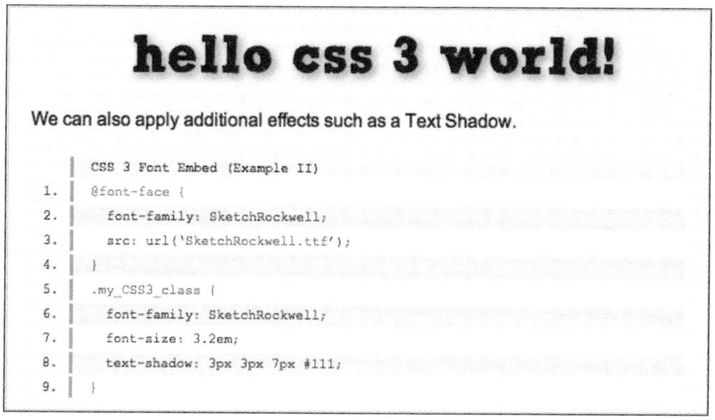

© Zen Elements Limited. www.zenelements.com

Figure 7-17: CSS is capable of a wide variety of effects, including drop shadows.

Letter-Perfect Type Design

*P*erhaps more than any other detail, your font choices say a lot about the level of your graphic-design skills. People who don't have any design training seem to gravitate toward the fun, frilly fonts and — like a kid in a candy store — try out every font on their system. You have to be careful with fonts, however, because they have a powerful effect on the look and feel of your website. Of all the graphic elements that go into a website, your font choices can make the biggest impression. Fonts have the uncanny ability to make people start listing off adjectives to describe your site like "cheerful" or "serious," or worse, "amateur."

In web design, you work with two different kinds of text:

- *HTML text,* which comprises the bulk of all text in your website, and as such, will be the focus of this chapter

- *Graphic text*, which is actually an image you create in a graphics program such as Fireworks or Photoshop

In this chapter, I discuss basic typography design rules and techniques for creating great-looking HTML and graphic text for the Web. In addition, I discuss text readability, what fonts to choose for different purposes, and how to use CSS to apply custom styles to make your text not only look great but also stay consistent throughout a website. After reading this chapter, you'll be able to wield fonts around your web page with confidence.

Text That You Can Actually Read

Whether a website uses graphic or HTML text, reading text on the computer screen can be uncomfortable on the eye: You squint from the glare while trying to read the small text. You can minimize the torture, however, by limiting the amount of text you include on each web page. By breaking copy into small chunks (as opposed to long paragraphs), and choosing the right fonts, colors, and sizes, you can make your page much easier to read on a computer monitor.

Print designers have the luxury of working with all sorts of fonts and font sizes. This is because they can print with a high *resolution* (fine dot size) on paper — even if the text is very small, readers can still easily see the detail. Images displayed on a computer monitor, however, are a different story. The smallest dot of light on a monitor, called a *pixel*, is 1/72-inch wide, or 72 dots per linear inch — which, without making you get out your ruler, I can tell you is not that small when compared to standard printing resolutions like 150 and 300 dots per inch.

For example, take a look at the type sample in Figure 8-1. This text is 10-point Syntax in bold on the computer. It has been enlarged so you can see that only a few pixels make up each letter. Such a small number of pixels makes the text appear clunky and unreadable — especially when magnified like this. Ten-point type size is a common font size on business cards, so as you can see, what works for a business card doesn't work as well on the computer screen. Of course, some fonts in this size work better than others on the Web, but you get the general idea.

Figure 8-1: A monitor's pixels are too big to render 10-point type effectively.

In addition to fonts and font sizes, other factors contribute to text legibility on a web page. You can do three things to make your text more readable (regardless of what font you choose):

> ✔ **Typically, dark text on a light background is more legible than the reverse.** As mentioned in the previous chapter, if your web page has a lot of text that you want people to read, choose a light-colored

background with dark text for good contrast. I like to use a dark, muted color rather than black text for body copy. A dark, muted color softens the effect, making the text not so glaring and stark as black text on a white background.

✔ **Try widening the *leading* — the space between the lines of text — to make the text more readable.** Increasing the leading helps the eye to find the next line of text. Compare the visual effect of the three text blocks in Figure 8-2. The text in the left block is too cramped, whereas the middle block of text is much more readable — especially on the dark background. The loose leading in the right block gives an entirely different, more decorative feel to the text.

✔ **Try to limit each body text column's width to no more than about 450 pixels.** Because web pages have more horizontal space than vertical space, you may be tempted to make each line of text run across the entire page to get as much above the fold line as possible. (*Above the fold line* means within the browser-screen space that the visitor first encounters.) The problem with this tactic, however, is that after your eyes get all the way across the page, you can't easily find the next line. Limiting each column's width to no more than about 450 pixels helps your visitors' eyes zigzag down the page quickly and accurately. Typically, web-page layouts account for two to three narrow columns of text instead of one wide one.

Using a significant amount of leading only works well for smaller blocks of text — not for entire pages of body text. You can use a lot of leading to make a lead-in paragraph or a quote stand out from the main body, as shown in Figure 8-3.

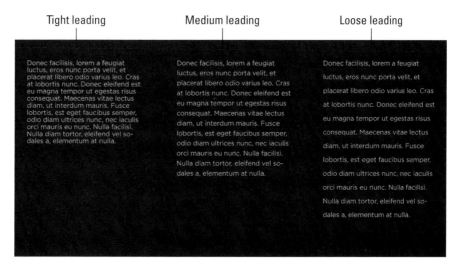

Figure 8-2: Different amounts of leading can lend interesting design effects to your text and affect its legibility.

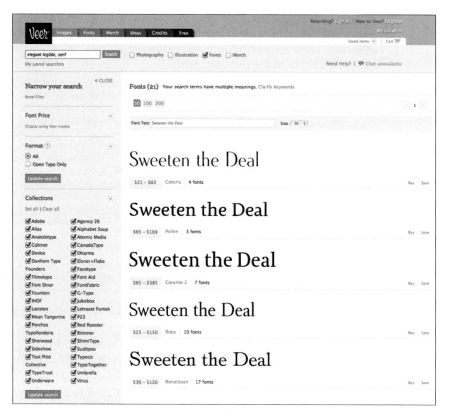

Figure 8-5: Veer.com is an excellent resource to find both unique and common fonts that may be suited for your project.

Easy to read font for body text

Decorative font for headings

Quisque ultrices mi ut enim vulputate quis dignissim ante mollis. Nam id euismod urna. Aliquam tristique sagittis augue, quis scelerisque felis imperdiet id. Pellentesque erat metus, volutpat venenatis gravida non, feugiat porttitor metus. Phasellus dapibus, sem sed suscipit suscipit, est neque pretium tortor, vitae elementum leo ipsum et tortor. Fusce adipiscing dui id metus gravida cursus. Aenean accumsan cursus tristique. Nam adipiscing vulputate massa, id rutrum tellus lobortis eget. Nunc sit amet viverra ligula.

Buisque ultrices mi ut enim vulputate quis dignissim ante mollis. Nam id euismod urna. Aliquam tristique sagittis augue, quis scelerisque felis imperdiet id. Pellentesque erat metus, volutpat venenatis gravida non, feugiat porttitor metus. Phasellus dapibus, sem sed suscipit suscipit, est neque pretium tortor, vitae elementum leo ipsum et tortor. Fusce adipiscing dui id metus gravida cursus. Aenean accumsan cursus tristique. Nam adipiscing vulputate massa, id rutrum tellus lobortis eget. Nunc sit amet viverra ligula.

Figure 8-6: The font on the left, Garamond, is designed for legibility in large blocks of text; the font on the right, Homework, is best reserved for short phrases and headings.

If you examine any font, you notice that the thickness varies in each letter. For example, take a look at the letter *m* in Figure 8-7. The letter is set in a few different typefaces for comparison. Some fonts, such as Kepel Bold (the example on the far left), change drastically between the thick and thin areas of a single letter. At a small point size, for the letter *m*, all you see is a blob of three bold strokes — the thin strokes disappear altogether. When choosing fonts for small-point-size text, therefore, find versions that don't have a big variance in the stroke thickness — for example, the middle and right examples in Figure 8-7. Also, avoid the "lightweight" editions of fonts — they're too thin to read at a small point size. (Most font families come in a variety of thicknesses, ranging from light for the thinnest of the set to bold, black, and ultra for progressively heavier line weight.)

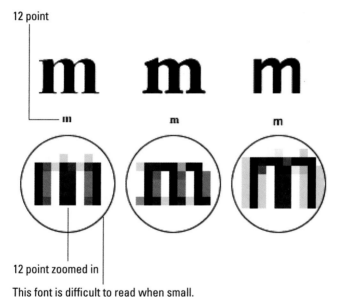

Figure 8-7: The font on the left differs dramatically between the thick and thin areas.

Serif versus sans-serif

Your font education won't be complete until you know the difference between serif and sans-serif fonts. As Figure 8-8 illustrates, a *serif* is the little ledge that adorns the tips of a letter. *Sans-serif* fonts, on the other hand, don't have these ledges. Some modern sans-serif fonts do have little embellishments on their tips, making you look twice, but they're still considered sans-serif fonts. Both serif and san-serif fonts can be used for larger blocks of body copy. Typically, serif fonts give the page a more conservative, classy, or newsy look — while using san-serif fonts yields a cleaner, more modern feel.

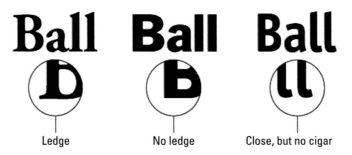

Ledge	No ledge	Close, but no cigar

Figure 8-8: The letters of serif fonts have ledges on their tips. Sans-serif fonts do not.

TIP

Figures 8-9 and 8-10 list serif and sans-serif fonts that read well on the Web. The fonts on the list all survived the *10-point test*: They are all readable when set at just 10 points, which is the smallest font size for text that you should ever consider for body copy in web design (best to set at 11 points at least).

TIP

Try mixing serif and sans-serif fonts together. For example, use one style for headings and the other style for the body text. Choosing a set of two to three fonts for your website — one for each different kind of type element — helps to add visual interest to the page as illustrated in Figure 8-11.

System san-serif fonts:	Example:	Custom san-serif fonts:	Example:
Arial	Lorem ipsum dolor sit amet, consectetur adipiscing elit. Morbi dolor diam, facilisis interdum elementum nec, adipiscing a nisl. Integer vehicula libero ligula.	Avenir	Lorem ipsum dolor sit amet, consectetur adipiscing elit. Morbi dolor diam, facilisis interdum elementum nec, adipiscing a nisl. Integer vehicula libero ligula.
Verdana	Lorem ipsum dolor sit amet, consectetur adipiscing elit. Morbi dolor diam, facilisis interdum elementum nec, adipiscing a nisl. Integer vehicula libero ligula.	Gotham	Lorem ipsum dolor sit amet, consectetur adipiscing elit. Morbi dolor diam, facilisis interdum elementum nec, adipiscing a nisl. Integer vehicula libero ligula.
Helvetica	Lorem ipsum dolor sit amet, consectetur adipiscing elit. Morbi dolor diam, facilisis interdum elementum nec, adipiscing a nisl. Integer vehicula libero ligula.	Helvetica Neue	Lorem ipsum dolor sit amet, consectetur adipiscing elit. Morbi dolor diam, facilisis interdum elementum nec, adipiscing a nisl. Integer vehicula libero ligula.
Geneva	Lorem ipsum dolor sit amet, consectetur adipiscing elit. Morbi dolor diam, facilisis interdum elementum nec, adipiscing a nisl. Integer vehicula libero ligula.	DIN	Lorem ipsum dolor sit amet, consectetur adipiscing elit. Morbi dolor diam, facilisis interdum elementum nec, adipiscing a nisl. Integer vehicula libero ligula.
Tahoma	Lorem ipsum dolor sit amet, consectetur adipiscing elit. Morbi dolor diam, facilisis interdum elementum nec, adipiscing a nisl. Integer vehicula libero ligula.	Akzidenz	Lorem ipsum dolor sit amet, consectetur adipiscing elit. Morbi dolor diam, facilisis interdum elementum nec, adipiscing a nisl. Integer vehicula libero ligula.
Trebuchet	Lorem ipsum dolor sit amet, consectetur adipiscing elit. Morbi dolor diam, facilisis interdum elementum nec, adipiscing a nisl. Integer vehicula libero ligula.	Eurostile	Lorem ipsum dolor sit amet, consectetur adipiscing elit. Morbi dolor diam, facilisis interdum elementum nec, adipiscing a nisl. Integer vehicula libero ligula.
Lucida	Lorem ipsum dolor sit amet, consectetur adipiscing elit. Morbi dolor diam, facilisis interdum elementum nec, adipiscing a nisl. Integer vehicula libero ligula.	Myriad	Lorem ipsum dolor sit amet, consectetur adipiscing elit. Morbi dolor diam, facilisis interdum elementum nec, adipiscing a nisl. Integer vehicula libero ligula.

Figure 8-9: Sans-serif fonts for body copy that pass the 10-point test.

System serif fonts:	Example:	Custom serif fonts:	Example:
Georgia	Lorem ipsum dolor sit amet, consectetur adipiscing elit. Morbi dolor diam, facilisis interdum elementum nec, adipiscing a nisl. Integer vehicula libero ligula.	Garamond	Lorem ipsum dolor sit amet, consectetur adipiscing elit. Morbi dolor diam, facilisis interdum elementum nec, adipiscing a nisl. Integer vehicula libero ligula.
Times New Roman	Lorem ipsum dolor sit amet, consectetur adipiscing elit. Morbi dolor diam, facilisis interdum elementum nec, adipiscing a nisl. Integer vehicula libero ligula.	Goudy Old Style	Lorem ipsum dolor sit amet, consectetur adipiscing elit. Morbi dolor diam, facilisis interdum elementum nec, adipiscing a nisl. Integer vehicula libero ligula.
Times	Lorem ipsum dolor sit amet, consectetur adipiscing elit. Morbi dolor diam, facilisis interdum elementum nec, adipiscing a nisl. Integer vehicula libero ligula.	Baskerville	Lorem ipsum dolor sit amet, consectetur adipiscing elit. Morbi dolor diam, facilisis interdum elementum nec, adipiscing a nisl. Integer vehicula libero ligula.
Palatino	Lorem ipsum dolor sit amet, consectetur adipiscing elit. Morbi dolor diam, facilisis interdum elementum nec, adipiscing a nisl. Integer vehicula libero ligula.	Bookman	Lorem ipsum dolor sit amet, consectetur adipiscing elit. Morbi dolor diam, facilisis interdum elementum nec, adipiscing a nisl. Integer vehicula libero ligula.
		Cochin	Lorem ipsum dolor sit amet, consectetur adipiscing elit. Morbi dolor diam, facilisis interdum elementum nec, adipiscing a nisl. Integer vehicula libero ligula.

Figure 8-10: Serif fonts for body copy that pass the 10-point test.

© Swiss Water Decaffeinated Coffee. www.swisswater.com

Figure 8-11: This website features an excellent use of type design.

Not too big; not too small

Unless you're going for an unreadable artistic effect, avoid body text that is less than 10 points in size. Ideally, body text is set at 11 to 12 points. Some fonts do better than others at these sizes, so you have to test and see what works best. On the flip side, don't make your text so big and "horsey" that your web page looks like an eye chart. (By the way, *horsey* is a fussy designer term for large and clunky.)

For headings, use 14- to 24-point sizes. You have to use your judgment for each situation, but headings larger than 24 points approach the horsey territory unless you have a good handle on type design and know what you're doing. Take a look back at Figure 8-11, which successfully mixes different fonts and font sizes to create an elegant and unique design.

It's better to use even-numbered point sizes like 10, 12, 14, 16, and so on — especially for sizes in this range. Computer fonts are typically *hinted* (manually crafted) to look good on the screen in these specific point sizes, in even-numbered sizes. If you specify an odd size like 11-point (which I love to do anyway), an algorithm is often what "hints" the font — and which can tweak its appearance.

Controlling Text Display

Your web page may contain two types of text: graphic text (which is really just an image) and HTML text (which is either in the HTML code or coming from a database). HTML text is also called *live text* because it is fully editable — just like the text in your word processor. You can apply various font and size settings to live text using CSS styles, or even just with HTML, and you can update the text easily, making live text the ideal choice for your website.

Graphic text versus HTML text

While live text gives you more flexibility to edit and update, it does have limitations. Your choices of fonts and visual effects are relatively limited, and you must rely on good coding to ensure that your text looks the same in *all* browsers, platforms, and devices. Graphic text, however, is just an image — essentially a picture of the text. Therefore you can apply any font you have in your toolbox — and any kind of effect — to create a cool-looking headline. While that sounds great, live text is the clear winner when it comes to the Web — because the ability to edit and update text far outweighs the ability to look cool. In addition, live text has the added benefit of making your page more search-friendly because search engines can read what it says.

Language localization

Another reason it makes sense to use live text for all copy elements is because many sites need to account for language *localization* (lingo for *translation*). If you're developing a site that will support multiple languages and character sets, you cannot afford to use any graphical text (not counting text that is part of photography and content graphics, like an image supporting an article). It's much more practical to maintain a database of live copy components translated for all the languages you support, and dynamically populate your web pages with the right content based on the country and language that a user selected.

Font specifications

In the past, live text was limited to display in boring system fonts. There are now different ways to utilize custom fonts in your website designs. One of the first methods was sIFR (salable *I*nman *F*lash *R*eplacement), an open source solution designed to replace short phrases (like headlines) by overlaying the original text with a Flash movie that displays the text in the assigned custom font. The replacement happens in a blink of an eye, but requires that Flash is installed in the browser. Remember, Flash does not work on Apple's mobile devices.

Now, most designers are using either the `@font-face` CSS method, or a type-embedding service such as Adobe Typekit (`www.typekit.com`), shown in Figure 8-12, or Google Web Fonts (`www.google.com/webfonts`) to expand the array of fonts available for live text. Designers will use these custom fonts for short phrases, navigation, and headlines, but often stick to the standard system fonts like Arial or Georgia for body copy. As these font-embedding technologies settle in and browsers extend more support for them, the trend will probably shift toward using all-custom fonts in traditional websites and mobile sites.

Have a font-fallback plan

Even if you're using an embedding-font technology, whenever you specify a font in either HTML or CSS, you're assuming that the font can be found. If the server that houses your embedded font is down, or the user's browser does not support the font format (see Table 8-1), your font will not display properly. If you're using standard system fonts (see the list again back in Figures 8-9 and 8-10), and for whatever reason the user doesn't have the ones you specify, your page will not display properly. The browser will find a substitute font. This can wreak havoc on your page layout and design, because as you may know, fonts vary a great deal in size and width — even when set to the same point size.

© Adobe Systems Incorporated. www.typekit.com

Figure 8-12: TypeKit is an online font-embedding service that allows you to utilize custom fonts in your websites.

Table 8-1	Font Formats and Browser Compatibility	
Browser	**Font Formats Supported**	**Font File Extensions**
Internet Explorer	Embedded OpenType	.eot
	Web Open Font Format	.woff
Mozilla (Firefox)	OpenType Font	.otf
	TrueType Font	.ttf
	Web Open Font Format	.woff
Safari and Opera	OpenType Font	.otf
	TrueType Font	.ttf
	Scalable Vector Graphics	.svg
	Web Open Font Format	.woff

Browser	Font Formats Supported	Font File Extensions
Chrome	OpenType Font	.otf
	TrueType Font	.ttf
	Scalable Vector Graphics	.svg
	Web Open Font Format	.woff
Apple mobile devices (Safari)	Scalable Vector Graphics	.svg
	OpenType Font	.otf
	TrueType Font	.ttf

A safeguard that you can take is to specify a list of fonts in your HTML or CSS code. For example, when you write the code defining the font, list the preferred font first, and then follow it with an alternative list of fonts to use if the first font isn't available or found. This prioritized list is called a *font stack*. When someone loads the page, the browser scans the list until it finds a match — ideally finding the first font in your list. Here's an example of CSS code defining the font-family property with a font stack:

```
font-family: Georgia, "Times New Roman", Times, serif;
```

In this case, `Georgia` is the first choice, followed by `"Times New Roman"` (it's in quotes because the name is three words) and Times. The last entry, `serif`, tells the browser to insert any available serif font on the system if it doesn't have the first three.

The other browser compatibility work-around when using the CSS @font-face method is to point to the various sources of multiple font formats to make sure you're covered.

Working with CSS

Cascading Style Sheets (CSS) technology allows you to define a set of font styles, which you can use consistently throughout your website. For example, imagine that you're designing a fairly large website and you want to ensure a consistent look for all pages: All headings should be set in Arial Narrow Bold, 18-point (you can use real point sizes in CSS), and a dark red color. All captions should be Verdana Italic, 11-point, and steel blue. The advantage of CSS is that it saves you time by allowing you to apply consistent settings quickly to *all* text elements throughout a website. Making a global style change to your website, therefore, is as easy as changing a single line of CSS code.

CSS comes in two flavors: *external* style sheets and *internal* style sheets, as described in the following two sections.

External style sheets

For external style sheets, you define a bunch of text styles in one CCS file like `mystyles.css`. Each style can have a custom name of your choosing like `.BigHeadline`, `.SectionHeadline`, and so on, as long as there are no spaces and the name is preceded by a period. A style like this is called a *class* in CSS terminology. (See Figure 8-13 for a CSS code example of two classes I've defined, and how they render in the Safari browser.) After defining the class with a custom name, you open brackets and include a list of style properties such as font choice, color, and size, as in the following example:

```
.BigHeadline {
  font-family: Arial, Helvetica, sans-serif;
  font-size: 24px;
  line-height: 30px;
  font-weight: 800;
  font-variant: small-caps;
  color: #900;
  Letter-spacing: 2px;
  Text-shadow: 2px 2px 3px #999999;
  }

.SectionHeadline {
  font-family: Arial, Helvetica, sans-serif;
  font-size: 18px;
  line-height: 22px;
  font-weight: 600;
  color: #333;
  Text-transform: capitalize;
  }
```

See Table 8-2 for a list of common CSS properties you can define for your text style; note that this table contains just a partial list of properties and potential values you can define.

When using an external style sheet, each of your web pages references this single `mystyles.css` file for their font styling information. This is accomplished through placing a line of code in each web page that tells it where to find `mystyles.css` online. Then, any text elements on the web page that are assigned one of your custom style names (such as `.BigHeadline`) will render as you have coded.

This way, if you ever have the need to make a global font change — say, change the `.BigHeadline` color from dark red to blue — you make the change *once* to the class in the `mystyles.css` CSS file, and all web pages with text that use the `BigHeadline` style will update instantly.

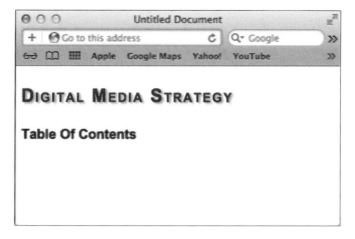

Figure 8-13: These are two examples of custom CSS classes I've defined to govern how my headlines and section headlines should look.

Table 8-2	Common CSS Text Properties and Values	
CSS Property	*Translation*	*Code Sample*
`Font-family`	Defines the common system font you assign, such as Arial or Helvetica. You can define a list of fonts separated by a comma. If the first font is unavailable, it tries the next one in line. Note that you can include a custom font in your list, but to do so you'll need to use the @font-face property.	`Font-family:` `SketchRockwell,` `Georgia, Palatino,` `"Times New Roman",` `serif;`
`@font-face`	This code allows you to define the name of a custom font (in the example, it's `SketchRockwell`) and then point to the online font resource.	`@font-face {` `font-family:` `SketchRockwell;` `src: url(http://` `example.com/fonts/` `SketchRockwell.` `ttf);` `}`

(continued)

Table 8-2 *(continued)*

CSS Property	Translation	Code Sample
font-size	You can specify the text size in points, pixels, ems, or percent. *Ems* define relative font sizes. If the default font size is 12pt, for example, 1em would equal 12 points and 2em would equal 24 points.	font-size: 12pt; font-size: 150%; font-size: 1.5em;
font-weight	Font *weight* is the boldness factor of your text. You can specify a value between 100–900, where 400 is normal and 900 is boldest on a relative scale. Or, you can simply type "bold" as the value.	font-weight: 800;
font-style	Use this property to define italic text.	font-style: italic;
Font-variant	Use this property to turn your text into small caps.	Font-variant: Small-caps;
Color	You can define the color of your text. There are a few colors like "white" and "red" you can specify just with their natural names. Otherwise you must select a hexadecimal color code.	Color: #333333
Letter-spacing	Like kerning, this property defines the space between letters, using whatever unit of measure you define. In this example, I'm using pixels, as indicated by px.	Letter-spacing: 2px;
Line-height	Like leading, this property defines the space (in pixels or other unit of measure you define) between lines of text.	Line-height: 24px;
Text-align	Text align allows you to align text right, left, centered, or *justified* (fits each line to the same width).	Text-align: center;

CSS Property	Translation	Code Sample
Text-decoration	Use this property to add a strikethrough or an underline.	Text-decoration: underline;
Text-indent	This property allows you to specify the amount of indentation. Negative values are also allowed so the first line of a paragraph could hang off to the left if you like.	Text-indent: 50px;
Text-shadow	You can add a shadow to your text element. The first value is the horizontal offset, the second is the vertical offset, the third is the amount of blur, and the last entry is the hexadecimal color of the shadow.	Text-shadow: 2px 2px 3px #999999;
Text-transform	This property controls the capitalization of text; you can specify uppercase, lowercase, or capitalize.	Text-transform: capitalize;
Vertical-align	You can define whether your text sits at the top, middle, or bottom of a contained area.	Text-align: top;
Word-spacing	This property increases or decreases the amount of space between words.	Word-spacing: 30px;

Internal style sheets

Internal style sheets are CSS styles that you define for only one page — not for the whole website. Internal style sheets are convenient for small nuances found only on one page, although it's not the best practice to use them. If all your CSS codes are scattered across different web pages, it poses a site-maintenance burden: your team must dig to find where all the codes reside. It's better to have all your CSS consolidated together in one easy-access file.

Internal style sheets, if you do decide to use them, are found inside the <head> tag and override external style sheets that the page may also be referencing. The class name and its property values go in the top <head> section of the HTML code, as shown in this example:

```
<head>
<meta http-equiv="Content-Type" content="text/html;
          charset=UTF-8" />
<title>Example of internal CSS styles</title>
<style type="text/css">

.Headline {
  font-family: "Arial Narrow Bold", Arial;
  font-size: 16pt;
  font-weight: 800;
  color: #990033
  text-transform: capitalize;
  }
.Caption {
  font-family: Verdana, Arial, Helvetica, sans-serif;
  font-size: 11pt;
  font-style: italic;
  color: #333366
  }
</style>
</head>
```

In this code, you can see that the `.Headline` style is Arial Narrow Bold
in 16-point. The `#990033` number after `color` is a hexadecimal code that
creates a dark red. As you add headings to your web page, you can quickly
format them by applying the `.Headline` style that you defined for the page:

```
<h1 class="headline"> Headlines are a cinch to format </h1>
```

9

Understanding Web Color, Resolution, and File Formats

In This Chapter

▶ Understanding the RGB color system

▶ Working with 24-bit and 8-bit color depth

▶ Demystifying hexadecimal color

▶ Understanding web-image and monitor resolution

▶ Surveying common web-image formats and compression schemes

*U*nderstanding the roles that color, image and monitor resolution, image compression, and file formats play in websites is essential to being an effective designer. Admittedly, the way that color works on the computer screen may be one of those mysteries that many folks just appreciate without really caring how it actually works. Designers — even many web designers — just want their stuff to look good. But in the print world, designers must know how the color printing process works in order to get the most out of their designs, and to ensure they prepare them properly. The same rule holds true in web design — you simply can't get around the technical stuff. Color is just one component. To fully understand your craft, you must also know how to account for the discrepancies between image resolution and monitor resolution, and to know not only what image-file formats are available to you but also when to use them.

If you read this chapter in its entirety, you'll understand the mechanics behind the designs you create. The goal is to arm you with the information you need to make your website not only look great, but also fast and efficient.

The Secret World of RGB

The secret to all the colors you see on your computer monitor is a system called *RGB color*. This system uses just three colors (red, green, and blue) combined together to create all the colors (including black and white) on your monitor. Although this sounds like quite a feat, consider that the system works in a way similar to natural daylight. When the sun is up, you see white light. When the sun goes away, it's pitch black outside. Only if you use a prism to break up the spectrum can you see all the colors contained within white light. Like sunlight, RGB color is an *additive* color process. The CMYK printing process, with its judicious use of *C*yan, *M*agenta, *Y*ellow, and a *K*ey color (black), is a *subtractive* color process. I explain the difference in the following section.

Subtractive and additive colors

When you mix two or more colors together to create a new color in any medium — whether it's in print or on a computer screen — the method you use is either an *additive* or a *subtractive* process. These terms refer to the way you produce the color white.

In printing, you achieve the color white by mixing no colors at all. By removing (subtracting) all colors, you leave the color of the plain paper — which is presumably white — shining through. Therefore the print process is a subtractive color process. The way to achieve white is by printing nothing at all — subtracting all colors from the page.

Combining cyan, magenta, yellow, and black inks in various proportions creates all the other colors. The color we perceive on the page is the result of the different spectral colors that the inks absorb.

At the other end of the spectrum (pardon the pun) is the computer's *additive* process. To create white on a computer screen, the display mixes all three colors — red, green, and blue — together at full strength. Just as if you switched on a light bulb, all colors of the spectrum come together to make white. And just as if you turned off a light switch, removing all the RGB colors leaves you with black.

Gazillions of colors

How do you mix all the colors of the rainbow using this *additive* system of just three colors? As with the CMYK process, the answer is to use different amounts of the three component colors. The RGB color scheme contains 256 *levels* (variations numbered from 0 to 255) of red, 256 levels of green, and 256 levels of blue.

To *generate* (or mix) a color, you take one level of red and mix it with one level of green and one level of blue. For example, to make a nice turquoise color, you can mix red number 75, green number 199, and blue number 211, as shown in Figure 9-1.

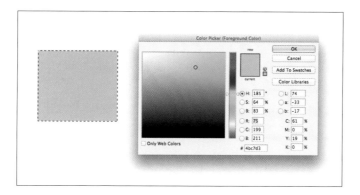

Figure 9-1: To make a turquoise color, mix red, green, and blue light at various levels.

If each of the component red, green, and blue colors has 256 possible settings from zero to 255 (as illustrated in the sliding bars of Figure 9-2), how many colors can you mix with the RBG system? Those of you who are mathematically inclined know that the number of colors is 256 x 256 x 256, or 256^3. This number amounts to a whopping 16,777,216 different color combinations — many more than you and I can see with our eyes!

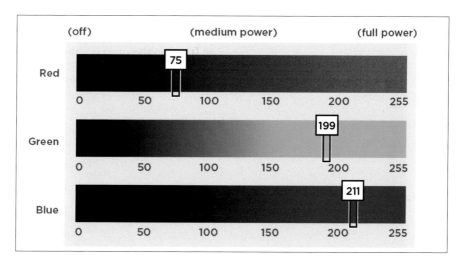

Figure 9-2: You can create more than 16 million colors by mixing all possible levels of red, green, and blue.

Color Bit Depth

Although the computer's RGB system is capable of mixing over 16 million different colors, the monitor is not always capable of *displaying* all these colors. Also, an image that contains all these colors can end up being a large file size — larger than is practical for web delivery. This leads us to the discussion of image color bit depth, color palettes, and monitor displays, all of which are important to the art of designing websites.

A *bit* is a tiny segment of computer information — it's like the atom of computer data. Without getting too technical, a lot of bits are needed to make colors appear in an image. The more colors that an image contains, the more bits of data it has — thus the greater its *bit depth*. For example, a 1-bit image has just two colors. An 8-bit image can have up to 256 colors — two color possibilities to the 8th power — 2^8. And finally, a 24-bit image can have up to 16,777,216 colors, or 2^{24}.

Limited color palettes

The web images you produce will ultimately have a bit depth associated with them, and different web file formats (discussed later in this chapter) require different uses of bit depth. As already explained, a computer uses 8 bits of data to show 256 colors. Each of the red, green, and blue primary colors has 256 levels. So does this mean that an 8-bit image is monotone, showing all 256 possible levels of red? The answer is no — an 8-bit image simply uses a limited palette of up to 256 colors. These colors are a subset of all 16,777,216 possible colors. Table 9-1 shows color bit depth and the maximum number of colors that each can have in its palette.

Table 9-1	Color Bit Depth	
Bit Depth	*The Math*	*Number of Colors in Palette*
1 bit	2^1	2
2 bit	2^2	4
3 bit	2^3	8
4 bit	2^4	16
5 bit	2^5	32
6 bit	2^6	64
7 bit	2^7	128
8 bit	2^8	256

When you reduce the number of colors in your image to keep the file size small, you can choose any number of colors up to the maximum for the given bit depth. Typically, you'll choose a set of colors that are best adapted to render the image. For example, you can choose a custom palette of just 200 colors. The image is still 8-bit, but because it uses only 200 colors in its palette, the file is smaller than it would be if you used the maximum number of colors (256) allowed for an 8-bit image.

Here's how to use a graphics editor such as Adobe Fireworks to experiment with reducing an image's color palette and compare the differences in quality, file size, and download times:

1. **Launch Fireworks.**

2. **Choose File⇨Open from the menu bar.**

   Navigate to any photo image you have on your computer and open the file.

3. **At the top of the document window, there are several icons. Click on the 4-Up icon to split the image's view into four panels.**

   As shown in Figure 9-3, Fireworks allows you to compare different palette and file format settings side by side so you can compare quality and download speeds.

4. **Click on the top-right quadrant to select it. Open the Optimize panel located in the Window menu.**

   It may already be open as a collection of panels to the right of the screen.

5. **In the Optimize panel, select the GIF format, Adaptive palette, and the 256-color option (which is an 8-bit color palette).**

6. **Click on the lower-left quadrant and, in the Optimize panel, select the GIF format as well as the Adaptive palette, but this time select just 64 colors.**

   Notice the decline in image quality.

7. **Click the lower-right quadrant and, in the Optimize panel, select the JPEG format and set the Quality to 60%.**

In this exercise, the noticeable difference in quality from the original image (top-left quadrant) to the two GIF format quadrants shows what a limited number of colors can achieve. The grainy appearance is called "dithering." As with pointillism, different colors from your limited color palette are placed near each other to simulate the effect of the missing color (it's like visually mixing orange by placing yellow and red dots next to each other).

Hexadecimal Color Code

When you specify colors in HTML or CSS code, you don't use their RGB numbers. Instead, you use something called a *hexadecimal code*. For example, plain old white is 255,255,255 in RGB, but it is #FFFFFF in hexadecimal code. In hexadecimal code, the first two digits define the red color, the next two digits define the green, and the last two digits define the blue of the RGB system. Using the #FFFFFF example, the first two digits FF equal 255. So this color is R=255, G=255, and B=255. All three colors at full power (255) make white.

Imagine that you're designing a website for a company that has a handful of company colors that they want you to use throughout the site. Often times, these colors are specified as PMS colors (*Pantone Matching System*). So just how do you go from PMS or RGB to hexadecimal color codes?

Instead of using a super-duper decoder ring to translate color values into hexadecimal code and vice versa, you can retrieve the code in both Adobe Photoshop and Adobe Fireworks. (Otherwise you really do need a special hexadecimal calculator, and they do exist online!)

Here's how to use Adobe Photoshop to find the hexadecimal number of a sample color, or of a known PMS or RGB color:

1. **Launch Photoshop.**

2. **Choose File⇨Open from the menu bar.**

   Navigate to an image you want to sample a color from and open it.

   If you don't have an image to sample and just need to translate an RGB or PMS color value, you do not need to open a file.

3. **Click on the Foreground color swatch at the bottom of the Tools panel.**

   As shown in Figure 9-5, a pop-up palette appears, offering a Color Picker for you to use. Note as well that your cursor turns into an eyedropper.

4. **Move your cursor over your image, and click on the color you want to sample.**

   Notice the hexadecimal readout updates in the Color Picker.

Figure 9-5: Using the Photoshop Tools panel, you can sample colors or enter a PMS or RGB color to find its hexadecimal value.

5. **Select and copy the hexadecimal code within the Color Picker before clicking the OK button to exit, then paste the code into your CSS code, or into your style guide.**

6. **To translate a PMS color, do the following:**

    a. Click the Color Libraries button in the Color Picker.

    b. Quickly type your PMS number, say 375, to see your color swatch appear.

    c. When you find the right one in the list, click the "Picker" button to return to the Color Picker.

    Notice the hexadecimal code appears for your color; you can now copy and paste it as you like.

7. **To translate an RGB color, simply enter the R, G, and B values in the Color Picker and see the hexadecimal number update accordingly.**

Image and Monitor Resolution

If you've ever watched a movie on your computer or on a high-definition TV, you can really notice the difference in detail compared to a standard TV. This is because HDTVs and computer monitors have a higher screen resolution than normal TVs. *Resolution* refers to the number of pixels squeezed into a linear inch. Standard computer screen resolutions vary from 72 to 96 ppi (*pixels per inch*) — that's a lot of detail. An old-school TV, on the other hand, is nearly half of that, and because most broadcast TV is analog and not digital like your computer, the image is all blurred together.

Monitor resolution

Why should you give a hoot about monitor resolution? Because the monitor is your web-design canvas. Although the monitor is a fixed resolution (after all, it is a piece of hardware), graphics come in varying resolutions. In web design, your graphics must *match* the screen's resolution.

Although monitors vary from 72 to 96 ppi, the web-graphics standard is 72 ppi. The professional lingo is *72 dpi*, which stands for *dots per inch,* a carry-over from the print industry.

Image resolution

Here's a frequently asked question: Won't a higher resolution image look better on my web page? The answer is no, because even though a 300 dpi image looks great in a printed piece, the fixed 72-to-96-dpi monitor isn't capable of showing all this detail. Regardless of the image's resolution, the browser simply shows it by its physical pixel dimension, say 200 pixels wide by 200 pixels high.

Both images in Figure 9-6 contain the same number of pixels. Because the left image is 300 dpi, each dot is smaller, so more dots can be squeezed into an inch. That's why the whole image shrinks (the figure on the right) when you print it. The computer monitor, however, isn't capable of displaying such tiny dots, so it blows each dot up to 72-dpi size. So you're back where you started — higher-resolution images don't improve the quality. Ergo, it's best to just stick with the default 72-dpi resolution in the first place.

Figure 9-6: At 300 dpi, this image's dots are zoomed up to fit the 72-dpi monitor resolution when viewed onscreen. When printed, the image comes out pretty small.

Bitmap versus Vector Graphics

All the graphics you encounter on the Web are either bitmap or vector graphics. The basic difference between the two is how they're drawn on your screen. This simple detail affects everything from image resolution to file size and format.

Bitmaps: A fabric of pixels

When explaining bitmap images, I can't help but think of my old childhood toy, the Lite Brite. Those of you who were pampered enough as children to play with this toy remember that you plugged little colored pegs into a grid and then flipped the switch to light them up.

Bitmaps work pretty much the same way. In simplistic terms, a *bitmap* graphic is a grid filled with tiny colored pixels, as shown in Figure 9-7. To draw a bitmap graphic onscreen, the computer lays out a grid, say 100 by 100 pixels, and then *maps* a color to each individual pixel. That's 10,000 pixels to draw! Remember, a pixel is ¹⁄₇₂ inch across. Therefore, if an image has a resolution of 72 dpi and is 100 pixels wide, it appears just over an inch wide on the computer screen.

Vectors: For the mathematically inclined

If you don't remember the Lite Brite, then surely you remember "Connect the Dots." Vector graphics employ a similar strategy. A mathematical formula places *points* on the screen and then connects them with *paths*. For example, to draw a triangle-shaped vector graphic onscreen, the computer simply lays down three points, connects them, and then fills them with a color. In Figure 9-8, you can see a handful of points — some with handles coming off of them. These handles control the curve of the path between two points — known as a *Bézier curve* to those in the know.

If you're thinking that vectors can draw graphics onscreen far more efficiently than bitmaps, you're right. Vector graphics have extremely small file sizes, making them ideal for online delivery. Both vector and bitmap graphics, however, have their pros and cons.

Figure 9-7: Zooming in on a bitmap reveals hundreds of colored pixels all working together to create an image.

Figure 9-8: Vector images are a leaner brand of graphics defined by a series of points connected by curves.

The vector-bitmap showdown

As a web designer, you should know a few things about the ups and downs of vectors and bitmaps before you push your first pixel:

- **Bitmaps are highly prevalent on the Web.** All JPEG, GIF, and PNG graphics that you encounter on the Web are bitmaps. Ironically, many of these graphics began life as vectors before they were converted into bitmaps. Why design with vectors? Because drawing graphics and interesting effects with vectors is often faster and easier than creating the same effect with bitmap graphics. It's also much easier to make changes to vectors because you just move a point and the line follows. And if you need to scale the graphic up or down, vector graphics can do so without losing image quality. To make changes to bitmaps, you often need to redraw parts of them.

  To become GIFs, JPEGs, or PNG files, vector graphics must be converted to bitmaps. Usually this is the last step; designers always save the vector source art in case future changes are necessary. The next question is, why convert vector graphics into bitmaps at all? The answer is browser compatibility. The SVG vector format for web graphics (discussed later in this chapter) is pretty complex; therefore it's been slow to catch on. Most new browsers support much of the SVG standard, but not all of it. Additionally, SVG is best suited for simpler, cartoonlike graphics.

- **Bitmaps can't maintain quality if they are resized.** Bitmap graphics have fixed resolutions. As I state earlier in this chapter, bitmap graphics are laid out on a grid of pixels. Like half-inch-grade chicken wire, this grid is a fixed size. And like chicken wire, if you stretch the image, you end up with a contorted mess. While it's possible to use HTML code to enter new heights and widths for an image, all this does is stretch and

GIF format

GIF (depending on whom you talk to) is pronounced either as it sounds — *giff* (my personal favorite), or *jiff* (as in Jiffy Pop® popcorn), and stands for *G*raphics *I*nterchange *F*ormat. This older format is still often used for images that have a lot of flat-colored areas (like illustrations) or sharp, contrasting edges (like a text headline on top of a solid background). That's because the GIF compression scheme can handle several patches of solid-colored areas very well.

The GIF compression scheme reads an image row by row, so if your image contains a gradient, a top-to-bottom gradient compresses drastically better than a horizontal gradient. Why? The GIF format reads each horizontal row of pixels in your image and records the color changes. In a top-to-bottom gradient, each horizontal row has the same color of pixels. In a left-to-right gradient, each pixel's color changes as you go across the horizontal row.

Keep in mind that the GIF format requires that your image be 8-bits or less; this means your 24-bit source file will first need to be reduced into a limited palette of 256 colors or less before you can save it as a GIF. Always save a copy of your 24-bit source file before reducing the palette. You cannot go back and recover those colors once they're lost (unless you immediately use the Undo feature).

The web-safe palette versus adaptive palettes

The Fireworks exercise earlier in this chapter experiments with reducing an image's color palette down to a specified number of colors that are best suited for the image. This is known as an *adaptive* palette and is most commonly used today because modern monitors can display thousands, if not millions of colors (16-bit and 24-bit "true color" display monitors, respectively).

In the past, designers often used what was referred to as the *web-safe* color palette. This was a set of 216 standard colors that worked on both Mac and PC browsers running on older 8-bit monitors that could not display custom palettes properly. This so-called web-safe palette, though largely forgotten, still may be something to consider if you're targeting 8-bit displays.

Single-color transparency

The GIF format also allows you to designate a single color in the palette as the transparent color. For example, if you prepare a button graphic like the one in Figure 9-11, and place it on top of a solid bright color not used in the image, you can select that bright color to be transparent. If that bright color *does* appear inside the image, however, parts of the image also become transparent. Think of single-color transparency as working like a "green screen" in film production.

Figure 9-11: The GIF format supports single-color transparency. In this example, the green background disappears when viewed on the Web.

Aliased versus anti-aliased graphics

Your computer graphics education would not be complete without understanding the concept of aliased and anti-aliased graphics. Because pixels are square, and the computer screen resolution is just 72 dpi, your graphics can easily look chunky, especially those with rounded edges where you can visibly see the stairstepped edges (as illustrated in Figure 9-12). That harsh, stairstepped edge is called an *aliased* edge.

To soften this effect, graphics programs like Adobe Photoshop or Fireworks will automagically add a tiny trim of semi-transparent pixels to make a smooth transition from the edges of the image to whatever background it sits on. This process is called *anti-aliasing*. Notice the difference of edges in Figures 9-12 and 9-13.

One caveat to be aware of is that single-color GIF transparency and anti-aliasing don't play nicely together. The reason is that during the creative process, anti-aliased edges are semi-transparent to make a transition from the image edges to the background. But if you reduce an image's color palette, those anti-aliased edges become opaque colors. Therefore when you select the single background color to become transparent, the transparent effect stops short at the anti-aliased edges and drop shadows, leaving a halo around your image. That halo will be okay on the web — as long as your image sits on the same color background as your transparent color. If it sits on anything else, you'll see the halo light up like a Christmas tree. (See Figure 9-14 for an example of what I'm talking about.)

Figure 9-12: Aliased graphics have no blending on their edges — making the curved areas look like stairsteps.

Figure 9-13: Anti-aliasing places a tiny semi-transparent rim around curves to blend them softly into the background color.

Figure 9-14: What happens when single-color GIF transparencies and anti-aliasing don't play nicely together.

GIF animation

The GIF format also supports simple animation. A single GIF file can contain a series of graphics that you can display in a timed sequence; the animation works like a flipbook. You can, for example, set up the images to change every 2 seconds. You can also determine whether the images play through once and then stop or play in a loop. For these reasons, a lot of advertising banners you see on the Web are GIF graphics. Both Adobe Photoshop and Fireworks allow you to create and export animated GIF files.

JPEG format

The JPEG format (*J*oint *P*hotographic *E*xperts *G*roup) was designed to *compress* (shrink the file size of) photographic images for web delivery. Therefore, your images remain in 24-bit color and do not need to be reduced into a color palette before saving.

The compression scheme that JPEG uses has a blurring effect. The more you compress, the more blur you get. You can also save JPEG images with no compression. If you save them at 100% quality, the image looks perfect, with no distortions, but the file size will suffer. Because of the blurring effect, the JPEG format is not recommended for images that have sharp edges, a lot of text, or flat-colored areas. With such images, the danger is that you'll see odd granular intrusions called *artifacts* introduced into your image, as shown in Figure 9-15.

Try using the side-by-side comparison feature in Fireworks to try a few different JPEG compression settings to see which one works best. I like to try quality settings between 60 and 85 percent.

Figure 9-15: JPEG compression can introduce artifacts (visual noise) into images, especially on flat-colored areas.

PNG format

The PNG (*P*ortable *N*etwork *G*raphics) format, pronounced *ping*, is the most flexible of the web-graphic formats. As with a JPEG, you can save your image as a 24-bit image and preserve its quality, or you can downsize its palette and save it as an 8-bit image. PNG allows you to utilize transparency in your images, but you're not limited to a single color! You can specify degrees of transparency — 256 such levels — in an 8-bit format. This *8-bit transparency* comes in handy.

You may have noticed, for example, that Photoshop gives you the option of saving a PNG as a 32-bit image: In addition to your 24-bit image, you can include an *alpha-channel mask* that provides 8-bit transparency. The mask is basically a grayscale image: Where the mask is black, the image is completely transparent. Where the mask is white, the image is completely opaque. Gray colors in between make the image appear at varying degrees of transparency. See the example in Figure 9-16: On the top-right you see the source file in Photoshop with a soft drop shadow. On the top-left, you see that image exported as a 32-bit PNG appearing in a web browser. Notice how the soft shadow blends nicely against the changing backdrop of the web page. Keep in mind that while the PNG format affords you a lot of creative flexibility, you need to use them judiciously, as they can be large in terms of file size, causing them to download slowly.

SVG format

SVG (*S*calable *V*ector *G*raphics) is a code language for creating vector web graphics in XML. If you recall, vector graphics are defined by a series of points plotted on two dimensions connected by lines and curves, and then filled with a color. These graphics have a major difference from the bitmap graphics we've discussed so far: They can be described in an editable (and relatively compact) text file. Thus you can edit SVG graphics with a stroke of the keyboard, scale them up or down without loss of quality, print them at any resolution, animate them, or apply scripts to them. Because they are text-based, they're even discoverable by search engines. No wonder all the newer editions of the major browsers support this format. Due to the complexity of the SVG standard, however, designers still favor utilizing bitmap graphics, but I think we'll start to see a shift toward vector web graphics as new tools make working with them easier.

Figure 9-16: The PNG format allows you to include 8-bit alpha-mask transparency.

The SVG format is suitable for graphics that are more illustrative in nature. For example diagrams, models, or designs that you might create in Adobe Illustrator are appropriate. In fact, Illustrator allows you to export your illustrations in the SVG format via the Save for Web & Devices function found in the File menu.

The Usual Software Suspects

Before you begin designing, you should become familiar with the industry standard web-graphic software tools. While there are a number of tools on the market that may be more suited to the weekend warrior, the ones I list here are the professional-grade standards used by all agencies and in-house shops. They are expensive, and can be purchased separately or bundled in suites. Notice that all the products listed here are from Adobe Systems. (Adobe has systematically bought up the thoroughbreds of web-design software.) If you wanted to purchase all five of the programs listed in this section, look for the Adobe Creative Suite: Web Premium or Design Premium online or at your nearest Apple or computer store.

Photoshop

For creating, editing, and manipulating bitmaps, no other tool on the market holds a candle to Photoshop. The problem with Photoshop, however, is that learning to use it to its fullest is akin to learning to fly a jumbo jet. In addition to the years it may take to fully master Photoshop's power, you also have to deal with a steep price tag. A less-expensive alternative to Photoshop is Adobe Photoshop Elements, but I cannot vouch for its viability as a long-term investment.

Most web *comps*, as page designs are called in the industry, are built in Photoshop. It is the agency and in-house standard; most developers expect to be handed Photoshop comps before they build the actual website. Typically, there is one Photoshop file per web-page template. Photoshop allows you to make extensive use of layers and layer sets, keeping distinct (and helping you organize) all the components that make up your design. Take a look at Figure 10-1 for a peek at the numerous layers and layer sets that go into making one web page.

It's a best practice to name and organize your layers so that other designers can make sense of your document.

The file extension for native Photoshop source files is `.psd`.

Fireworks

One of my personal favorite graphics software tools is Fireworks because it is purpose-built for creating web comps. Unfortunately, it just has not really caught on as a standard at design agencies and in-house departments. (I'm sure it's because the designers are well vested in Photoshop.) That's a shame because a single web-page comp — with all its layers — in Photoshop can be 24–100mb file. (The Hansen's Home page comp shown back in Figure 10-1, for example, is a 26mb file.) I can design that same exact page in Fireworks and the file would be lucky to push 3mb because it utilizes a mix of vector and bitmap graphics. That is a file I could e-mail as an attachment to clients and developers.

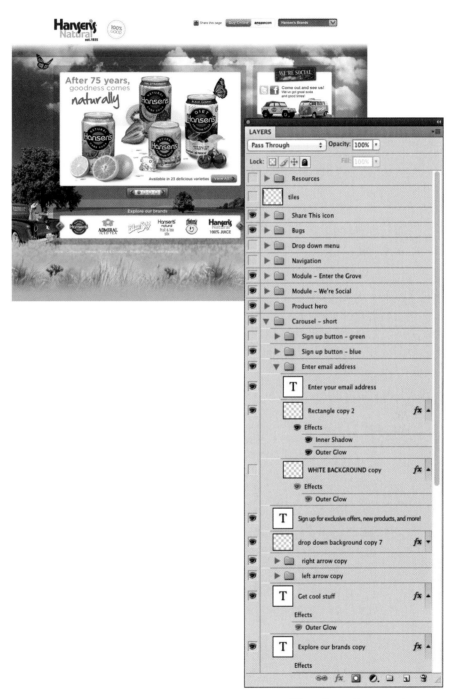

Figure 10-1: A web-page comp utilizes a number of Photoshop layers.

Not only is Fireworks a fantastic tool for creating web graphics, it also empowers us non-techies to add interactivity to our graphics — for example, links, rollover buttons, and drop-down menus that we can load and test in a browser at the click of a button. That's a great way to demonstrate proposed menu designs to clients, or to generate click-through user tests quickly.

The only edge that Photoshop has over Fireworks is in bitmap image enhancement and manipulation. However, you can do all those things in Photoshop and then import the result into Fireworks to work into your web layout. You can also export your Fireworks file as a Photoshop layered file, or import Photoshop layered files, so it has some good versatility.

When you save a Fireworks source file — with all its layers, interactivity, frames, and pages (yes, there is a "page" dimension to Fireworks that allows you to develop more than one web comp in a single file), you save it as a special flavor of .png file. This is not to be confused with the single-graphic PNG format you use on the Web; this particular .png file is a custom version of the PNG file format that Adobe uses to embed a lot more data.

Illustrator

I mention Illustrator here only because it is the standard for producing vector graphics. Often you'll need to create custom icons, buttons, or illustrations in web design — and it's easiest to use Illustrator for such tasks. You can then import these illustrations into Photoshop or Fireworks to fold into your web comp.

All web comps are built and assembled in either Fireworks or Photoshop. Illustrator merely contributes graphic pieces or is used to create individual web graphics you may export in various web formats, including SVG, PNG, and JPEG.

Flash

Flash allows you to create highly interactive web applications with ActionScript — its robust scripting language — and design animations that leverage the tight file sizes as well as the scalability of vector graphics. Flash files are output as .swf files such as the one shown in Figure 10-2, and can be embedded directly in your web page. Flash *movies* (as .swf files are often called) can be so interactive and complex that you can build an entire site experience just with Flash. The HTML page just presents the Flash file and Flash takes over from there.

The downside to Flash is that it requires end users to have the proper Flash plug-in and version installed on their browser to view (although most people have some version of it installed). Also, the Apple iPhone and iPad Safari browsers do not display .swf files — and as of this writing, do not plan to do so.

© California Milk Processor Board. www.gettheglass.com

Figure 10-2: This web experience is built entirely in Flash.

Dreamweaver

Dreamweaver is not a graphic-design tool; it's for building HTML pages and CSS files. What many people get confused about is that, on the one hand, you have your web-page comp designed in either Fireworks or Photoshop to look exactly the way your web page is going to look online — down to the last details of your scroll bars and footers. Then, on the other hand, you have developers who must re-create your comp designs in HTML, often using a tool like Dreamweaver.

Why do developers have to re-create your designs? I wish it were so that you could simply pull some levers in Photoshop and say "export this page" as an HTML file, but the truth is that in order to gain maximum page efficiency, developers must rebuild your page. Your comps serve not only as the piece-meal art source and layout to follow but also as the color, button, border, and text source needed to derive CSS styles.

I found a company that provides such a comp-to-HTML-page service. The company, called W3 Markup, takes your Photoshop or Fireworks layered comps and turns them into HTML pages with supporting CSS. They charge on a page-by-page basis and their fees are reasonable. Go to http://w3-markup.com for details.

Mood Boards: Setting the Tone

I know you want to jump in, already, but one step you might consider — especially when you're working with new clients, new brands, or new products — is to create a set of mood boards. A *mood board* is simply a collage of font choices, colors, and imagery (of anything from other websites to print ads) that captures a tone or a feeling. The idea is to explore tones that might inform the direction of your web designs.

I like to name each mood board for added effect, with something a little intriguing such as "Enhanced Reality," and include descriptive words that capture the tone. Figure 10-3 is one of four mood boards I created for a new Disney site. This board ended up not being chosen because the client liked the down-to-earth human and emotional component conveyed in a different board. That's great feedback and just saved me the effort of developing a set of web-design directions with a fantasy feel to them.

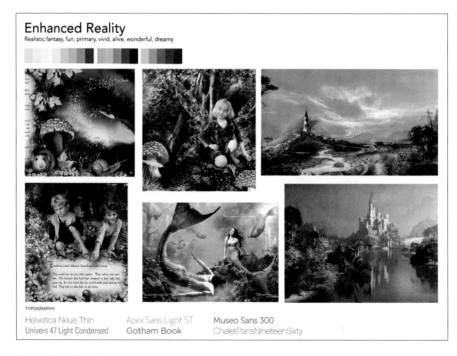

Figure 10-3: Mood boards are a collage of colors, fonts, and imagery designed to convey a tone that can inform your web design.

Because most web projects have a lengthy up-front information design phase, clients are often itching to see something visual. Mood boards are a great way to put early visuals in front of impatient clients and get a sense of what they like, what they don't like, and why — *before* you dive into creating design directions. In addition, many clients have trouble verbalizing the visual look they're going for, so mood boards are a great way to kick-start the conversation.

Design Resources

When you do finally sit down to explore different web-design directions, you're not on your own when it comes to tracking down the assets and resources you'll need to complete your designs. A number of online design resources can come in handy during the creative process. I use each and every one of the resources listed in the following sections.

Stock photography and illustration

You can find virtually any kind of photo or illustration — including icons — that you need for a project (even video and audio clips) at one of the many online stock-media companies. For instance, you can go to my favorite, www.istockphoto.com shown in Figure 10-4, and search through thousands of images based on handy criteria such as color profile, subject matter, and even image orientation.

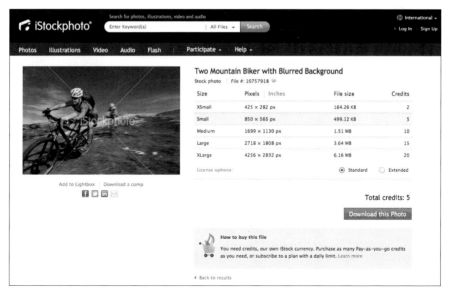

© iStockphoto IP. www.istockphoto.com

Figure 10-4: A great online stock media resource is istockphoto.com.

It's very inexpensive to purchase web-resolution images to use in your comps, and it's well worth the money. Istockphoto.com works on a credits system, whereby each credit is just over $1.00. Fortunately for web-design purposes, you only need one of the smaller images (each image has a few size options). By *small*, I mean 700 x 1000 or so pixels, and 72 dpi. What you *do not* want to do is utilize the free trial versions of images that have the copyright notice emblazoned on them. That is such a distraction to clients, and it makes your designs look unpolished.

If you do download the free placeholder versions of images just to make sure they'll work for your designs, generally each one comes with an image number in its filename. Keep that code number in the filename! If you do need to go and purchase the image later (or a higher-resolution version of it) you can search for it by its code.

Digital photography and scanning images

Why do I love my iPhone? Because it has an amazing built-in camera that, in a pinch, can capture great-quality images that I can e-mail to my desktop machine, adjust and resize in Photoshop, and plop into my web design in minutes. High-end digital cameras are great too, but just have the added step of hooking up the memory card or attachment cord to get the images out of the camera. Or, if you engage a professional photographer, you'll usually get a DVD of all the images to sort through. The good news is that because you're working with just 72 dpi, digital images are pretty fast and easy to work with.

The other option is to scan images using a desktop flatbed scanner. For desktop scanners, always scan at roughly twice the resolution you need. For web graphics that need to be 72 dpi, scan the images at 150 dpi. This way you capture enough detail to make editing easier. You can zoom into detail you need and crop away the rest, and you can always shrink it down, which eliminates the scan's graininess. (Scaling down images causes them to lose detail — including detail that highlights imperfections.)

Typography

I have mentioned before that when creating web-design options, it's best to use "greek" text as a placeholder for all body copy. You do not want a client focusing on reading text within your comps. You can generate the Greek text you need from www.lipsum.com and then copy and paste it into web comps.

For decorative headlines, I like to try out different fonts at www.veer.com. (See Figure 10-5.) You can type in your own phrase, adjust the size and color, and see how it looks in an assortment of fonts. What's even better, if you right-click (PC) or Control-click (Mac) the custom text you create in Veer, you can save the sample as a transparent PNG file. Notice that when you do so, the font's name is included in the filename so you can keep track of which font is what. You can then place the text into your web layout and see how it works, even change its colors or apply effects to it. The text itself is a bitmap image, but this is a great way to "try before you buy."

Figure 10-5: At Veer.com, you can enter custom text, adjust its size and color, and then right-click to save it as a transparent PNG file to place in your web comp.

Photoshop brushes

Photoshop excels at allowing you to create unique textures and effects to use in your designs. You may think that you need to download these textures as images from stock photography companies, but actually there are a ton of free and inexpensive Photoshop brushes that you can download online that create virtually any type of texture from splattered blood to Disney pixie dust. If you simply do a Google search for "Custom Photoshop Brushes," you'll get a wealth of websites to choose from. Or you can search for specific brushes like "pixie dust Photoshop brush." Of course, you still need to invest a lot of money to purchase Photoshop first!

Widgets

Widgets are standard components of computer and browser interfaces — scroll bars, system buttons, radio buttons, cursors, check boxes, and such. You'll often need to represent these in your web designs to indicate components that will be system-generated. Rather than taking screenshots and cutting out the pieces yourself, you can use some online resources that provide widgets already cut out on transparent backgrounds, ready to be placed in your designs. One site that can get you started is Designer's Toolkit at `www.webdesignerstoolkit.com`.

Web-design templates

If you need help getting ideas or getting started, a number of online resources offer free or pay-per-download web-design templates of varying quality. There are so many sites offering these templates that if you just do a Google search for "web-design templates," you'll be well on your way. (One site you can try is `www.templatesspot.com`.) Even if you don't buy online templates, they are a great resource to get design ideas. These templates are generally Photoshop layered files that are already set up in terms of resolution and dimension, and now it's just a matter of tinkering with them and customizing. Prices range from free to around $65 per page template.

Building a Web-Page Template from Scratch

The standard tool across digital agencies and in-house departments for building web graphics is Adobe Photoshop. Although Fireworks is optimized and purpose-built to produce web-graphic source files, it just has not caught on, probably because of the massive re-training effort it would entail to make whole departments make the switch. So I'm assuming that you, too, will be using Photoshop to develop your web comps. In this short step-by-step, I show you how to set up a new web-comp template and will discuss how to organize your layers and guides.

1. **Launch Photoshop.**

2. **Choose File⇨New.**

   In the dialog box that appears, enter a canvas dimension of 1,200 pixels wide by 1,000 pixels high. Resolution should be set to 72 dpi (*pixels* per inch, actually). The color mode should be RGB color. The background color can be white. Click OK.

3. **From the Photoshop menu, select Preferences⇨General.**

   On the left, select the Units & Rulers option. Then, in the main window area, for Rulers, select "pixels" from the drop-down menu. Click OK.

   You will be using guides. To do so, you must first turn on the Rulers from the View menu, as shown in Step 4.

4. **Select View⇨Rulers from the menu.**

   After you see the rulers, click the left side ruler and drag a vertical guide and drop it at the 100-pixel mark, as shown in Figure 10-6.

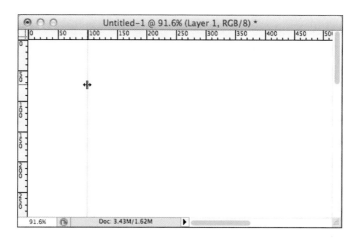

Figure 10-6: Drag out a vertical guide by clicking and dragging from the left ruler.

5. **Reset the 0,0 marker.**

   In the very top-left corner of your document, at the intersection of the two rulers is a small square with dotted lines in it. Click that square and drag to your guide at the 100-pixel mark, but be careful to stay at the tippy-top of the page. What you're trying to do is keep 0 at the top of your page (where it is now), but set your current 100-pixel guide mark to 0 instead. If you do it properly, you'll see the numbering update in your top ruler.

6. Set the second guide marker.

Click the left ruler again and drag out another guide. Drag this new guide across the page and drop it on the 1,000-pixel mark. If you've done Steps 1–6 properly, you should have a 100-pixel margin on either side of your two guides. Save the document.

I want to share a few notes before we move on in this exercise. First, you'll notice we are setting up a web page that will be 1,000 pixels across, with a skirt of 100 pixels on either end. Your design may be less than 1,000 wide, but these guides are a good start and keep you from going too wide. Just for comparison, the Apple.com navigation bar measures about 950 pixels wide.

The reason I want you to have a skirt of at least 100 pixels on either side is because I want you to think about your web page's background. When users with large monitors view your page, there is nothing worse than an unconsidered background that has no connection to the design of the page. At the very least, you should set a complementary solid background color — which can be white if that's what makes the most sense, as in Apple's case. Often designers use a large graphic as a backdrop or a smaller repeating tile *in conjunction* with a solid background color; CSS and HTML allow you to set both these properties.

7. Turn the background into a layer.

In the Layers panel, you should have just one layer called "Background" in italics. Double-click it to turn it into a layer that's capable of transparency, and of being moved into layer sets that you'll create. In the window that appears, leave the name as Layer 0 for now and click OK.

8. Create four layer sets.

At the bottom of the Layers panel you'll see a folder icon. Click it four times to create four distinct *layer sets* (folders that can contain layers). They're a great way to help keep you organized. Here are the steps:

 a. *Double-click the* Group 1 *text of the bottommost layer set and rename it to* **BACKGROUND** *in all caps.*

 I like to use all caps for folder names and lowercase for layer names to help distinguish them.

 b. *Click and drag the* Layer 0 *layer into the BACKGROUND layer set.*

 c. *Double-click the* Group 2 *text and rename it* **FOOTER**.

 d. *Rename the other two layer sets* **CONTENT** *and* **NAVIGATION**.

Your Layers panel should now look like Figure 10-7. These layer sets are just your starting point, and you may need fewer or more as you go. Save your template.

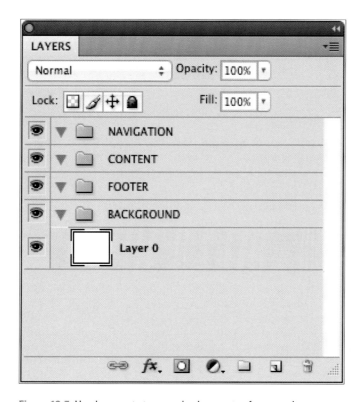

Figure 10-7: Use layer sets to organize key parts of your web comp.

You now have a blank canvas ready for your creative inspirations. As you create new layers to work on different parts of your comp, name them right away and make sure they are dragged into the appropriate layer set. Not only will that help you stay more organized, any other designer who picks up your comp to make changes — as well as the developer who has to use it to build the HTML version of it — will be better able to make sense of it.

Web Background Graphics

Designing a nice background for your website is an important detail that can add a lot of polish to your design. Considering that you do not know what sort of monitor people will have when viewing your site, you must account for all scenarios. While it's important to ensure that all main content and navigation fits within a 1,000-pixel-wide space, what happens to your site when it's viewed on a large cinematic monitor? Here are a few suggestions and examples for you to consider:

✔ **Pick a solid, complimentary background color.** At the very least, choose a solid color for your site's background that compliments the design. Don't just leave the background white because you simply forgot about it. If white is appropriate, then choose white.

Generally, more muted colors are better. If someone widens the browser window and gets a blast of bright orange, it's probably not the best user experience.

✔ **Use a repeating background tile.** Create a small graphic (can be any size, actually) that can seamlessly repeat across and down the page.

There's a bit of a trick to making a pattern that has no visible seams. Use Photoshop to place four copies of your tile end-to-end around the original tile's perimeter to see how all the edges line up. The advantage to using tiles is that regardless of whether you're using CSS code or HTML, one relatively small graphic is all it takes to fill a large area. This saves on download time.

✔ **Create a background tile that is a long, skinny horizontal strip.** With CSS, you can determine that a pattern repeats in just one direction: either *x* (horizontally across the page) or *y* (vertically down the page). If you create a tall, thin strip, say a gradation, you can have it repeat across the page only. You should then compliment this by setting a solid background color that matches the bottom color of your tile. That way, if users scroll down the page, they cannot see where your tile ends and the background color begins. (See the example in the Hong Kong Disneyland website shown in Figure 10-8.) We designed a thin decorative strip that ends in the color #badfef (the hexadecimal code for a light blue color). The page's background is set to this solid blue color. The tile sits on top of this color and repeats, or tiles, across the page. Because the tile ends in the same blue color as the background color, the effect is seamless.

✔ **Create a background tile that is much larger than your web page.** Many people think of background tiles as small, square graphics that work like a floor tile in a house. This isn't necessarily true. You can create a background tile that is (a) much larger than your web page, (b) is of any proportions, and (c) doesn't even repeat. This is a great way to create an "environment" behind your website, and reveal a nice surprise for people who widen their browser windows. Look again at Figure 10-1. The clouded-sky design with the red truck and grass is a single large background image that does not repeat. This background sits on top of a different background which — like the Hong Kong Disney site — uses a thin, repeating gradation tile that matches the large image's colors.

Figure 10-8: A thin, decorative background tile repeats across the Hong Kong Disneyland website, ending in a color that exactly (seamlessly) matches the underlying page color.

Developing Design Directions

After the information-architecture phase and an optional "mood board" presentation (see Chapter 10), the first visual presentation to your client is the "Round 1 Design Directions" presentation. This is a highly anticipated event in all web-design projects; it's when the client gets to see your proposed ideas for what the website could look like — both on a computer and on a mobile device.

Your comps should be complete graphical mock-ups of web pages — including all the HTML components, such as forms, text, and buttons. The idea is to show visually what the final page will look like without building the actual page in HTML.

Best practice here is to develop not one but at least three different design options that you can present to the client. Some agencies like to include slight variations on some of the options — in font, layout, or color scheme — to extend the presentation to include about 5–7 designs for the client to choose from.

Each design direction that you present should include a set of two pages — the home page and one sub-level page. This way, the client can see how the proposed graphic treatment works throughout the site. (It also forces you, the designer, to ensure your design can accommodate the rest of the site.) The designs should also show how the navigation works. After you prepare a few different designs, you can organize them into a polished presentation, which I'll discuss in the next chapter.

Working from wireframes

When you set out to develop your design options, you'll be working from the *wireframes* — the diagrams showing the page's structure, content, and navigation. Since you'll develop both a home page and a subpage, take these two wireframes and use them as your guide — much the way a builder refers to blueprints. Remember, the wireframes should be pretty much locked in, or at least at 90 percent complete, by the time you start on your design directions. The wireframes can serve as a checklist of website aspects for your design to accommodate — from navigation to content elements.

It's important to note that a designer should not be confined to the exact layout and proportions represented in the wireframes. You are not relegated to simply "coloring inside the lines." Use the wireframes to inform yourself about what's important, how much content to accommodate, and how the navigation works. The way you present these items visually is up to you.

Putting multiple designers on the task

Because you must create at least three different "looks" for the client to choose from, I like to put at least three different designers on the task. Typically, agencies will put together a creative brief and have an internal kickoff meeting with the assigned designers so that everyone understands what the client is looking for. The creative brief contains all the necessary background information that a designer would need — the goals of the project, the creative input from the client, the existing collateral, client preferences, and so on. In this meeting, you supply each designer with the wireframes and the creative brief as well as any other relevant material. Armed with this same input material, it's amazing how a range of designers can come up with a diverse array of creative solutions, as shown in Figure 11-1.

© Front Row. www.frontrow-studios.com

Figure 11-1: Here are two very different design directions created by two different designers using the same wireframe as a reference.

Gathering Design Input

The big question: Where do you start? The knowledge that you have to produce not just one but as many as three or more different designs is sure to conjure up the evil creative block that so often plagues writers. To ward off the block and start the creative juices flowing, I often look outward, not inward, for ideas. Here are three places to look:

- ✔ **Ask the client.** One of the simplest ways to find inspiration is to ask the client for ideas. To better understand the desires and expectations of your clients, discuss what websites they like (and sites that they don't like) and why. This helps shape your creative thinking toward something that the client ultimately appreciates.

- ✔ **Look at the client's existing materials.** An obvious and crucial place to look for inspiration is the client's current set of marketing materials. Most companies probably have a number of published materials (whether on paper or online) from which you can base your designs. For example, as shown in Figure 11-2, design elements from the company's products and packaging design, marketing collateral, and brand style guide are great resources to consider when developing your designs.

- ✔ **Look online.** Another source of inspiration is to look online at various award-winning websites. This chapter will explore a few examples to get you started.

© Specialized Bicycle Components. www.specialized.com

Figure 11-2: Specialized's product catalog has a refined brand look that can inform the design of their new website.

Creative inspiration

I asked John LaCroix, Associate Creative Director at LEVEL Studios, how he finds inspiration for new design projects. Here's what he had to say:

Q: How do you stay fresh in web design?

I visit a lot of websites that I find through social media and random web surfing. I constantly share these sites with others and ask their opinions, often standing over them when they visit for the first time. I'm looking for unfiltered, emotional reactions. As a designer, I find that I often take for granted the features and details that some users absolutely love and others violently hate. Websites are made for people; so I'm motivated to make them better by watching people, not designers, use them.

Q: How do you go about getting visual ideas for a particular project?

Great ideas come from unexpected places. As we interact with more and more devices in our daily lives, I try to remember that nearly anything we interact with is an interface that was designed by somebody. Sometimes I just take a walk and look around contemplating how I'd redesign everything I see. I've found myself looking at a chair and getting great ideas for how to design buttons on a website.

Q: How closely do you follow wireframes? Where do you take artistic license and why?

Wireframes are only one stage in the design process. Clients tend to have difficulty visualizing the final look and feel from wireframes, so this gives you an opportunity to take liberties with the organization of elements and continue to refine as needed. When images, colors, and fonts are brought into the mix, it can change everything. It's up to you to recognize this and make the design work without changing too much from the wireframes.

Q: Anything else you can think of that is important to the topic?

Compare apples to oranges. Find sites with greatly contrasting objectives to the one you're working on and break down exactly what makes that site interesting or useful. Your clients may also offer examples that seem irrelevant at first, but if you take a closer look it may spark one small, unlikely idea that can inspire a great, innovative design. Your clients will love you because you hit the mark while making them a useful part of the brainstorming process.

Getting Ideas for Visual and Interaction Design

One of the best ways to get ideas for the visual appeal and interaction strategy of your website is, well, to peruse the Web. There are several websites that aggregate great design examples in various categories and industries, such as e-commerce or health care. (For a quick look at some of them, just use the names of those industries as search words.) While it's helpful to look at websites within the same industry as your client's, good design ideas come from everywhere. You must learn how to isolate design approaches, break them down to essentials, and see how you can utilize them to influence your own designs.

Cinematic websites

One of the more popular trends is to design *cinematic* websites: A large *hero image* serves as a literal backdrop for the website, taking up the entire browser window. This dramatic approach really "romances" the product and forces the designer to come up with a visually clean system of supportive navigation. In such sites, interface elements and main navigation float on top of the backdrop, often with a degree of transparency so as to retain the larger-than-life look.

A lot of cinematic sites use Flash to accomplish the seamless look, such as the Specialized microsite shown in Figure 11-3. Notice, by the way, how the design feels similar to the Specialized print catalog in Figure 11-2, creating a unified family of marketing material.

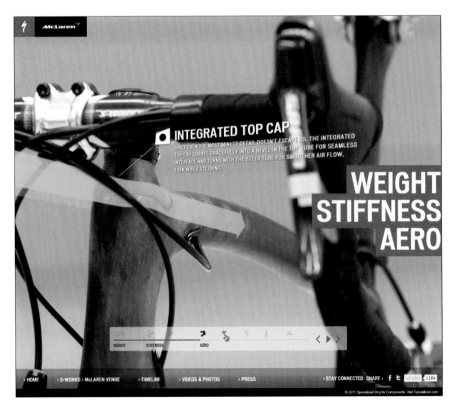

© Specialized Bicycle Components. venge.specialized.com

Figure 11-3: The Specialized Venge Flash-based microsite employs a dramatic cinematic approach.

What is unique about the Specialized example is that the large photo back-drop is the content itself: The minimalistic, transparent, overlaid elements of the interface reveal different parts of the bike or offer access to video segments about the making of the bike. There is also a mobile-friendly version of the site (since Apple devices don't support Flash animation). This version is slightly different in its presentation but shares the same look and feel, as you can see in Figure 11-4. (The mobile-friendly version could be improved upon by making the type much bigger and having a better plan for the main navigation, which is way too small for mobile viewing.)

© Specialized Bicycle Components. www.specialized.com

Figure 11-4: This mobile-friendly version of the Venge site is only slightly different in presentation.

Another good example of the cinematic approach is The Frye Company website shown in Figure 11-5: The rotating hero images fill the browser window for an immersive experience. This cinematic website does not rely on Flash and so it works well on mobile devices. However, it has not been optimized for the smaller display — and, as with the Venge site, the interface display is too small.

Arrows on either side of the hero space allow users to click through the images, but otherwise they auto-rotate. This site also has elegant drop-down menus that reveal a featured product at the bottom. What I don't like are the three big transparent overlay buttons at the bottom of the hero area. These three buttons activate a "drawer" that slides up to reveal more info and clickable links. Because they're used in this fashion, the three buttons could be half again as tall, and just have enough visual "affordances" so that users intuitively know that they are clickable. (As discussed in Chapter 5, affordances are design cues that suggest how a user should interact with an element.)

Innovative interaction design

Any way a designer can make efficient use of screen real estate — and, at the same time, keep users mentally grounded in terms of where they are in a website — is innovative and good design. Two examples in this section illustrate a creative use of two common ingredients: maximizing a content area and *scrolling* (up and down) or *panning* (side to side) within a controlled space.

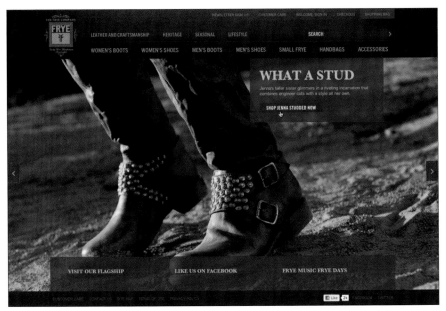

© The Frye Company. www.thefryecompany.com

Figure 11-5: The Frye Company has a cinematic website and elegant main navigation system that uses standard HTML and CSS coding.

One of the more unique means of navigation I've been seeing recently is a creative use vertical scrolling. The scrolling happens in a controlled, animated fashion, based on the user's click. For example, the Features portion of the Tesla Model S website (shown in Figure 11-6) starts users at the top of the page and presents six elements to explore. The content of all six are stacked on this page, and clicking on one of the buttons jettisons you down the page to reveal that portion. This way, the users see how the page is structured, and they can scroll up and down manually to visit all six panels. This is a great way to collapse several pages of content onto just one page. The minimalistic interface design also drives a user's focus to the product and the content. A similar example of this style of interaction design can be found at the Mea Cuppa website shown in Figure 11-7. This site even has a Start Scrolling cue at the top of the page.

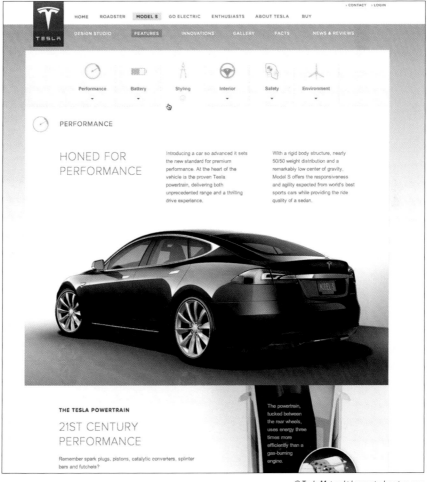

© Tesla Motors Ltd. www.teslamotors.com

Figure 11-6: Six buttons on the Tesla Model S Feature's section animate users up and down the page. The single page essentially has six vertically stacked content panels to explore.

Another excellent example of interaction and visual design is the Salt Lake City Public Library System website, show in Figure 11-8. This simple, clean site has two areas that are maximized in terms of their content display. The top portion has a rotating hero area (not uncommon); what's nice is that unlike many sites that use this convention, the open, layered visual approach breaks up the region so it doesn't look boxed in. The lower portion has two design features going on: Not only does a tabbed system allow the user to flip among four categories of content display (Movies, Books, Graphic Novels, and Zines), but also each tabbed display scrolls horizontally, revealing a nicely designed collage of products. Upon rolling over a product, the user sees a pop-up display offering more information, plus a link to the detail page. The compressed interaction in this design approach can provide quick access to hundreds of products, in one small portion of a page.

www.meacuppa.be

Figure 11-7: The Mea Cuppa website exists on one large web page that scrolls vertically.

Figure 11-8: This web page is divided into two content regions that can quickly and efficiently provide access to and more information about hundreds of products.

Capturing the brand experience

The ultimate goal of your visual-design efforts is to capture the essence of the brand experience. For example, when you walk into a Hollister store, the sights, décor, smells, and textures are a completely unique, immersive retail experience that is unlike walking into most other clothing stores. This is the Hollister *brand experience.* It would be a missed opportunity to apply the brand if the website did not offer an e-commerce version of that same extraordinary experience. As you can see in Figure 11-9, the Hollister website is right on target. The site supports a lot of information and products — but the visual design is richly textured and reprises the offline retail experience.

www.hollisterco.com

Figure 11-9: The Hollister website design reflects a branded retail shopping experience.

Another site that is beautifully designed yet houses a lot of information is the Sheffa Foods site shown in Figure 11-10. Notice how simple and clean the interface components are designed. If you were to remove the photography, as you can see in Figure 11-11, the site template design is actually very plain and monochromatic. That is the key to this design strategy. By keeping all support components simple and using just a few colors, you allow the content itself to take center stage. In this case, the content features bold photography that reinforces the Sheffa Foods brand image of fresh, high-quality products.

© Sheffa Foods, Inc. www.sheffafoods.com

Figure 11-10: The Sheffa Foods website is an elegant blend of simple interface components combined with dramatic photography and excellent typography.

Figure 11-11: Stripping out the content shows a simple Sheffa Foods web-design template, which lets the content stand out and create impact from page to page.

Designing a Mobile-Friendly Version of Your Site

When designing or redesigning a website, you must also consider creating alternative, mobile-friendly versions of the site. These versions are not to be confused with native applications that live on your smart phones (the ones you download from app stores). Smart phones all have web browsers and can render your website with varying degrees of success. Essentially, you must make a list of what devices you will support, and design alternative sites to meet these multiple targets. Other than that, the most obvious constraint they all share is the small screen size of phone browser windows.

You can add code to your site that detects a user's device and redirects them to the appropriate version of your website. With so many devices to choose from, developers typically create various *device profiles* and lump many devices into one of a handful of these profiles. Profiles are usually driven by screen size:

Microscopic: 132 pixels or less wide

Tiny: 240 pixels or less wide

Small: 320 or less wide

Given these small screen spaces in which to deliver your web experience, there's no getting around the need to provide alternative designs. In the following sections, I cover the key points to take into account when you're designing a mobile-friendly version of your website. For more in-depth information, take a look at *Mobile Web Design For Dummies* by Janine Warner and David LaFontaine.

A new way to look at pixels

What's unique to devices is that we are not dealing with 72-dpi pixels anymore. Many of these devices have higher resolutions. This is where things get tricky, because for websites and CSS, you must still define elements in pixels that are 1/72 inch wide. This measurement has nothing to do with the pixel density of devices, so the pixel is now a relative unit of measure. There is a great article online that explains this mind-bending phenomenon in detail (search "A pixel is not a pixel" by John Gruber or go to www.quirksmode. org/blog/archives/2010/04/a_pixel_is_not.html).

Nevertheless, if you were to set up a Photoshop template to simulate an iPhone screen space, you'd use 640 x 960 at 72 dpi. This screen size gives you the right "retinal display" detail you'll get on an iPhone. But don't be tempted to squeeze a lot of text and images into this space. This is clearly a much larger canvas size than the phone. To get a sense of how your design will actually display on the phone, zoom out your Photoshop document to 50 percent.

Simplify the navigation

Remember, there is no mouse to move around. Many mobile users have either a keypad or a touchscreen. There isn't a lot of space to show all the navigation elements you might normally include in the main site. For this reason, mobile versions of sites often have a stripped-down navigation scheme. If you look at the CNN mobile site for iPhone in Figure 11-12, you'll see three main buttons, a drop-down list, one feature story, an ad, and a weather button. This is a lot more compact than the main CNN website shown in Figure 11-13; it has to be.

Often, these reduced sites are frustrating to users who are on the go and need to access a certain area of the normal site. That's why it's a best practice to include a link to view the main site.

Figure 11-12: The mobile-friendly version of CNN is a highly simplified version of the normal site.

Figure 11-13: The regular CNN website is much richer in content and navigation features than its mobile counterpart.

Reduce file sizes

When they're not using Wi-Fi to browse the Web, mobile devices cam rack up a lot of megabytes on a user's data plan, which may have a monthly limit. Therefore, the more you can reduce the file size and dimensions of interface and content components, not only will your site download faster on cell networks, but it will tread lightly on the user's monthly data transfer allocation budget. You can also remove unnecessary code, comments, and optional tags to speed things along.

The easiest way to reduce file sizes is, once again, to simplify the site. Making the user wait (and pay) to download too much content and navigation features that are too small to see — or use effectively — is just a waste on all fronts.

Horizontal and vertical orientation

Mobile browsing is a fluid environment. Between the variety of pixel densities and the ability to view sites in both horizontal and vertical orientations, it's best to approach your mobile-friendly website with a flexible layout, as opposed to a fixed-width layout. By not specifying the site's width and letting it fill up the available space naturally — and by working with percentage widths for content regions and "ems" for type — you adapt your site more effectively to the mobile viewing environment. (One em is the height of a capital "M" in the browser's default font setting as set by the user, and so can be a variable height.) Additionally, use CSS color and tiled graphics, instead of pixel-bound single images, to fill your components.

Use a single-column layout

Even though smart phones are larger than their predecessors, they're still not big enough to effectively support more than a single-column layout when displaying content. This is a significant design alteration to make to your main web design, but well worth the effort in terms of the usability boost. A single-column content layout that uses the entire width of the screen (in whatever orientation) avoids the need for a user to pan back and forth or zoom in. Let the *content* expand down the page instead. Users are much more accepting of scrolling down the page than they are of having to move side to side and zooming in — or all three at once.

The Crew Clothing Company mobile site, shown in Figure 11-14, is an excellent example of a complex e-commerce mobile site that uses a simplified navigation system and a single-column layout to pack in a lot of functionality. In addition, they also provide a clear link to view the main site in case users need additional functionality that has been stripped out of the mobile version.

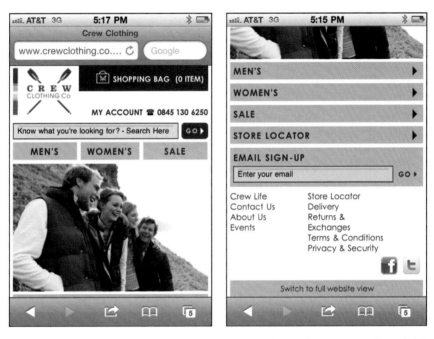

© Crew Clothing Co Ltd. www.crewclothing.co.uk/mobile

Figure 11-14: The Crew Clothing e-commerce mobile site is a simplified single column with a lot of bang for the buck. At right: what users see as they scroll down the home page.

Presenting Your Design Masterpiece

Gaining client approval at every milestone is an indispensable part of being a web designer, producer, or developer. How you present your designs plays an integral part of your success in selling your designs.

Whether you are presenting in person or remotely, there are a few underlying commonalities that I've found work best. The first is to present options. Clients get nervous if you come in for a big presentation and have only one idea on the table. If they don't like it, they'll have serious doubts about continuing with you. First, presenting options to your clients shows that you're open and flexible and are looking for their input at a critical crossroad. Second, your presentation must be polished and professional. Finally, your attitude while presenting must be deferential and never defensive. When you put your work out there, treat it objectively. Look at it from the viewpoint of the client, as if together you're judging the work of another agency — discussing the merits, the pros, and the cons of each idea.

In this chapter, I show you how to prepare a presentation so clients can best judge your work. I also show you how to print your designs and mount them on boards. Together, an online and a printed presentation help clients better understand your design ideas, which enables them to choose a direction for their site. I also give you tips for pitching your work to clients and guiding them toward the design solution that you think is best.

Assembling an Online Presentation

With all your design directions in hand (as spelled out in Chapter 11), your next creative task is to figure out the best way to present them to the client. I find that a good strategy is to develop both an online and an offline presentation. The online presentation gives the client the chance to see, in the browser, how the various designs will look on the computer and on devices. The offline presentation is a series of printed pages, mounted on nice boards for a polished effect. The printed portion of your presentation allows the client to quickly compare different designs side by side, as well as to refer to certain designs for discussion. Overall, the online/offline combination gives your presentation a powerful one-two-punch.

This particular section focuses on how to create online presentations. Offline presentations are discussed later in the chapter.

Presenting your designs online

The best way to showcase all the design directions online is to build a special project website just for the client. Ideally, this website is password-protected so no one but you and the client can enter; however, if your resources are limited, a *hidden web address* should suffice. A hidden web address is one so arcane that only you and the client could ever find it without knowing the direct path. An address like *www.yourcompany.com/clientname/projectname* should do the trick.

You should save each mock-up as one giant JPEG file, with 100% quality (no compression), and show it in the browser window. As the screenshot in Figure 12-1 shows, this technique makes the page look real and shows where the cutoff points are that require a user to scroll. By showing a non-functioning JPEG that looks real, the client can get a sense of how the website will look before you commit to actually building it in HTML.

The project website is a design repository for everything from the approved sitemap and wireframes to the design directions. As you make your way through a project, you'll find that you'll want to present more than one round of design directions; the project site is also a good place to store past rounds so that a client can see the design's evolution. In addition, clients like to be able to refer back to this project site and share designs with co-workers.

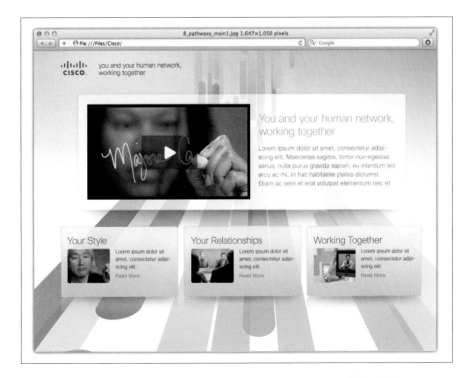

Figure 12-1: This design option created for Cisco by LEVEL Studios fits nicely within a 1,000-x-800-pixel browser size.

Organize a project index page that provides links to the pages of each design direction. Figure 12-2 shows one such client project site created by David Solhaug of www.sgrafik.com. In addition, I find it useful to give a descriptive name to each design direction, such as "Direction 1: colorful, geometric," to make it easier to refer to them. Because clients will be looking at the project site without your guidance, I also like to provide a short paragraph or bulleted list that explains the logic and the benefits of each direction.

The online presentation not only allows you to efficiently organize all the design directions in one convenient location, making it easy for a client to see all the directions, but also allows you a chance to include your own branding on an index page, or design a nice frame with your name and logo around the client comps for that extra professional touch.

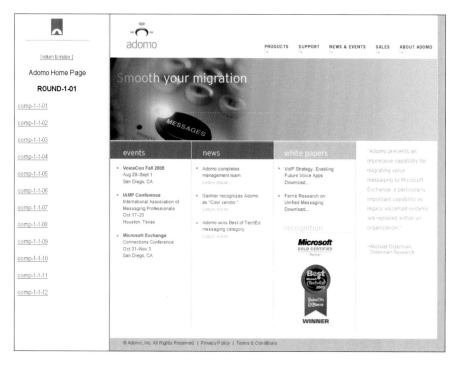

Figure 12-2: This project site developed by Solhaug Grafik offers his clients access to all current and past design directions, wireframes, and versions of the sitemap.

Constructing working and non-working prototypes

For the most part, you don't need to provide working HTML prototypes for your client presentations. Simple JPEG images should suffice to give a client a good idea of how the site will function. If you need to show how a complex interaction will work, you may consider showing a series of mock-ups in storyboard form rather than spending the extra time to make the online component really work.

In some cases, it may be worthwhile to make a small portion of the page actually function. In such cases, you can fake it by using minimal HTML and various technologies that are quick and easy to implement. For example, you may find that in the bidding stage of a project, you may have to invest time in a semi-working, animated presentation simply for the wow factor, to help win the project in the first place.

Remote presentations

The Internet allows you, as a web designer, to work with clients all over the world right from your home office. In fact, I never met the good folks at *National Geographic* in person, even though I designed at least three separate sites for them. All our presentations were carried out over the phone along with online presentations.

A great way to run remote presentations is to use a tool such as WebEx (www.webex.com) or GoToMeeting (www.gotomeeting.com). These tools allow everyone to call into a conference line (or in the case of WebEx, it calls you to add you to the call), and a web link allows clients to see my screen as I move the cursor around to point out various elements.

Creating Sizzling Printed Presentations

In addition to an online presentation (described earlier in the "Assembling an Online Presentation" section), you should have a color printed presentation — if only for backup purposes. Just imagine not having access to the Internet during your client meeting, or some other technical troubles. Aside from having a good backup, it's always a good idea to surround the customer with visuals. For one thing, unless you have access to an oversized monitor or projection system, it's hard to have the same impact with a small monitor when presenting to even a small group of people. Besides, on the computer screen, the client can see only one screen at a time. Comparing two design options side by side is impossible unless you have printed copies.

Creating black-and-white copies of the designs for each client present at the meeting is also a good idea. This way, they can take notes during the presentation and mark up ideas right on the design. Along with the black and white prints, include a copy of the site map and wireframes so clients can refer to them in the meeting.

In living color: Printing your mock-ups

These days, printing beautiful photographic-quality prints of your mock-ups is a simple and affordable process. The price of high-end desktop color printers has come down remarkably in the last few years while the quality has increased ten-fold. For $300–$500, you can buy a great desktop color printer that gives you more than enough quality. I currently own an Epson that is capable of printing on the large 13-x-19-inch paper size or on rolls.

When printing your mock-ups for a presentation, don't worry that your comps are just 72 dpi. Just print them at size, or perhaps a little larger. If you alter the resolution, you run the risk of making them appear blurred in the printout. In addition, as shown in Figure 12-3, print all your designs in the same orientation — either landscape or vertical, whichever orientation works best for your set of designs. I like to print the designs centered on either oversize 11-x-17 paper or "Super B" paper, which is 13 x 19. (Standard 8½-x-11-inch paper is too tiny to make an impact.) Printing all in the same orientation and on same-size paper creates a polished, professional presentation with impact.

Always use the more expensive photo-grade glossy paper for your prints. If the paper isn't glossy, the ink soaks into the paper too much and the designs look dull. When this happens, you can often see the row lines of the ink dots — cheapening the effect of your presentation. Also, matte paper has a tendency to warp and curl when saturated with a lot of ink. When you print, look in the Print dialog box for the paper type settings and make sure to choose the Glossy Paper and Best Quality options for your output settings. If you don't choose the correct paper in the print settings, the results aren't as good, and you waste a nice piece of expensive glossy paper!

Figure 12-3: Print your web-design mock-ups centered on a larger piece of paper with all designs in the same orientation, either landscape or vertical.

Mounting your work on boards

Like a flimsy handshake or a wilting business card, your nicely colored prints just won't have maximum impact unless you mount them on sturdy boards. The standard in the web-design industry is to use black boards that are black all the way through. Don't use black-colored boards that have white interiors shining through along the cut edges. These boards have a tendency to fade even before you get to the presentation.

I like to use quarter-inch black foam-core boards. They are light and sturdy and won't warp. You can buy them at any art store, and usually you can have them cut to a consistent size for you right at the store. Otherwise a good straight edge, a cutting mat, and an X-Acto™ knife will do the trick. I find it best to mount each design on its own board. That way, the boards are not unmanageably large, and clients can easily pass selected designs around the room.

Adhesive-schmesive

You may think I'm being a bit (ahem) retentive, but the sticky stuff that you use to mount your boards makes a big difference — not only in the final look but also in the flexibility you have for remounting. Rule Number One: Never use glue! If you use glue, the boards and the print are ruined afterward — you can never separate them from one another and reuse the boards. In addition, the drops of glue leave discernible lumps under your print.

The best adhesives to use are either 3M Spray Mount or a lightly adhesive, ultra-thin, double-sided tape. These allow you to remove your prints for remounting (in case you mess up) or you want to reuse the boards for a future presentation. Spray Mount comes in an aerosol spray can and is pretty easy to use. Always use it in a well-ventilated area and use it *sparingly*. A little goes a long way.

If you use Spray Mount, don't spray the board! The spray goes everywhere and makes everything sticky. Instead, spray your print, face-down, with an oversize sheet of paper underneath to catch all the extra spray. Hold the can one to two feet away and make *one* pass over the entire back of your design. Let it dry for a minute and then mount the print to your board. If you use double-sided tape, place one strip at the top and one at the bottom of your print and then mount it to the board.

Consistency

One of the most important details in your presentation is to make sure everything is consistent. Use the same boards, use the same glossy paper, and make sure everything is cut to the same size! As shown in Figure 12-4, you don't want one board to be 11 x 14 while the rest are 14 x 17. Consistency ensures that the focus is on the designs and not the irregularities in the presentation.

designs, and if they don't like any of the designs, to at least find elements they like and dislike from each. Let them know that the second round is usually driven by a combination of elements from these designs.

✔ **Ask clients to select which design is best.** It's rare that clients love one of your first round designs. Let clients know that this is normal before they even look at your designs. If in fact they do love one of the designs as-is, that's great — otherwise ask them to select one that is closest to the target. You can then use this design as the basis for the next round of development.

Here we go again: Round two

More often than not, your designs won't hit the nail on the head the first time around. Be prepared for the client to like certain aspects of each design and ask you to do another round that combines the various elements into one new design. I call this second design round the "Frankenstein round."

This is actually a healthy process, believe it or not, because you're still the designer and can control how the various aspects are combined into one cohesive design. Plus, at the end of this round, you should be that much closer to something the client loves.

The worst scenario, however, is to let clients try their hand at assembling the Frankenstein round of designs themselves. This can truly result in a monster of unbridled proportions. When clients dig in with their own hands, their hearts and their egos get involved, too. The resulting design is likely to be a horrific mess that needs a lot of help. Unlike you, with your professional distance, a client might not take kindly to honest criticism, and there you are, stuck with their mess.

The other "gotcha" is to let the client request too many design changes. I have worked for large corporations that noodle a poor vendor's designs over and over. Not only does this make timelines slip, it also makes profit margins slip. Be upfront in your initial proposals about the number of design revisions included in your bid. Be sure to tell clients that any noodling past the second or third round incurs hourly rate charges above and beyond the fixed bid amount.

Part IV
Producing the Final Website

The 5th Wave — By Rich Tennant

@RICHTENNANT

TOWN BANK

MR. LUGGAT

"We have no problem funding your Web site, Frank. Of all the chicken farmers operating Web sites, yours has the most impressive cluck-through rates."

*A*t the end a complex working day, when all the designers go home for their well-deserved rest, the HTML and programmer folks come in — lattes in hand — and begin final assembly of the website. Although website design is a team activity, everyone on the team must know a little bit about everyone else's job in order to make the whole process go smoothly. As a web designer, you must know enough about HTML, CSS, and what goes on behind the scenes to be able to design a site that makes best use of all those juicy technical capabilities — and is easy to maintain once the site goes live.

For example, if you design a graphics-heavy interface with a weird, slanted layout, the HTML people will have a hard time implementing the design and making it look the way you intend. Additionally, the site will be hard to maintain, take too long to download, and won't be search engine friendly.

Chapter 13 steps you through what can be done with HTML and CSS. Chapter 14 discusses the critical behind-the-scenes topics of platform selection, content strategy, and site analytics. Lastly, Chapter 15 goes into business-oriented considerations such as database, social media integration, and global strategies (including support for multiple countries and languages).

Building the Presentation Layer

*E*very web page has two sides — the nice-looking side that visitors see, and the underlying HTML and CSS side that holds everything together. Collectively, the HTML and CSS coding that makes websites look, animate, and interact the way they do is referred to as the *presentation layer*. You're going to need to familiarize yourself with this less-glamorous coding side if you want to be a more effective designer. Note that I'm not saying that you *must* know how to write HTML and CSS code, but you do need to know how these two languages are structured, what is possible and not possible, and under what circumstances you can copy and paste chunks of code (my favorite form of coding).

Mastering HTML and CSS is really not that difficult, but does take dedication. The Web itself makes learning HTML and CSS tricks, tips, and shortcuts from other web pages easy because your browser enables you to take a sneak peek at the HTML coding behind any web page. In addition, there are many online tutorials and resources. Writing presentation layer code is also not too hard with the help of software tools like Adobe Dreamweaver that tend to have easy-to-use interfaces and show you the results of your coding in real time.

ERWIN *de* **RUITER**

Ik ben Erwin, 28 jaar en houd me vooral bezig met online development en design. Ja ik weet het: een zeldzame combinatie. Daarnaast houd ik me bezig met het uitdenken van technische innovaties. Ik ben een ochtendmens en je mag me 's nachts ... er maken voor een bak zwarte koffie met een ... stuk pure chocolade. Ook ben ik altijd in ... or een potje Mario Kart.

In this chapter, you get a bird's eye view of basic HTML and CSS — a designer's sense of how they work together and what their capabilities are. So, without further ado, put on your propeller cap and take a look under the hood and into the world of presentation-layer coding.

HTML: The Glue That Holds a Page Together

Everything that you see on a web page is held in place by a page-layout language called *HTML* (*HyperText Markup Language*). Since the time that HTML was first introduced, it has evolved from a simple way to display and link documents on multiple types of computers to its current capabilities — which include support for complex CSS page layouts, rich interactive media, and programming languages such as JavaScript and PHP. HTML essentially provides the structure of a web page.

A browser, such as Mozilla Firefox or Internet Explorer, interprets the HTML code and draws the nice-looking side of the page that we all know and love.

The first graphical web browser on the scene, introduced in 1993, was called Mosaic. This little program was an overnight success and, just one year later, evolved into Netscape under the code name "Mozilla."

Within the browser window, HTML is sort of like the "man behind the curtain" in *The Wizard of Oz*, pulling off an amazing display of graphics, animation, and media, all without being seen — that is, of course, until you take a peek (as shown in Figure 13-1). The HTML and CSS code behind any website you visit is accessible by selecting View⇨Source from your browser's menu.

When you first take a look at a page's HTML code, you may think that you're looking at specs for a rocket launcher, but it's really not that complex. HTML uses a system of *tags*, bits of code that define every type of element (from text blocks to links and images) on a web page. All these tags are marked by a set of opening (< >) and closing (< / >) characters. For example, the <a> HTML tag is the *anchor tag* used for linking to other pages or to parts of the current page. So, to make the text Click here to see our sales items into a link that goes to the page sales.html, you use opening and closing anchor tags as follows:

```
<a href="sales.html">Click here to see our sales items</a>
```

Notice how the opening anchor tag is not just a simple bracketed "a" like <a>. It has an *attribute* inside the brackets — href — that gives the browser more information. Because the <a> link can either go to another page or to a portion of the current page, you have to specify which location you have in mind. In this case, I want the link to go to another page, so I use the href attribute and give it a value of ="sales.html".

You are not limited to just one attribute to help define an HTML tag. You can add a whole bunch of attributes and values in the opening tag. Look again at Figure 13-1. On line four, the opening anchor tag has *four* attributes.

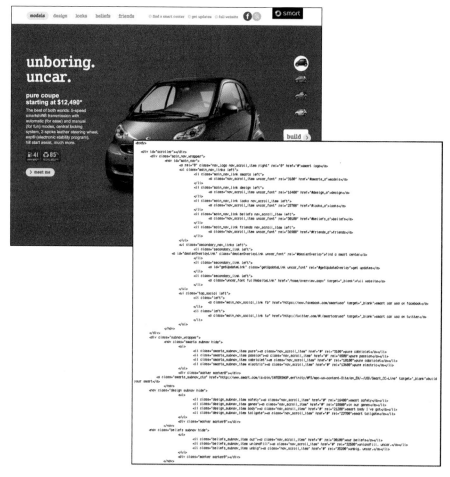

© *Daimler Vehicle Innovations USA LLC. www.smartusa.com*

Figure 13-1: A peek at the HTML and CSS code behind a website.

Learning HTML is mainly about learning all the various tags and where they go in the code structure. If you can remember this much, you can get pretty far in your copying-and-pasting career. You can literally build web pages by copying and pasting tags from other pages and then modifying them slightly for your own purposes.

Sneaking a peek at the source code

As I mention earlier, web browsers enable you to view the HTML and CSS source code of a page. Sneaking a peek at the source code of a web page is a great way to see how it's built — and to see how you can do something similar.

To see the HTML code behind a web page, follow these simple steps:

1. **Go online and open a web browser, such as Mozilla Firefox or Internet Explorer.**

2. **Go to any website by typing the URL of any web page whose HTML source code you'd like to see.**

3. **Look at the HTML source of the page:**

   • In Firefox, choose View⇨Page Source from the menu bar.

   • In Internet Explorer, choose View⇨Source.

   You'll see a new window with the HTML code for the current page you are viewing. (Refer to Figure 13-1 for a more schematic representation of what goes on.) If you glance through the code, you'll see the text content of the page and all the <a> tags for each link. You can select and copy the whole page or any portion of it.

The source window shows you just the HTML code, not any externally linked CSS documents. If the page uses CSS, the <head> section at the top of the HTML code will contain the URL path to the CSS file, as shown in Figure 13-2. You can copy the path and paste that into your browser's location field, like typing in a web address, and see the CSS code that the page uses.

In the Figure 13-2 example, the CSS link is written as a *relative* path — relative to the http://www.smartusa.com/ path already in the web browser. To complete the path you need to append /unassets/css/smart_min.css to the URL that shows in the address bar at the top of the screen. Your complete path to access this CSS example is

http://www.smartusa.com/unassets/css/smart_min.css

```
<!DOCTYPE html>
<html manifest="/unassets/cache.manifest?cb=1773862274" xmlns:fb="https://www.facebook.com/2008/fbml" lang="en">
<head>
    <meta charset="UTF-8">
    <meta http-equiv="X-UA-Compatible" content="IE=9,chrome=1">
    <title>eco-friendly. high mpg micro cars. smart USA</title>
    <link rel="stylesheet" type="text/css" href="http://fast.fonts.com/cssapi/61485a38-09bc-4d06-8a77-2f618bd7352d.css" />

    <link rel="stylesheet" type="text/css" href="/unassets/css/smart_min.css" />

    <meta name="description" content="Unbig. Uncar. Official site of smart USA featuring high gas mileage and electric micro cars that embody innovation and
efficiency." />
    <meta name="keywords" content="smart car, smart cars, electric car, eco friendly cars, electric smart car, smart car body kits, smart car mpg, smart car price,
smart car fortwo, micro cars, smart car gas mileage" />
    <meta name="apple-mobile-web-app-capable" content="yes" />
    <meta name="apple-mobile-web-app-status-bar-style" content="black" />
```

© Daimler Vehicle Innovations USA LLC. www.smartusa.com

Figure 13-2: At the top of the HTML source you see URL links to CSS code files.

When you finish adding the relative path to the URL, you press or click Enter to access the CSS; if you're running Windows, the CSS shows up in a Notepad file that opens automatically onscreen. Figure 13-3 shows the extracted CSS code behind the Smart Car website. I cleaned it up in Dreamweaver (separating each code snippet) so it's easier to read.

```
article,aside,details,figcaption,figure,footer,header,hgroup,menu,nav,section
{display:block}

blockquote,q
{quotes:none}

blockquote:before,blockquote:after,q:before,q:after
{content:'';content:none}

ins
{background-color:#ff9;color:#000;text-decoration:none}

mark
{background-color:#ff9;color:#000;font-style:italic;font-weight:bold}

del
{text-decoration:line-through}

abbr[title],dfn[title]
{border-bottom:1px dotted;cursor:help}

table
{border-collapse:collapse;border-spacing:0}

hr
{display:block;height:1px;border:0;border-top:1px solid #ccc;margin:1em 0;padding:0}

input,select
{vertical-align:middle}

body
{font:13px/1.231 sans-serif;*font-size:small}

select,input,textarea,button
{font:99% sans-serif}

pre,code,kbd,samp
{font-family:monospace,sans-serif}

html
{overflow-y:scroll}

a:hover,a:active
{outline:0}

ul,ol
{margin-left:2em}
```

Figure 13-3: By copying and pasting the CSS URL path in a browser window, you can view a page's CSS source file.

Learning (borrowing) from others

When you've had a peek behind the curtain, you can bookmark the next interesting web page you see when you're surfing around the Internet, and come back to it in the future to see what makes it tick. I've found that the best way to teach yourself HTML and CSS is to study the structure of pages you see every day. After looking at a number of these pages and picking them apart, you start to understand the basic structure of the code and the order in which tags should be laid out on a page — crucial stuff to know before you start copying, pasting, and modifying code.

Like the wings of a butterfly, the opening and closing HTML tags mirror each other in terms of their position on the page. For example, the first line of a web page opens with the <html> tag. The last line is the closing </html> tag. In between are all the object tags. As seen in Figure 13-4, the tags are nested like Russian dolls inside each other. If one tag pair is out of position, the object won't render correctly in the browser.

```
<html xmlns="http://www.w3.org/1999/xhtml">

    <head>

        <title></title>
        <meta http-equiv="Content-Type" content="text/html; charset=iso-8859-1" />
        <meta http-equiv="Content-Language" content="en-us" />
        <link href="Global.css" rel="stylesheet" type="text/css" />
        <script src="Scripts.js" type="text/javascript"></script>

    </head>

    <body>

        <div id="globalContainer"></div>
        <script type="text/javascript"></script>

    </body>

</html>
```

Figure 13-4: Opening and closing tag sets are nested inside each other, mirroring each other's relative location in the page structure.

After you know the basic structure of an HTML page, you understand what parts to copy from other web pages — and where to paste them into your own page for further editing and experimenting.

No two browsers interpret the same HTML code in the same way. Building a web page that looks horrible in one browser and perfectly fine in another is entirely possible. There are a lot of online resources for "workarounds" to help troubleshoot these discrepancies. One such resource can be found at http://websitetips.com/css/solutions/.

HTML editing with power tools

When you're just starting out, one of the best tools for writing HTML and CSS code is Adobe Dreamweaver. This software application allows you to see a split-screen view (as shown in Figure 13-5) so that you can see your visual design at the same time you're coding. Any code changes you make are immediately reflected in the visual design view. This is a great real-time illustration of how things work. Even seasoned professionals like to use Dreamweaver because it offers a lot of short cuts to faster coding and fewer errors. (Missing even just one character can throw off your whole design.) For example, Dreamweaver has an auto-complete feature; as you type code, it offers suggestions. CSS also has panels that allow point-and-click visual interfaces to configure CSS styles.

Another company that offers HTML and CSS coding software tools is CoffeeCup at `www.coffeecup.com`. Its tools also offer an auto-correct feature to help keep your code clean and error-free.

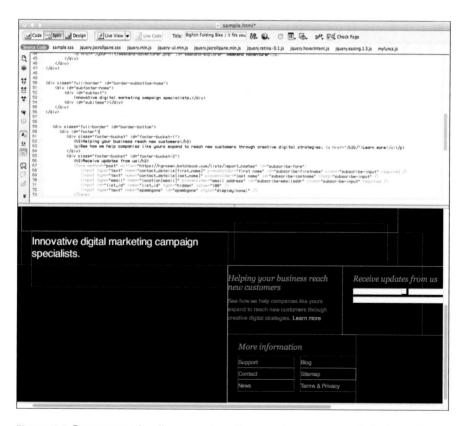

Figure 13-5: Dreamweaver's split-screen view allows you to see your page's design and its source code at the same time.

Web standards

Through the years, HTML and CSS constantly evolve to support an increasing appetite for richer content and interactive displays. Additionally, different companies have developed browsers that interpret both HTML and CSS — some better than others. Because of all this constant innovation on two fronts, the issue of *standards* is naturally at the forefront of web industry discussions. Leading the standards charge is the W3C organization, an international community of developers who work together to ensure the Web evolves to the best of its potential.

The World Wide Web Consortium, at `www.w3.org`, is sort of the keeper of the World Wide Web kingdom — approving all new HTML coding standards and just about every technology that integrates with HTML. Their website offers a lot of in-depth explanations if you are looking to learn more. Another website resource that offers a lot of code samples — and pointers on how to use them — is `www.w3schools.com`.

HTML5

The newest evolution of HTML is HTML5, which takes all of us leaps and bounds forward. This generation offers an expanded set of elements and properties — allowing for cool new design and interaction possibilities. It cleans up a lot of the browser "workarounds" mentioned earlier — and acknowledges the way coders use elements. For example, amazingly enough, a new — and long-awaited — `nav` element defines navigation components (previously coders would have had to create special *containers* for those, using other elements). Because HTML5 also supports mobile web devices, it has rapidly become the new standard and is by now supported by all major browsers (although Internet Explorer does require that the web page include a *code shim* — a redundant code segment written in a way that Internet Explorer can understand).

A mobile and device-friendly solution

With the introduction of HTML5, one particularly thorny issue may have finally been laid to rest: achieving cool animation effects on Apple devices without the use of Flash. The Apple device platform has never supported Flash. This refusal was more about Flash hogging battery-and-bandwidth resources than about company rivalry with Adobe (the makers of Flash). Whatever the case, any websites that used Flash for anything whatsoever — say, navigation, interaction, or animation effects — would simply not work on iPhones or iPads. One website (before we redesigned it) was entirely reliant on a complex utilization of Flash. When the company's CEO opened the website on his iPad, a blank black screen was all that appeared. HTML5 came to the rescue. We found we could replicate the cool interactive and animation features of the site with HTML5 and drop Flash altogether.

An animation alternative

With the introduction of the new <canvas> element in HTML5, we now have a container (similar to the CSS div element) that can hold cool JavaScript animations and interactive functions. Because JavaScript is a powerful scripting language and can do a lot of what Flash can do, this canvas-plus-JavaScript combination presents a real alternative approach to web animation supported on both desktop and mobile browsers. For example, Figure 13-6 shows a typical home-page hero-image rotation — complete with cool, animated transition effects — done entirely with HTML5, CSS3, and JavaScript.

© Apple Inc. www.apple.com

Figure 13-6: The hero image on Apple's iPhone landing page has animated transitions between panel displays, thanks to the new HTML5 <canvas> element.

The downside, of course, is that you'll have to tame JavaScript to make all this neat stuff happen — and JavaScript is a pretty robust language! The upside is that the sky is the limit. With JavaScript, you can create fancy user interfaces, draw diagrams with basic shape elements, scale and rotate items, and load external images in and out. To use the <canvas> tag, you take two actions: You include a <canvas> tag in your HTML and create a JavaScript that targets the canvas.

Touchscreen support

In recent years, the advent of touchscreen devices has forced us designers to rethink the way we design interfaces. Designers can make use of several *touch events*: finger on something, finger moving across an element, and finger removed — or (in more technical terms) touchstart, touchmove, touchend, and touchcancel. These HTML5 native events work in WebKit (which are the Chrome and Safari browsers) and enable almost any kind of finger interaction such as drag, pinch and zoom, and rotate.

Geolocation

In the past, to get a user's geographical location, you'd have to use an IP detection script that accessed a database and make a reasonable guess about the user's general whereabouts, accurate to a regional level. HTML5 now supports retrieving more specific geolocations: Using JavaScript, you can find longitude and latitude information through GPS (for mobile devices) and Wi-Fi router info (for laptop and desktop computers). You can even obtain altitude and a time stamp on the location. Of course, the user must agree to release that location information. (I'm sure you've seen mobile applications like Yelp that ask whether they can access your location when you "check in" to places. Same principle.)

Now, a user's longitude and latitude points are only useful to retrieve in the context of a map — so you have to integrate this data with Google's Static Map API. (More about APIs in Chapter 15.)

The other thing to note is that once the browser knows your position, it's possible to track your position as well! That might sound Big Brother-ish, but imagine a mobile application that knows where you are in a shopping mall and serves up coupons for stores you are in or near as you move about.

Powerful content handling

Several upgrades in HTML5 allow designers more control over various content elements on the page. For example, the new contenteditable attribute can be assigned to any element that you want the user to be able to edit — say, a text field that has example text that the user can replace with purpose-specific text.

Another upgrade that HTML5 provides is an expansion to the form-design toolkit. Now you can add range sliders, a search field, an option to insert default text into input fields such as find books, a pop-up calendar for date selection, and even a color selector that opens the computer's color picker. Also, HTML5 offers native support for required form elements. You can simply add the required attribute to an input, select, or text area element. In concert with this new required component, CSS allows you to target these required fields and give them a unique look and feel.

DHTML, JavaScript, jQuery, and Ajax

As you get knee-deep in web design and development, you'll invariably hear terms like DHTML, JavaScript, Ajax, and jQuery come up in technical conversations. One of these, JavaScript (mentioned earlier), is a robust scripting language that is capable of complex animation and interaction effects. You pretty much have to be a dedicated programmer to turn out good stuff in JavaScript, but for our designer's purposes, just know that if you want something to move on the page (say, a menu to drop down and fold out, or a layer to expand and collapse), you're looking at a *dynamic HTML* (DHTML) implementation that integrates JavaScript programming into your HTML. DHTML is not an actual language; rather, it's an artful combination of HTML, JavaScript, and CSS capabilities to accomplish all these wonderful effects.

jQuery is a lightweight form of JavaScript that focuses on the commonly used interactions between JavaScript and HTML. A library of open-source jQuery scripts is available on the Web to customize for your own purposes. One such online resource is `http://docs.jquery.com`. With jQuery, you can accomplish many of the popular web animation and interaction design effects with a lot less code than would be required in JavaScript. And, because it exists as a library of code snippets, it saves developers a lot of time. Common effects like drop-down menus, sliding panels, accordion navigation, carousel navigation, and drag and drop, and even the product image zooms you see on many e-commerce sites, as seen in Figure 13-7, are all part of the jQuery script library. You can simply search for jQuery scripts online to find a variety of sources.

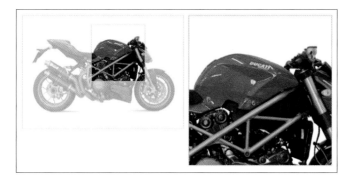

Figure 13-7: Here mousing over an image makes a jQuery script display a zoomed portion of the screen in a new window that dynamically appears.

The last in this section's technical bunch is Ajax: *A*synchronous *J*avaScript *a*nd *X*ML. All this fancy nomenclature really just means that this code allows the website to perform functions "in the background" — without affecting the current display of the web page. For example, without having to refresh your browser window, Ajax can push content updates (such as new articles and headlines) to certain parts of the page.

CSS

CSS, or *C*ascading *S*tyle *S*heets, is code that controls not only the visual appearance of your individual HTML elements but also where the elements appear in relationship to one another, and sometimes how they interact and animate. Between HTML, CSS, and JavaScript, you code the entire presentation layer of a website. *Powering* the site to perform dynamic functions or connect to a CMS (content *m*anagement *s*ystem) database requires additional code such as PHP. The next two chapters offer a closer look at PHP — for now, time to take a brief look at CSS, how it works, and what it can do.

CSS has evolved its capabilities dramatically in the last few years; it's now possible to design visually rich websites — with (for example) rounded-corner boxes, simple gradients, and shadowed text — without using bitmap graphics at all. All these cool effects can be defined as code snippets and then applied to whatever HTML object you feel needs some gussying up. If you ever require an across-the-board change to your website, updating one CSS line of code will do the trick. Figure 13-8 is a beautiful example of CSS and HTML5 working together to create a visually interesting site that optimizes a mix of bitmap and CSS-driven graphics. (Point your IE browser right now to `http://www.frontrow-studios.com` to see the example "live.")

How CSS works

To get your CSS capabilities off the ground, you start by defining a series of styles for each element you want to affect, whether it's an HTML component (like a link or a headline) or a CSS element (such as a `div` container). You *can* do all this defining within the HTML document itself, but it's more common to define your styles in a document separate from your HTML page. Note as well that you can define a series of modifiers, called *classes*, that you can call upon in your HTML code to further affect the way elements appear — it's similar to how adjectives help specify the noun(s) they're attached to.

Here's an example of CSS code that makes all your HTML `<h1>` headlines appear red and set in 18-point Arial:

```
h1 {
color: #e80f0f;
font-family: Arial, Helvetica, sans-serif;
margin: 20px 20px 32px;
line-height: 22px;
font-size: 18px;
}
```

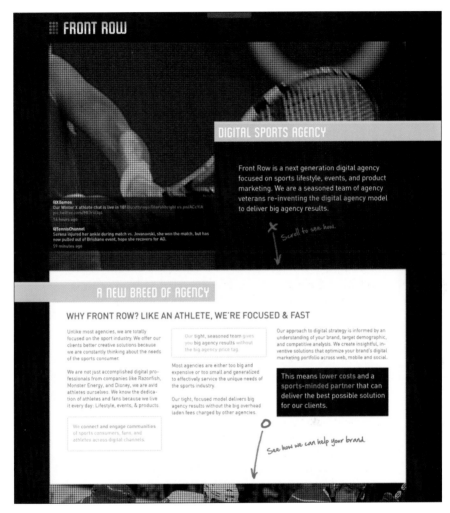

© Front Row Studios. http://www.frontrow-studios.com/

Figure 13-8: This beautiful website for Front Row utilizes CSS and HTML5 to optimize its use of graphics.

This code is saved inside a separate document — in this case, a document called `sample.css`. The HTML page refers to this external document up in the head section of the page, as shown in Figure 13-9. Then, anywhere on the page that I use the `<h1>` tag, the text that follows will render with the settings that I configured back in the CSS document.

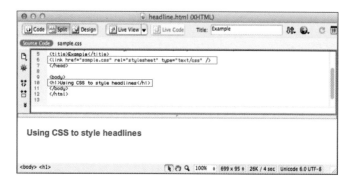

Figure 13-9: This split-screen view in Dreamweaver shows the HTML code in the top panel and the resulting formatting in the bottom panel.

Now, if I wanted to have a special-case headline that made certain headlines larger with an even brighter red, I could set up a custom CSS class to handle that task and append it to the <h1> tag in my HTML. You can name a class anything you'd like — just make sure it has a period in front of the name and has no spaces in the name, like this:

```
.big {
font-size: 24px;
line-height: 26px;
color: #e80f0f;
}
```

As shown in Figure 13-10, the first <h1> headline appears as my CSS code has defined. The second <h1> headline has the .big class appended to the <h1> tag so the result is a larger, brighter headline.

Notice that in my CSS .big class code example given earlier, I don't have to repeat the font and margin preferences. These settings are already accounted for in the original <h1> styling. I need only outline the changes. The word *cascade* in Cascading Style Sheets means your styles are passed along (*inherited*) by style sheets that get their instructions from your original preferences — in this case, those you set up in the class. Basically, when you set up a style, any element that gets assigned that style "cascades through" to the other styles, as directed by your settings, unless you apply a change.

You create visual effects in CSS like this by using approved properties such as font-size, margin, and color, as used in the examples just given here. Therefore, as you might imagine, the key to getting a handle on CSS (and on what you can and can't do with it) lies in studying all the available CSS properties and experimenting with what sort of values you can enter for each one. You can find pretty comprehensive lists online if you search *CSS properties list and values*. Specifically, www.w3schools.com is a good place to start.

In Figure 13-10, the first `<h1>` tag appears with the normal CSS styling, whereas the second `<h1>` tag has the `.big` class appended to it so the text appears both larger and with a brighter red color.

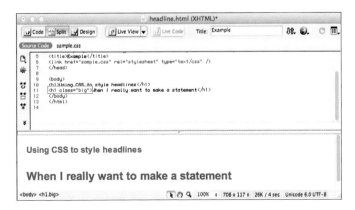

Figure 13-10: Here the first <h1> tag has normal CSS styling and the second <h1> tag has the .big class appended to it.

With the basics of how CSS works out of the way, it's time to take a look at some of the newer properties available in CSS3, the latest edition of CSS.

Color gradients, transparency, and reflections

CSS3, the latest edition, introduces advancements in design handling. Of these, some new capabilities that define color gradients, degrees of transparency, and even reflections are definitely worth checking out!

In the past, if you wanted a color gradient, you had to design bitmap images for the purpose. Now CSS allows you to fill containers with linear and radial gradients that make an even transition from one color to another, or from one color into several colors. You can also control how the gradient fills the container.

Most interesting is the fact that you can now use CSS gradients as image masks that incorporate alpha-channel transparency, as discussed in Chapter 9. By defining the image you're using as a mask — and associating that image with an element or another image *as part of the definition* — you can make that element gradually fade out in appearance, revealing whatever background had been hidden underneath. This capability allows for some interesting layered effects in your website design.

To create a reflection (where the image appears to be mirrored off the surface below) using just CSS, you need to use a combination of transformation settings and containers, but the net effect is nonetheless a reflection effect, as shown in Figure 13-11. Essentially, you create two containers — one for the main image and one for the reflection. By applying transform effects to the reflection container that first turn the image upside down then squash its height and then add a transparency mask, you end up with a convincing reflection. The beauty is that, with this technique, you have one normal graphic with the option to include a reflection — a reflection that is dynamically configurable — all without the use of Photoshop.

Figure 13-11: Some clever CSS coding is all it takes to achieve a dynamically configurable reflection.

Shadow effects

It's now possible to use CSS to add drop shadows to elements — another very cool effect. Before CSS3, semi-transparent shadows were only possible with bitmap image, specifically using the PNG format that supports transparency.

The examples in Figure 13-12 show that both the text and the box element can have a drop-shadow effect or a letterpress effect (lighter-color drop shadow) — all by modifying a line of CSS code. Simply by adjusting the colors and the amount of offset and blur, you can create very different effects. For the <h2> HTML text, I'm using the CSS text-shadow property. Notice that in the case of the box-shadow (the third image in the figure) it's necessary to have two lines of code immediately following — one for WebKit and one for Moz. These are to support the Safari and Firefox browsers, respectively.

Rounded corners

Also shown in Figure 13-12 is an example of the new CSS3 border-radius property in action. By defining a value for this property — check out the last two lines of the CSS code in the figure, where the value is set to 10 pixels — you control how large the corner curve appears. Before the introduction of the border-radius property, rounded-corner effects were possible only through the use of bitmap graphics.

✓ **JSP** (Java Server Pages) is a web development platform introduced by Sun Microsystems (now part of Oracle) to compete with PHP and ASP. NET. Like ASP, it is a server-side technology, meaning that the code is first compiled and then executed as an application by the web server.

Other development platforms may offer tempting features, but beware: If you stray too far from the more common ones, it's harder and more expensive to find people who can maintain the site. For instance, one company developed its site on a powerful platform that was not very well known. After the site was launched, finding engineers to make even the simplest fixes to the site was next to impossible. Engineers who knew the platform well were rare enough that they could charge three times the standard hourly rate for their services. The situation was like getting an oil change for a Maserati. Our team fixed this company's site by keeping the front-end design but switching to a PHP platform — maybe less exotic, but easier to fix because more people knew it at the nuts-and-bolts level. As I like to say, our team ripped out the Maserati engine and put in a reliable Honda under the hood!

Content Management

An effective business website must be flexible enough to *scale up or scale down* (quickly add and/or subtract new pages) and update its content (change ads, change promotions, change prices, and so on). The way to do this is to rely on just a handful of page templates — such as a category page, a landing page, and a detail page — and populate them dynamically with appropriate content that resides in a database. For example, if a user is browsing an online store and visits the Gardening section, the single category-page template displays the images and text and any promotions associated with the Gardening department. If the user visits the Home Décor section next, that same category page template updates with the new content.

The real task for this online store example, therefore, is managing the content that resides in the database. The company database must allow effortless access and fast updates — on a daily, if not hourly, basis. Of course, databases don't have the friendliest of interfaces — so websites often have a middle layer between them and their databases called a *content management system*, or CMS for short. A CMS is often a separate, secure website that only administrators have access to. An administrator logs in to the web-based CMS, makes changes to the content, and pushes the updated content to where it has to go: either to a *staging server* (a private preview website where the company can verify the information) or to the live main site. A successful CMS interface is neatly organized and easy to use — like the example shown in Figure 14-1 — which empowers a team of non-technical people (such as brand managers and product managers) to manage their content efficiently.

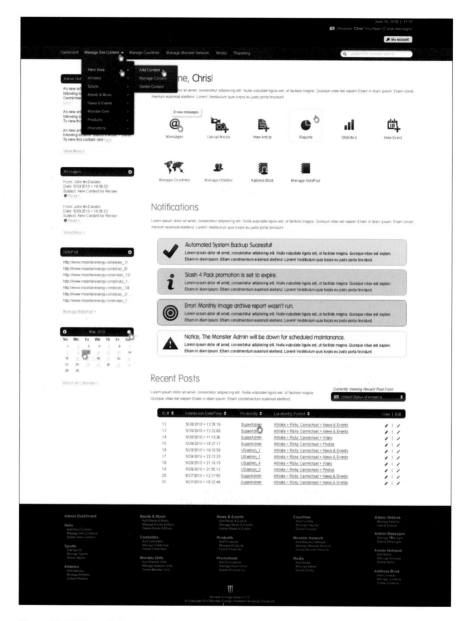

Figure 14-1: This web-based CMS neatly organizes all the site content, making it easy for non-technical administrators to keep the site fresh.

Custom versus off-the-shelf solutions

There are a lot of factors to consider that drive what type of content management system is right for the new site. Some factors to consider are as follows:

- **Platform:** What development platform is the site being built on? And here are a couple of related questions: What databases are you drawing content from, and where is the site being hosted? Can the CMS you're considering integrate well with all these technical factors?

- **Language:** Should the website support multiple countries and languages? Will administrators around the world need to manage translated content and custom products — and the accompanying imagery — for their respective regions or countries?

- **E-commerce:** Does the website need to tie into the company's existing product or sales databases? Does the site need to integrate with multiple systems? Does it need to tie into SAP — the business software platform used to manage products, supply chain, sales, and inventory levels?

- **Administration:** Do you need to set up multiple levels of site administration access? For example, will some users be able to change fundamental site structures, while other users can only change the content of certain pages?

- **Unique product or services:** Does the website offer unique products and services (for instance, a site that lets users create and distribute their own online books) that don't fit the mold of off-the-shelf content management systems?

Many off-the-shelf solutions are available that may be just fine for the size, scale, and content of the site you're building. Popular ready-made solutions such as Drupal (www.drupal.org, shown in Figure 14-2), Joomla! (www.joomla.org), WordPress (http://wordpress.org), Concrete5 (www.concrete5.org), and Plone (http://plone.org) are customizable enough to make them economical choices for most sites. One reason these solutions are popular is because they're open source: Any developer can access the source code and use it to create custom modules that extend functionality. These modules can then be made available to everyone else who uses the source code. The result is an ever-growing library of features to draw from. Some open source modules are free; others are licensed — in the end, an open source solution generally results in a wide feature set to choose from or customize further. The only drawback, however, is that because open source applications are community-supported, you're not going to find the official tech support you see with proprietary solutions offered by Oracle and Microsoft.

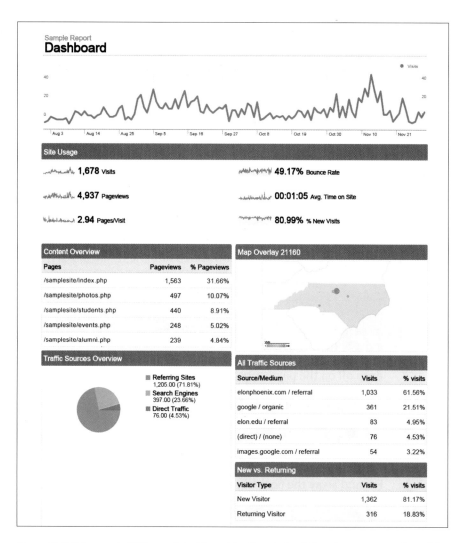

Figure 14-3: This sample PDF report dashboard for Google Analytics shows an overview of the things you can track, such as where your site traffic is coming from.

What can you learn about your site?

What exactly does Google Analytics track about each page of your site and how is it useful? Here is a handy reference with an explanation of each item.

✓ **Traffic sources.** For a given time range that you can set, Google breaks down where your web traffic comes from. *Organic* traffic means that someone found you via a search (whether through Yahoo!, Google, Bing or other search engines). *Direct* traffic means people entered your URL. *Referral* traffic shows you what sites are linking to you and what page they are linking to. This data is good to know when contemplating an online marketing strategy. If you see that the bulk of your traffic comes from (say) YouTube referrals, you may decide to focus your marketing there.

✓ **Browsers, platforms, and screen resolutions.** Of particular interest is Google's information on what browsers people are using to view your site, which platform (Mac, Windows, or mobile) they're using, and what screen sizes they have. This is invaluable data when it comes to optimizing your site to perform well and look good because you know what browser and screen sizes to give highest priority as marketing targets.

✓ **Top pages.** Interestingly, your home page is not always the first page — nor the most visited page — of your web site. Often an internal page is leaps and bounds ahead of other pages. It's always interesting to look at these top pages and understand what may be driving so much relative interest. Additionally, you can view your top pages by country (what countries are visiting those top pages). As Figure 14-4 indicates, for my watercolor site, I have an equal interest in a certain top page from both the US and India. You can also see how much time visitors spend on each page.

✓ **Demographics.** Google lets you see what countries (and even what cities) people are from that are visiting your site. Clearly, this is useful data because it lets you know where you might target offline advertising efforts. For example, as Figure 14-5 shows, I can see that Chicago is home to most of my site's visitors. If I were to invest in a print advertising campaign, I might target a local Chicago lifestyle magazine.

Figure 14-4: Google tells you what your top (most-visited) pages are and who's visiting them.

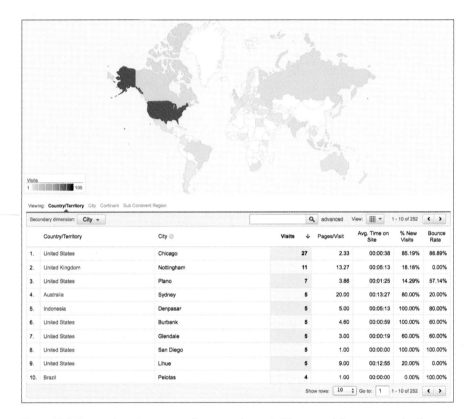

Figure 14-5: A map view shows you what countries and cities your visitors are coming from.

Real-time monitoring

A relatively new feature of Google Analytics gives you real-time activity feedback. You can see how many people are currently visiting your website, what pages they're viewing, what countries they're visiting from, how they got to your site (via search, directly typing your URL, or a link). This real-time data is interesting because you can spot trends when certain regions are visiting your pages, and you may be able to tune the content of those pages to suit their needs.

Where do people click?

If you really want to get a sense of how each page is functioning within your site — if, say, people are clicking on your Buy Now button (or in my case, which of my paintings are the more popular) — the In-Page Analytics view shows you where people are clicking. As shown in Figure 14-6, you can see an overlay covering each active link on a page, with a relative percentage of clicks that it gets. The color coding shows what links are "hot" (red and orange) and which ones are relatively "cold" (yellow and blue).

Figure 14-6: See what links on your page people are clicking on in Google's In-Page Analytics view.

Fee-based services

Google does offer a more robust premium service for an annual fee that allows you to track more data — and customize what you track. In addition to its around-the-clock support, the Google premium service, found at www. google.com/analytics/premium, is geared to the needs of large-scale global websites and cross-channel marketing campaigns. Adobe also offers a suite of tools available at www.omniture.com that you can use to track activity across a series of websites, social media sites, and mobile sites — as well as applications that offer a big-picture view of how your digital channels are performing together.

Search Engine Optimization

When you use a search engine to look for websites, you're actually searching through an index that the search engine keeps. This index is a giant database that is constantly refreshed. Search engines like Google use an army of *bots* (automatic search programs, also called *spiders*) to go out and scan the world's web pages. The bots make a note of each site's content (keywords) and, based on inbound and outbound links to that site, determine how important the site is relative to other similar sites. These factors determine where a website is listed in a search results page — on the first page, or pages back (where it won't immediately catch the eye of the web-surfing user). Figure 14-7 illustrates how Google search supposedly works — courtesy of the good folks at PPC Training. (You can find the original illustration at `http://ppcblog.com/how-google-works`.)

Many users find your website simply through their own search efforts. Therefore, the more you can make your site search-engine-friendly, the better. *Search engine optimization* (SEO for short) is the collective practice of understanding — and making savvy use of — the way search engines work and how they rank the importance of your content. More importantly, SEO offers insights into how best to utilize site keywords so your site has the best chance of being found.

On-page and off-page search

In SEO specialist circles, there are two categories of search efforts: on-page and off-page. On-page search efforts are those that you (as a developer) have immediate control over. Off-page SEO, on the other hand, relies on external factors such as user browsing patterns, social media links (included within Facebook posts and Twitter messages), and on other websites that may be linking to you.

Since you have limited influence over the external factors, or off-page SEO, let's focus on what you *can* do to improve your on-page SEO efforts. According to Google, who publishes SEO tips at `googlewebmaster central.blogspot.com` (see Figure 14-8), the first thing you can do to boost your site's search ranking (where it appears in the search results list relative to other sites) is to give *each* web page a unique and descriptive page title and description. It's amazing how many websites have short, non-descriptive page titles that do nothing for their site's search visibility, such as SoCal Mountain Biking home page — or worse, use the same title for each page such as SoCal. Page titles and descriptions are found in the <head> section of your HTML code, as shown in the following example. Note that the title can be more than 60 characters long, but that only 60 characters will display in a Google search result.

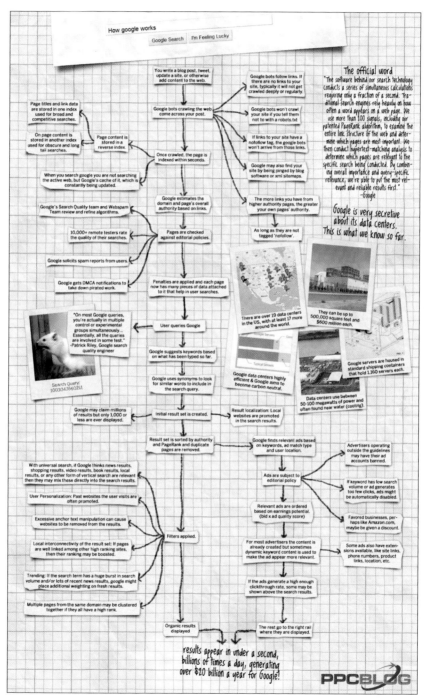

© PPC Training, Inc. http://ppcblog.com/

Figure 14-7: This detailed visual flow chart shows how the popular Google search engine works.

```html
<html>
<head>
<title>SoCal High School Mountain Biking League - Start a
        team in Southern California</title>
<meta name="description" content="The SoCal High School
        Cycling League was organized in 2008 to provide
        a well defined race season for high school
        (grades 9-12) student athletes and to promote
        the formation of teams at public and private high
        schools.">
</head>
```

Using the code example above, if a user searches for "high school mountain biking," this web page would have a good chance of appearing high in the results page. As Figure 14-9 shows, the page's title appears larger and underlined. The search terms that the user entered will appear in bold. The `<meta>` tag description *may* appear underneath the title. If there is no `<meta>` tag description, or Google's algorithm thinks there is more useful or descriptive content on the page itself, then Google will use that text instead of your `<meta>` description as the snippet under the page title. As Figure 14-10 illustrates, the actual page itself contains content that does not appear in the search result. In this case, Google is using the page's meta description instead of page content.

© Google. www.google.com

Figure 14-8: Google publishes a Tips blog at googlewebmaster central.blogspot.com.

SoCal **High School Mountain Biking** League - Start a team in ...

www.socaldirt.org/

The SoCal High School Cycling League was organizied in 2008 to provide a well defined race season for high school (grades 9–12) student athletes and to promote the formation of teams at public and private high schools.

Figure 14-9: The page's title and meta description appear in a Google search result.

Figure 14-10: Notice that the text within the Google search result is not necessarily contained within the actual website.

URL structure and file names

When you develop a website, you typically have multiple sections all neatly organized in your navigation system. When you click on a main section, say, gift baskets, it's important to give the page file a descriptive name such as giftbaskets.html as opposed to sectionthree.html or products.html. Not only can users remember the URL path better: www.*yourcompany*.com/gift baskets.html, but also search engines are better able to discern possible page content from specific words used in the file name. Also, URLs are listed in search results and any search terms a user may have entered will display in bold.

Often if you're using a Content Management System, (CMS for short) URLs are dynamically generated and look like a long, unintelligible mess of numbers and symbols like the example in Figure 14-11. Although that may be ok for detail pages and other lower-level pages within your site, try to set up a directory structure (folders on your server for each section of your site) that uses descriptive names where these pages can reside such as: www.*your company*.com/giftbaskets/1234weirdnumbers&symbols.

www.victoriassecret.com/ss/Satellite?ProductID=1265700853834&c=Page&cid=1265710536800&pagename=vsdWrapper

Figure 14-11: You can spot a database-managed website by a long URL of numbers and symbols.

Remedy duplicate URLs to the same page

Often there are multiple ways to get to the same page. For example, a user might type or click all the following URLs to get to a company's home page. Note that the long URL example in this list is one with a tracking code so the website owners can count how many people came in from, say, a QR code (short for Quick Response code; learn more at www.qrstuff.com) scanned in a print ad.

- www.company.com
- www.company.com/
- company.com
- company.com/
- company.com/?utm_source=Conference&utm_medium=QR&utm_campaign=Ad
- www.company.com/index.html
- company.com/index.html

Although users seem to be ok with navigating in multiple ways, such duplicate URLs pose a problem for search engines because they distribute the backlinks (more about these later in this chapter) across multiple sources, thereby diluting the page's search ranking. For instance, if a website links back to your site one way and another website uses a different link to the same page, the search engine sees a split. To remedy this, you can specify one official URL using the canonical link element up in the <head> section so that search engines know to credit that one link for all ways of getting to this page:

```
<html>
<head>
<link rel="canonical" href="http://www.company.com"/>
</head>
```

Prepare a search-specific Sitemap

There is a lot of talk, even in this book, about sitemaps. One flavor of sitemap is a document created during the information architecture phase of a website's development, as discussed in Chapter 3. Another flavor is an actual web page that lists all the site's sections. This type of sitemap (with a lower-case s) is designed to help your visitors better navigate the site.

A third type of Sitemap (with a capital S) is one that your users will never see. This type is made specifically to inform search engines about the pages on your site. It is an XML file, as shown in the example below, that lives on the root directory of your server (ideally, although not required) that contains a list of your site's URLs, along with additional data about each page, such as when it was last modified and its relative importance in your site's hierarchy.

Without a Sitemap file, search engines rely on the links already within your site (such as in the navigation system or embedded within page content) to all the various pages and make their best guess at what all the pages contain and their relative importance to one another. Having an XML Sitemap file does not guarantee that search engines will use them, but it does provide good data for them to do a better job. You can generate an XML Sitemap online at www.xml-sitemaps.com. For more information, visit www.sitemaps.org.

```
<?xml version="1.0" encoding="UTF-8"?>
<urlset xmlns="http://www.sitemaps.org/schemas/sitemap/0.9">
<url>
 <loc>http://www.example.com/</loc>
 <lastmod>2012-01-01</lastmod>  <changefreq>monthly</
          changefreq> <priority>0.8</priority>
</url>
<url>
 <loc>http://www.example.com/catalog.html</loc>
          <changefreq>weekly</changefreq>
</url>
</urlset>
```

To submit a sitemap to Google, follow these steps:

1. **Upload your Sitemap to the root directory of your site.**

   Typically the file is named sitemap.xml.

2. **Go to the Google Webmaster Tools home page at** www.google.com/webmasters/tools.

3. **Sign in to Google Webmaster Tools using the same account information you use to sign in to Google Sites.**

4. **If you haven't already done so, add your website to your list of Google sites: Click the Add a Site button, enter your site's URL in the field that appears, and then click Continue.**

   You will need to follow the online site ownership verification guidelines.

5. **When done verifying your ownership, click on the site that you want to work with.**

   A set of navigation links in the left column opens.

6. **Click the Site Configuration⇨Sitemaps navigation link.**

7. **Click the Add/Test Sitemap button in the toolbar that appears.**

8. **In the text box of the new dialog box that appears, enter the full URL path to your sitemap (for example, `http://www.company.com/sitemap.xml`).**

9. **Click the Submit a Sitemap button.**

More SEO strategies

So what are some other handy on-page SEO strategies that you can employ? Here's a list of tactics to consider in your search strategy:

- **Keywords and phrases.** Make a comprehensive list of all the words and phrases customers are likely to think of (such as vintage guitars) when they're looking for a service or product like yours. Also sprinkle in specific words and phrases as well such as Pre-CBS Stratocasters that users are likely to search for. Make sure you utilize these words as much as possible throughout your website copy. If you use Google Analytics, the reports will show you what terms people searched for before clicking through to your site. This will help in your efforts to hone down the list of keywords that you integrate into your site.

- **Keyword density.** Search engines will look at the frequency that your keywords and phrases occur throughout your pages and site — *keyword density*, in other words. The keyword density is a factor in determining a page's relevance to a user's search for these same terms. Be careful, however, to not overdo it. *Keyword stuffing* (as it's called in the industry), the cramming of irrelevant keywords into every nook and cranny of your site, is not only not cool, but also a ploy that search engines are smart enough to sniff out — which can result in the lowering of your ranking.

- **Headline tags.** Headline tags are used to structure a hierarchy within your page copy. For example, use the <h1> tag for all main top-level headlines. Use <h2> for sub headlines, and so on down the ranks to

<h6> for the lowest level headline text. Search engines look at the content associated with each of these tags and assume that their level of importance corresponds to their h1–h6 tagging.

- ✔ **New content.** Sites that always have fresh, new content are assumed to be more credible and relevant than stagnant sites that haven't been touched in ages. (Keep in mind that in the high-speed online world ages can mean a day or two.)

- ✔ **Image alt tags.** Every graphical image that you include in your web page can include an `alt` attribute inside the image tag. This is an opportunity for you to include a short, keyword-rich description. Go easy on these, however, because (as mentioned earlier) loading up on keywords can start Google's alarm bells a-ringing and adversely affect your search ranking. Additionally, people with screen readers will have to sit through listening to `<img alt>` tags in addition to the regular content on the page. If you have a ton of text inside your `<img alt>` tags, the result can be a bad user experience — and no return visit.

- ✔ **Meta keywords.** In addition to the meta description tag located in the `<head>` section of your HTML, you can add a meta keywords tag to enter a string of words and phrases that you think users will search for to find your site.

Because these are behind-the-scenes elements that the site owners control, search engines often put a lower priority on them.

Natural versus paid search

As discussed in the previous section, there are many ways to boost your on-page SEO through best practices that you can control. When a user finds your site as a result of your good SEO practices, it's referred to in the industry as natural or organic search, because you are not paying for your search result ranking. Purchasing keywords in an attempt to reach out to users that might be browsing for something similar to your products and services qualifies as off-page SEO.

In the web industry, your combined on and off page, paid and unpaid, SEO efforts to make your website found by the end customer is called SEM, or *search engine marketing.*

See Figure 14-12 for an example of a Google search of the relatively generic keywords *dark chocolate gift basket.* Notice that the circled area contains the top sites that come up organically as a result of their good SEO practices. The sites listed above and in the right column have purchased some of those generic keywords by using Google AdWords (`adwords.google.com`). If you click one of those sites in the paid area, the companies are charged a fee. This is known as PPC or *pay-per-click,* or CPC, *cost-per-click* keyword advertising. Fees for these clicks range in price depending on how valuable the keyword is. For example, it's more expensive to purchase the word *wine* than the word *whine* because there are more businesses interested in leveraging the power of *wine* as a user search term. In Google AdWords, prices are based on bids that companies are willing to spend on keywords, so the range could be anywhere from 50 cents to $3 or more. You can set the limit of how much you'll pay for a keyword click — say at $1 — and will not be charged any more than that; however, if someone bids more, their ad will appear above yours. Since it's hard to guess how much others have bid for the same keywords, you can also set up automatic bidding, which tells the system to work within your daily maximum budget.

For your paid search efforts, why should you use Google AdWords? Because, like it or not, Google has the lion's share of people using Google for search and for their e-mail (Gmail). When you use Google AdWords, your ads will appear not only on a Google search result (as in Figure 14-12), but also in their inbox as a small strip across the top, as shown in Figure 14-13.

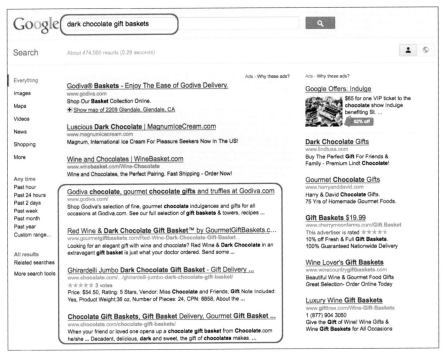

© Google. www.google.com

Figure 14-12: The Google search results page showing both paid and unpaid listings based on the keywords entered.

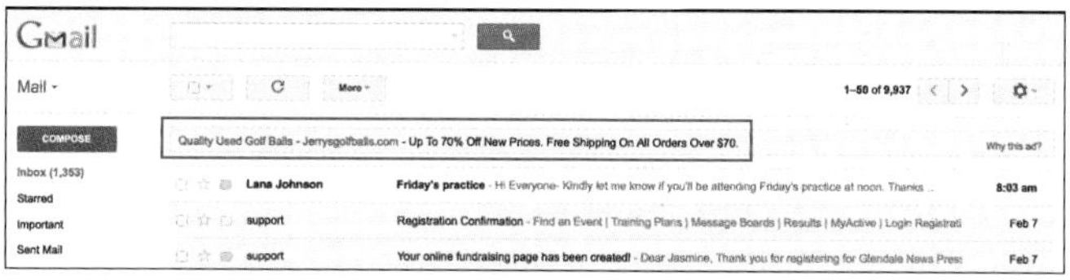

Figure 14-13: Google AdWord campaigns will show up not only in Google search results but also in people's Gmail inbox.

How do you know which keywords to purchase for your site? If you use Google Webmaster Tools, found at www.google.com/webmasters/tools, once you register your site, you are able to see what search terms people have been using to find your site. Interestingly, as Figure 14-14 illustrates, my watercolor painting website (dreadfully out of date) is found overwhelmingly by people typing in *paintings of love*. Another place to look is Google Analytics, which can include the search queries result from Webmaster Tools. As Figure 14-15 shows, you are able to see how many times your website appeared in the search results list (impressions) and how many actual clicks you received.

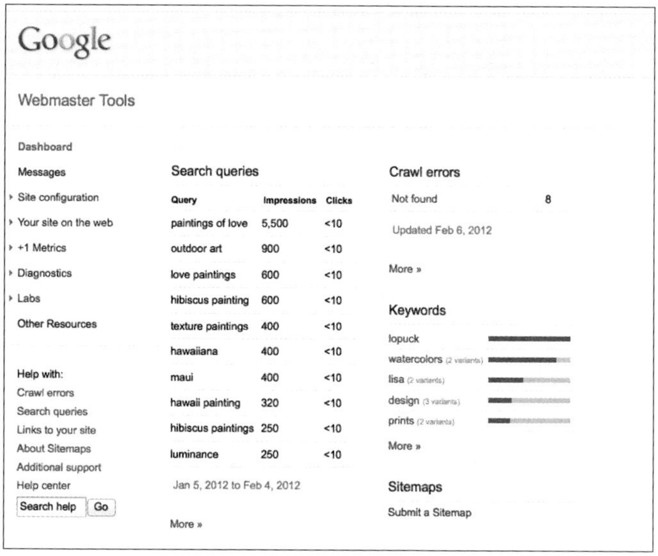

© Google. www.google.com

Figure 14-14: Google Webmaster Tools provides insightful data and allows you to manage aspects of your site such as Sitemaps.

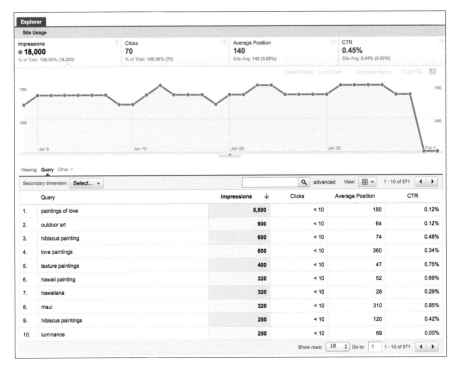

© Google. www.google.com

Figure 14-15: Google Analytics can import data from Webmaster Tools to inform you of which keywords and phrases people use to find your site.

Inbound and outbound linking

Two types of links have a direct impact on your search-engine ranking: inbound and outbound links. As their names imply, *inbound links* (also called *backlinks*) are links on other websites that lead to your website. *Outbound links* are the links on your site that go elsewhere.

Backlinks are of considerable importance to SEO because their number is a measure of how popular — therefore how relevant — your site is. The more credible the sources of your backlinks are, the better your page's ranking. For example, if Disney is linking to your website, your site will get a good score. If you have several sites like Disney linking to your site, your site will rank even higher. Thankfully, there is no penalty for bad sites linking to you. The worst that can happen is no ranking at all from an inbound link coming from a seedy site.

In addition to outbound links from websites, Google also looks at outbound links to your site contained within Twitter messages and Facebook posts. As in Google's analysis of a website's quality, Google's algorithm also tries to determine the credibility of such social media authors (likely by number of followers and fans) as a factor in weighting the importance of these outbound links.

Another factor that search engines consider is the similarity of content of the two sites. If the referring site has content similar to that of your site, the search engine assumes greater relevance than if the referring site has very different content. If the inbound link was attached to a keyword-rich phrase such as *Check out ACME's awesome chocolate gift baskets*, even better. Because it's difficult to get other websites to link to your site — let alone give you keyword-laden links for the user to click — search engines assign a lot of credibility to quality backlinks when they're determining your site's search ranking. It's worth mentioning that your site does not get any SEO boost from having a large number of outbound links to other sites. Neither the quality of the sites you link to nor the number of sites you link to will make a difference. For example, there are many websites that have a link resource page, such as a dog breed club that offers links to breeders, rescue sites, training sites, and event sites.

Websites on Steroids

In This Chapter

▷ Integrating third-party features through APIs

▷ Enabling e-commerce on your site

▷ Personalizing web pages with cookies

▷ Determining a user's global location

▷ Boosting website global performance through CDNs

*I*t's rare to find a major commercial website these days that's not using some form of technological steroids to boost performance. HTML and CSS (covered in Chapter 13) and an integrated CMS (covered in Chapter 14) are just the starting points. From there, developers must rely on heavy programming within the development platform of choice to create a living, breathing business machine.

...tion on canvas...

ART ▶

Fortunately, you may not have to do all the heavy lifting to get your behemoth to work right. Chapter 14 lists some of the many available open source solutions. Anyone that works well with your chosen platform can provide a solid starting point — and some basic modules you can build upon to power many of the features you'd like to offer. Additionally, through APIs (*application programming interfaces*), developers can utilize well-known features such as Google Maps and discussion boards to extend the functionality of their sites. Offering full-featured e-commerce on your site, however, requires additional certification — *and* a secure means of sharing user information with banks.

$30 Everday print, 12 x 12

| 1 | ADD TO CART ▶ |

$45 Keepsake box, laquered cherry finish , 4 x 6

| 1 | ADD TO CART ▶ |

50 Folded note card, 4 x 6

D TO CART ▶

In this chapter, I offer a bird's-eye view of the technological options you have available for giving your site some superpowers — along with what they do, and what sort of ramifications they could have for your site. I also fill you in on some ways you can optimize your site to deliver a great user experience — regardless of whether people are accessing your site on a mobile device in the next town or connecting from half a world away (in which case they'll prefer to see your site's content localized and relevant to their needs).

Extending Website Functionality

Long gone are the days when you could just whip up a simple website, slap it up on the World Wide Web, and expect results. These days the complexity of websites comes from several sources:

- Powerful advancements in HTML and CSS. (See Chapter 13.)

- Open source programming languages that provide basic platforms for so many features

- Integration of your site's features with those of popular sites such as Google and Facebook.

- APIs (application *programming* *interfaces*) are source code components that provide hooks — or "interfaces" — that web developers can utilize to connect to their systems, allowing the two to communicate. Translated, that means that companies like Google provide APIs so that web developers can add cool features like Google Maps, discussion boards, or live chat to their site.

Facebook Connect

One of the more popular trends is to integrate social media conversations and user-generated content into company websites. Additionally, more websites are moving away from a distinct process of user registration; instead, they're utilizing people's existing social media accounts as a painless, transparent way to "sign in" to their sites. That way users don't have to remember a bunch of different usernames and passwords — and website owners can still gather user data about their site customers.

Facebook Connect is a suite of APIs that Facebook offers so that Facebook members can log on to websites and mobile devices simply by using their Facebook identities. From the users' perspective, the first step is to share their Facebook personal data with a site they want to access. As shown in Figure 15-1, the website can collect a number of data points. Using the Facebook Connect API, developers can configure these data points to match what you want to know about your customers. After users agree to share the requested personal data, they can interact with the Facebook modules on the website as if they were on the Facebook site itself; Figure 15-2 shows an example of such a module in action.

Among the quickest Facebook features that you can integrate on your website are the social plugins such as the ubiquitous Like button. This button enables web visitors to share your page with their Facebook friends with just one click. This feature is easy to implement by using the following HTML:

```
<html>
<head>
<title>Website title</title>
</head>
<body>
<iframe src="http://www.facebook.com/plugins/like.
        php?href=www.yourwebaddress.com" scrolling="no"
        frameborder="0" style="border:none; width:450px;
        height:80px"></iframe>
</body>
</html>
```

Figure 15-1: The first step of connecting to a website with Facebook is agreeing to release certain information to the site.

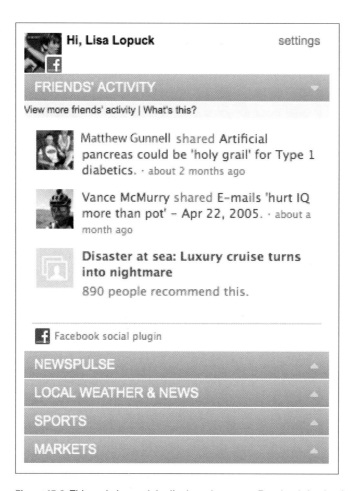

Figure 15-2: This website module displays the recent Facebook feeds of the user's friends.

You can customize this feature a bit further (as shown in Figure 15-3) by adding the names and faces of people who recently clicked your Like button. You can use the online Facebook tool found at the following URL to generate the necessary code:

```
http://developers.facebook.com/docs/reference/plugins/like/
```

Other social plugins such as Comments and Live Stream (which allow your web visitors to share comments in real time — great for webcasts and live web events) are a little more complex to integrate. These require the use of XFBML (*e*xtended *F*acebook *m*arkup *l*anguage), which are a set of XML components that must be included in your HTML page. Without getting too technical, these XML elements are processed by the JavaScript SDK (*s*oftware *d*evelopment *k*it) — a browser-side/client-side set of functions.

Figure 15-3: It's easy to add the Facebook Like button to your web page by using simple HTML code.

As mentioned earlier, Facebook allows its users to log in to websites using their Facebook identities. From a web developer's perspective, adding this feature to your site is a three-step process:

1. You register your website with Facebook and get an *App ID*. This ID ensures a secure connection between the Facebook user and your website.

2. You add the proper JavaScript to your HTML page that references your ID and processes the login request.

3. You add the Login with Facebook button in its own `<div>` tag, and the JavaScript SDK renders the button on your page.

After a user is logged in to your site via his or her Facebook credentials, you can personalize that person's web experience using the *Graph API*, a feature of Facebook's core logic that connects people with other people and their interests. For example, if Jane Doe has "checked in" to her favorite restaurant, your website has access to that info. There are all kinds of creative things you can do with that information, such as suggesting other cool things to do near her location.

Twitter

Like Facebook, Twitter also has an API that allows its members to use their Twitter credentials to log on to websites. Once signed in, users can send Tweets right from the host website or participate in general discussions, as shown in Figure 15-4. Twitter also allows developers to stream Tweets right on to a web page — see the example in Figure 15-5 — and include a Follow Me button to help widen the subscriber base.

Figure 15-4: Many sites allow users to sign in using their social media credentials so that they can participate in live discussions.

Figure 15-5: NationalGeographic.com integrates Twitter feeds and recent Facebook fan additions right on their home page.

Disqus

Many online news articles now have robust discussion forums at the bottom of the screen that I often find more interesting than the article itself. By including user commentary, you can add value to your site — for not a lot of extra effort — by integrating Disqus, which is one of the leading forum providers. As Figure 15-6 shows, Disqus allows users to authenticate with one of their existing accounts to join in on discussions — very convenient for the user. What's even better for the host website, however, is that the discussion dialog is searchable by search engines. If you have lively conversations happening on your web page, your SEO can improve due to the abundance of changing content and keywords. For more information, visit `disqus.com/api/docs/`.

Figure 15-6: Disqus is a popular tool used to power discussion forums on many websites. Users can sign in with an existing account to join in on the conversation.

Google Maps

The Google Maps API is a free service that anyone can integrate into his or her website. Not only can you embed maps on your page, but you can also customize the way the maps appear and add informative overlays specific to your business. If you want to take this capability up a notch, Google does offer a fee-based premier edition that comes complete with support and legal services — but for most web applications, the free service is all you need.

A myriad of APIs to choose from

So far we've just scratched the surface. Although Facebook, Twitter, Disqus, and Google Maps are popular features to integrate into a website, there's a vast range of other APIs to choose from. For example, YouTube, eBay, Flickr, and Blogger also offer APIs that you can customize and use to extend the feature set of your site. The advantages to integrating APIs are twofold:

- You don't have to engineer what is usually complex coding in order to add a cool feature.
- Users are already familiar with the user interface associated with these brand-name feature sets.

Programmable Web, at www.programmableweb.com/apis, offers a list of over 4,000 APIs that you can search by keyword or category as shown in Figure 15-7.

Figure 15-7: Programmable Web is a site that lists thousands of APIs that you can search by name or category.

E-commerce Websites

Building an online store is one of the more complex endeavors a web designer can ever face, because it requires tying into many different *back-end systems* — essentially the systems that do the actual work of the business. These range from product and user-account databases to merchant accounts and credit card processing. As with the Content Management System (CMS) solutions I discuss in Chapter 14, many open source e-commerce products are available that provide much of the base functionality; you can further customize them to suit the needs of your site. One example is a popular PHP solution for many small and large-scale business sites: Magento, found at `www.magentocommerce.com`. A popular .NET platform solution is StoreFront at `http://storefront.net`.

For smaller online commerce businesses, some do-it-yourself solutions include eCart from WebAssist (shown in Figure 15-8), or PayPal's offerings found in the business section of their site at `www.paypal.com`. These solutions are designed for the less technical people and help walk them through the process of configuring their online stores.

© WebAssist.com Corporation. www.webassist.com

Figure 15-8: WebAsist's eCart, part of their Super Suite product offering, steps you through the process of building an online store.

Secure socket layer

When you shop online, you'll notice that as soon as you begin the checkout process, a little lock icon appears in the URL string of your browser or on the bottom of the page. Also, the URL starts with `https:` instead of the normal `http:`. The lock icon and the `https:` in the URL string are your indications that you're on a *secure socket layer* (SSL for short) — which means the browser will encrypt your data when you submit it.

Another factor in data security is the *SSL certificate* — a small piece of software issued by a legitimate authority (such as VeriSign, DigiCert, or Entrust) that resides on your secure server and validates your website's identity and domain ownership. Although you can *self-sign* a certificate — configure your own SSL certificate to save time and expense — often self-signed certificates are not recognized by the browser. The major web browsers (Safari, Firefox, and Internet Explorer) come with a small set of root certificate authorities that they trust, and if your certificate is not issued by one of these companies, the browser may trigger a warning that the user will see, which can make your site look less secure and credible. Root certificate providers are VeriSign, Comodo, Entrust, GlobalSign, and GeoTrust among others. You can find a comparative list of credible SSL certificate providers at www. SSLshopper.com/certificate-authority-reviews.html. Cost-wise, you should expect to pay from $50–150 annually for your SSL certificate.

Payment gateways

In order to process online sales transactions, you need to arrange for the secure collection of personal information and credit card data from users (as discussed earlier), and then pass the collected data through a *payment gateway* — a software application that acts as the bridge between your shopping-cart application and the banks that are involved in the transaction. The payment gateway decrypts the data, checks the validity of the user's card, and makes sure the bank information is all in order. When the data is verified, the banks re-encrypt and process it. Popular payment gateway services such as Authorize.net, Amazon, PayPal, and VeriSign usually have a setup fee, a small monthly fee, and then a micro per-transaction fee. Note that the micro transaction fee is in addition to whatever VISA or MasterCard charges on the transaction. You can find a handy comparison chart of different payment gateway providers at http://payment-gateway-services-review. toptenreviews.com.

Building a simple shopping cart

If you'd like to build an online store yourself but don't know how to begin, try WebAssist's eCart software, available at www.webassist.com. It features a wizard-like interface that walks you through the process of building and customizing your store so you don't have to write code. Ample help documentation and examples guide you through the process, but it will still take a clear head to get it all figured out and hosted properly.

Two simple solutions to look into are Google's Checkout system and PayPal's system. These two web-based services do the hosting for you, so they are less complex to set up and integrate into your site. These can be found at https://checkout.google.com and the business tab of www.paypal.com, respectively.

Shopping cart design tips that boost sales

At the heart of your e-commerce website is the *shopping cart* — the user's collection of set-aside store items that he or she wants to purchase. Often a shopping cart takes two forms:

- ✔ A small area generally found up in the header of the website that keeps a running tally (often called a Quick View cart)

- ✔ A dedicated page where users can see and review their items before proceeding with checkout.

I have found this two-fold approach is best for usability because users visually see the contents of their shopping cart filling up as they shop.

In order to maximize sales, it's best to stick with conventional user interface conventions. Let's take a look at best practices for both types of shopping carts, the Quick View cart and the shopping cart page:

Quick View shopping cart design

A small link up in the header of your website (the upper right is the convention) that says "shopping cart" is not enough. As shown in Figure 15-9, it's best to at least show the number of items in the cart. A visual treatment such as including a small bag design or icon will help users find the cart, the means to purchase their items, and see how many items they've already set aside. When a user clicks a Quick View cart (as you can see in Figure 15-10), typically a small window opens and displays a summary of the items (hence the name "quick view"). The user can either click outside the window to close it and continue shopping, or click the Checkout button to proceed with the purchase. Often, the Quick View window has additional helpful elements such as a customer service link, a phone number, and icons for the types of payment accepted. One more nice touch is to provide the user with a look at the total amount in response to rolling the mouse pointer over the Quick View cart in the header (as Figure 15-11 illustrates).

Figure 15-9: E-commerce websites such as Bath and Body Works often have a Quick View cart located in the top header portion of the website.

Figure 15-10: A Quick View cart, such as this one at upper-right on the Lush site, gets its name from the small preview window that opens when a user clicks it.

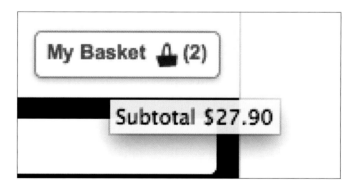

Figure 15-11: The Lush Quick View cart design displays the total cost when the user rolls the mouse pointer over it.

Shopping cart page design

When a user is ready to check out and clicks the link in the Quick View cart, the next page that appears is the dedicated shopping-cart page. This page shows a summary of all the elements presently in the cart. As Figure 15-12 shows, the best practice is to show a visual representation of all those items (the images should be clickable and take the user back to their respective detail pages) — and to give the user the option to edit the quantity or remove an item. Another useful element to include is a shipping calculator next to the subtotal. Shipping is often a huge barrier for users because they are surprised at how much it costs; it's best to give an estimate early on in the process. A lot of retailers offer incentives on shipping to help coax shoppers through this barrier.

Also, if you are offering a promotion, the shopping cart page is a great place to allow users to see how much of a discount they are eligible for. Offer a promotion entry field next to the subtotal (as in Figure 15-12), along with the shipping calculator, so users can get a sense of the actual costs they'll have to pay.

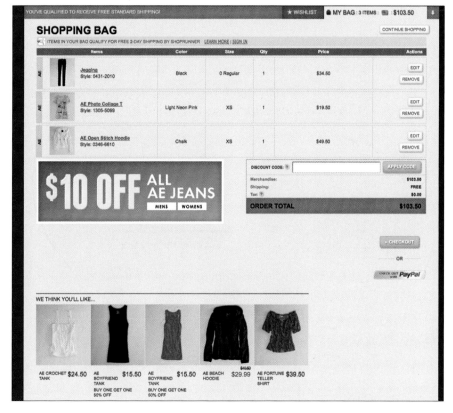

© AEO Management Co., www.ae.com

Figure 15-12: The American Eagle Outfitters shopping cart page offers a graphic view of your items and a means for entering your promotional code.

Offering different payment options is another good tactic to help funnel users through the checkout process. A lot of companies allow you to pay with PayPal in addition to credit card. The goal is to give a user as much total cost information upfront and show payment flexibility so they feel comfortable proceeding on to checkout.

Once you click the Checkout button to proceed with your purchase, many e-commerce companies provide two paths: You can either proceed as a guest or sign in and proceed as a registered user (as you can see in Figure 15-13). The idea of signing in before proceeding is that the website can pre-populate the information fields (name, address, and such) with the data it has on file for you, making checkout a faster process.

What you want to avoid at all costs is *forcing* users to register before proceeding with checkout. That's a sure way to lose customers. Always provide a guest checkout option. During checkout, you end up capturing most of the data you need to register these users anyway, so if registration is your goal, you can give people the option to add a password at the end of checkout, and voilá, you have a new registered user.

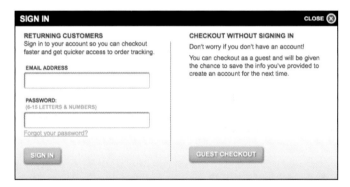

© AEO Management Co., www.ae.com

Figure 15-13: Good e-commerce sites allow users to check out either by signing in or by continuing as a guest.

Personalized Web Pages with Cookies

I'm sure you've visited a website that knows who you are and immediately greets you by name, even without you having to log in. The magic sauce that makes this sort of personalization possible consists of little bits of code called cookies.

In the web-design world, *cookies* are little pieces of data that a web page leaves behind on your computer — sort of like a trail of data crumbs. As you use the site (for example, to order a product), the cookie stores information about your computer, your preferences, your name, and so on. Cookies can be one of two types:

- **Session:** This cookie is only a temporary resident on your computer and stores information as you move from page to page. As soon as you quit the browser, the cookie is deleted, and none of your preferences are recorded for the next time you visit.

- **Permanent:** This cookie is installed on your computer and keeps a running tab of data, storing your name, preferences, and other information so that they appear automatically on the website the next time you come back — even if you've shut down and restarted your machine.

Users can turn off the cookie feature in their browsers, so if you plan to use cookies, make sure that your web pages can also work *without* them. The user's experience shouldn't rely on cookies, just be enhanced by them.

Cookies can also pose a security risk for users. Because they store personal information such as the user's name or website login information, cookies can be a target for other websites trying to get a user's personal information. Only the website that left the cookie on the computer is supposed to be able to retrieve data from it — but some folks have suspected that it's possible for other sites to hack into them. For more information on cookies, visit Cookie Central (www.cookiecentral.com).

Browser and Location Detection

When you visit a website on your mobile phone, many sites automatically display their mobile-friendly version. Behind the scenes, developers placed a script in the site that runs to determine what kind of browser you're using — iPhone, iPad, Android, Blackberry, or even desktop browsers such as Firefox and Internet Explorer. Depending on the queried result, the script then redirects the user to the appropriate website to guarantee an optimal experience. For example, it's not uncommon to have several versions of a website. In addition to a mobile-specific site, you may have a site optimized for newer desktop browsers, supporting many of the latest HTML and CSS features — and one simplified for older browsers.

IP and GPS detection

Depending on the nature of your products and services, a useful detail to detect is the user's general location in the world. Many sites, for example, are global sites that serve a lot of different countries and languages. It's possible to create a single website that displays entirely different content — in the user's native language — simply by using an IP (Internet Protocol) detection script that figures out the user's location. The way it works is that when someone gets Internet service, he or she is assigned an IP address. There are databases of IP address locations that the script can check against as a means of determining the general user location.

The MonsterEnergy.com website, for example, works this way. If you are in Spain and type *MonsterEnergy.com* into your browser, you get local Spanish news, events, and imagery captioned in Spanish as Figure 15-14 illustrates. The IP-detection script tells the site which country and language content to pull in from its content management system (CMS).

© Monster Beverage Company. www.monsterenergy.com

Figure 15-14: MonsterEnergy.com will automatically reflect the local country and language based on the user's location in the world.

While the IP detection method will give you a general region associated with the IP address, as discussed in Chapter 13, it is also possible to obtain a user's specific GPS location by using a combination of JavaScript and HTML5. The JavaScript method, however, does require that you first ask the user's permission (as per the Geolocation API specification at `www.w3.org/TR/geolocation-API/#privacy_for_uas`). While this method requires the extra step of asking permission from the user, it does give you pinpoint-accurate location results, while the IP-detection method is accurate only at a general regional level. Although most of us are familiar with a cellphone's ability to get GPS location data quickly by using Wi-Fi hotspot and cell-tower data, you might be wondering how your desktop computer can get such data. The answer is that your Internet-connected home and office computer shares its IP data with nearby wireless networks. In addition to nearby Wi-Fi networks, the Geolocation API makes use of several location information sources, depending on the device (smartphone or desktop) — including satellite data, radio tracking devices, and Internet hardware. Can you say "Big Brother is watching?"

Responsive design

A more recent trend is the notion of responsive design in which a web page can sense the browser size and screen resolution — even as it changes when a user resizes the browser window — and dynamically reconfigure its layout to accommodate the new size. The magic that makes this possible is the Media Queries portion of the CSS3 specification. A media query is a CSS code that detects the browser's size and, based on the result, tells the page to load the appropriate style sheet such as `widescreen.css` as opposed to `mobilescreen.css`. These different style sheets contain different layout systems, font sizes, and image optimization settings. Therefore, in theory, no matter how many different devices are introduced on the market, each with a unique screen space, it's possible to simply create a new CSS document that optimizes your website to accommodate it.

Take a look at Figure 15-15. When the website is viewed on a desktop, with a large browser window, it orients itself in a two-column layout. As I shrink the browser window (see Figure 15-16), the website automatically reorients itself into a single-column design. The same is true when this site is viewed on a mobile device such as an iPhone, as Figure 15-17 shows: I automagically see a single-column layout.

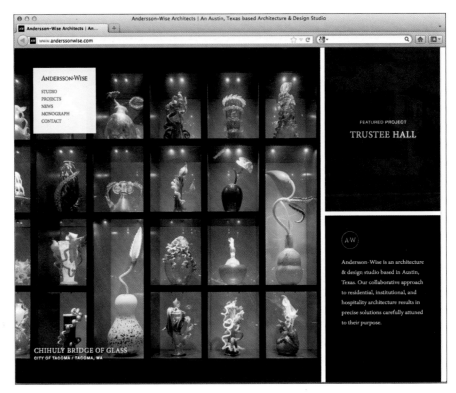

Figure 15-15: The Andersson-Wise website is an elegant example of responsive design. The site displays in two columns within large browser windows.

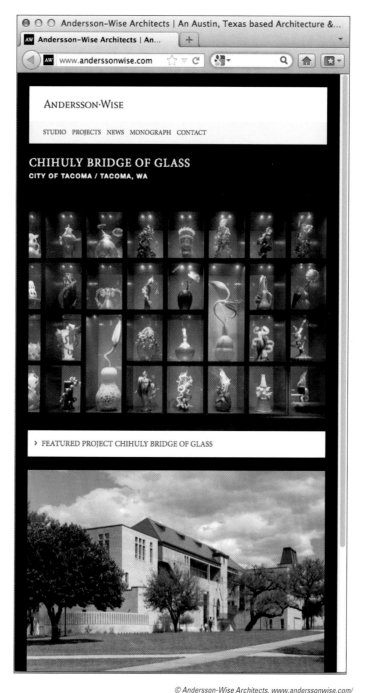

Figure 15-16: The same Andersson-Wise website reconfigures itself in real time to a single-column view when the browser window gets smaller.

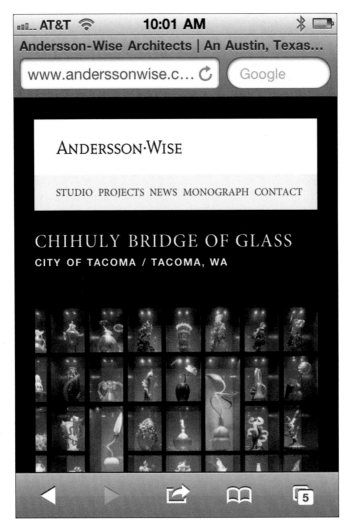

Figure 15-17: When viewed on an iPhone, the Andersson-Wise website displays in a single-column layout.

Global Website Performance

If you're building a global site that will serve users all over the world — such as the MonsterEnergy.com site — you'll have to pay some pretty specific attention to your site's performance early on. Typically, a website is hosted at a secure data center (with the hosting usually outsourced to a large, dedicated facility such as Rackspace) — but the host facility has a physical location *somewhere* in the world. Therefore, a significant lag time can crop up when a user accesses the site from some remote location (relative to the host site, anyway). Even at this higher-speed point in the digital age, it takes time to load a bunch of images, Flash elements, video, and information — and the time it takes is related directly to your location on the globe. This variable lag time, referred to as *latency* in the web industry, can be quite severe — especially in countries that don't have the widest bandwidth.

Another factor that has plagued websites of the past is traffic load. For example, if your site offered a sale at midnight, you might have too much traffic hit the web server all at once, crashing it. Most folks who've been online for a while have visited sites that suddenly went "down" for some unknown reason. Often the reason was, in effect, an online traffic jam.

To solve the problem of latency and balance the traffic load, most hosting services now offer *cloud computing:* They distribute copies of your website files to servers all over the world. This strategy is what's referred to as a *content distribution network* (CDN), which offers the advantage of a shorter distance between user and content. You can structure your website hosting in such a way that only content elements like images and video are hosted through a CDN service like EdgeCast (www.edgecast.com) — while the rest of the site is hosted at a data center. When users access your site on a CDN, they are actually accessing locally cached versions of your files that are nearest to their location, making the site load much more quickly and efficiently for them.

Part V
The Part of Tens

The 5th Wave By Rich Tennant

"The divorce was amicable. She got the Jetta, the sailboat and the recumbent bike. I got the servers and the domain name."

In this chapter, I offer tips on how to do the ten tasks that I've found most crucial for your web-design career, either when you're on your own or when you're working for a company.

Presenting Your Work

Whether you're going on a job interview to work at a company, presenting to an internal client, or presenting your work to your freelance clients, keep the following techniques in mind when assembling and presenting your portfolios.

Assembling a portfolio

Here are some tips for assembling your portfolio:

- **Build an online-portfolio website.** Often, a client asks for a list of URLs to websites you've designed. Rather than just e-mailing a list of URLs to the client, assemble samples of your work in one nicely designed online-portfolio site and e-mail just the URL of that site to the client.

  By making your own online-portfolio site, you can also show work that's no longer "live on the Web." Rather than providing a link to a nonexistent site (a *broken* link), you can show images you've saved from the site and provide a little blurb about the project. In fact, I like to show images (scaled down to about one-quarter size) of the website and allow people to click on them to see a larger version. Include a little paragraph that describes what you did, what design challenges you encountered, and how you solved those challenges. As shown in Figure 16-1, providing a little background on the project helps clients and employers better evaluate your designs.

  Some copyright legalities can crop up when you share client work in the context of your portfolio. Generally speaking, most copyright lawyers believe that reproducing work you've done for clients in your portfolio is considered "fair use." Displaying your designs in your portfolio is a common practice — and typically, the copyright owners don't make a stink about it. That said, keep in mind that some clients are more sensitive about this issue — but usually it's because they don't want their competition seeing what they're up to and who's helping them. Certainly you should never show a client's work that is not yet available in the marketplace.

- **Build an offline portfolio book.** In addition to your online-portfolio website, you should assemble a book full of printed editions of your work. You can choose and buy a cool-looking portfolio book at your local art (not craft) store for about $80. These usually have black paper in a binder-like book, so you can take the pages out and rearrange them as needed.

  You may be surprised to find out that a lot of employers at design agencies ask you to *send* your portfolio to them rather than bring it in personally. If you aren't present, your book is your only representation, so you've got to make sure it's polished, consistent, and professional.

Take screen shots of your work and print them at full size, in full color, on glossy paper. My feeling is that glossy paper gives you better color results than matte paper. You can decide whether to leave the browser interface in the screen shots, but whatever you do, do it consistently. Use a light spray adhesive (such as 3M Spray Mount) or double-sided removable mounting tape to adhere your prints onto the black paper of the book. Finally, make sure that your book is not too big and not too small — Super B (13 x 19 inches) is a good size to shoot for.

✓ **Put together a biography.** If you're an independent consultant, a client does not want to look at your résumé to get a sense of your qualifications. A client looks mainly at your portfolio of work. Still, providing a short paragraph that outlines your professional experience and accomplishments is a good idea. Remember, after you sell a client on your services, the client has to turn around and sell you to the other people he or she works with. If the client can rattle off a few fun facts about you to grease the skids, his or her job is a little easier.

In addition, a bio is helpful to include at the top of your résumé when you're seeking a design job at a company. A bio is like an executive summary that sums up your experience and gives you a chance to sell yourself before the potential employer drills into the job-history listings.

Taking screen shots

When building your on- and offline portfolio components, at some point you'll probably need to take screen shots of your online work. To take a screen shot, use either the computer's built-in capabilities or a special screen capture utility such as HyperSnap or Snapz Pro.

Mac users can press ⌘+Shift+3 to take a picture of the whole screen or ⌘+Shift+4 to draw a box around just a portion of the screen (with this latter option, the cursor changes to crosshairs, and you drag a marquee around the portion of the screen you want). The resulting screen shot is saved to your hard drive or to the desktop. (After it's on your hard drive, you can rename it to better remember what the screen shot represents.)

Windows desktop users can press the Alt + Print Scrn key to capture an image of the active window; some PC laptops require you press the Function (Fn) and the Print Scrn buttons at the same time. This key instructs the computer to take a screen shot and store it on the Clipboard. Next, open any graphics program such as Photoshop, Paint Shop Pro, or Fireworks, start a new file, and paste the screen shot from the Clipboard.

Neither of the built-in Mac or PC screen-capture methods will capture the cursor. If you want to include the cursor in your screen captures, you'll have to purchase and download a screen-capture utility (as mentioned earlier), either HyperSnap or Snapz Pro:

✓ **HyperSnap:** `www.hypersnap-dx.com/hsdx/`

✓ **Snapz Pro:** `www.ambrosiasw.com/utilities/snapzprox/`

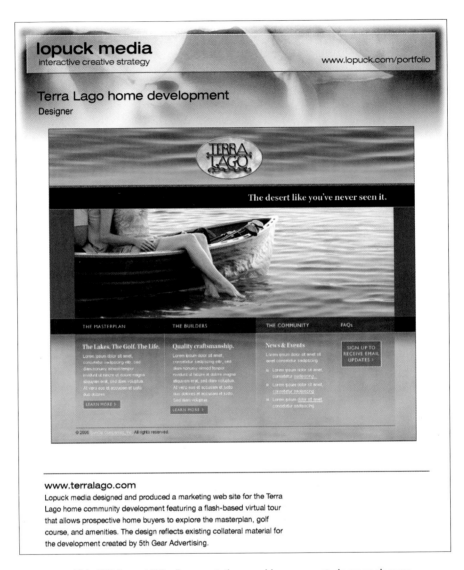

Figure 16-1: This PDF "capabilities" presentation provides a case study on each page.

Presenting your work

When you're ready to present your work in person, keep the following points in mind:

✔ **Have presence.** Presentation is half the battle. For the meeting itself, dress the part, have your material ready in all its forms — online and offline — and be bright, positive, and confident. Speak clearly and convincingly, make eye contact, and read and respond to the body language of the room. The worst thing you can do is come off nervous, soft-spoken, and unprepared. If by reading the room, you feel people are getting anxious, bored, or losing patience, change topics, or switch it around — acknowledge and appreciate their time and ask if there's something they'd like to focus on.

✔ **Be positive and informative about your work.** The biggest mistake that new designers make is being too humble about their work (or even making excuses for — or berating — their work). As I say, "If it's good enough to show, it's good enough to support." Talk positively about your work. Discuss design challenges you may have faced and how you solved them. This approach shows the thinking behind your design treatments, giving them context and relevance so the client is better able to judge them.

✔ **Don't be married to your work.** Don't be upset if your work is not well received, or another designer's work is chosen instead. As soon as you produce a design candidate, remove yourself emotionally from it. Present it objectively and never defensively. Being defensive is bad form, and it's not going to advance the project. Discuss the feedback and, together with the clients, think through ways to change it more to their liking.

Developing a Proposal

When clients want work to be done, they prepare an *RFP* (*Request For Proposal*). An RFP is a document that outlines the goals and scope of the project so designers can better prepare a proposal. Often, however, the clients themselves are not sure what they want or what can be done, so the RFP is not as helpful as you may hope.

Often the RFP outlines clear, sometimes strict, procedures for submitting your proposal, telling you what to include, when to submit it, and what to expect after that. For RFPs that are less specific, here's a list of things you should include in your RFP response:

✔ **Project summary.** Include a section that outlines the project, any specific ideas you have for the project, assumptions you have about the project, and any unique qualifications you and your team have for the project.

✔ **Project budget.** The most important aspect to include in your proposal is the bottom line: How much is this project going to cost the client? Provide an estimate for the project that covers the work assumptions and ideas you stated in the project summary and timeline. Clients often include a budget range in their RFP. If so, you can work backward from the budget amount and scale the production effort to fit. When the client does not include such info, you must estimate what the project will cost based on the scope of the work and the schedule you've outlined in your proposal.

When estimating, always add 20 to 25 percent more than you think that the project will cost. You can always impress the client by billing less, and if you end up needing the additional amount, you'll be thankful that you built in the extra padding. Regardless of how the project goes, asking the client for more money is always bad form unless the client has asked you to increase the scope of the project. Clients expect you to put enough time into the proposal to accurately predict your costs and profit margin.

✔ **Visual examples.** Clients usually respond better to visuals than to a lot of text. Wherever you can, include diagrams and sample designs.

✔ **Market and competitive analysis.** Depending on the nature of the project, it may be helpful to provide a market analysis section that shows competitive sites and discusses ways to differentiate the client's site. If you are developing a website for a commercial enterprise such as an online store, it's helpful to do a little research into similar websites to make sure that the design you propose is competitive.

✔ **Your company background.** Include a section that provides an overview of your design agency or consultancy along with case studies of relevant projects you've completed. Also include a short bio on you and other key team members.

✔ **Outline of content and special features.** Create a basic outline of the content and features you propose for the website based on what the RFP states and the brainstorming you've done with the client. For example, if you think that an interactive timeline would be a great addition to the website, list it as a special feature and describe how it would work.

✔ **Sample navigation ideas.** Along with a list of content and features, you may even go so far as to suggest how you'd organize the interface. For example, you can outline a list of main categories and subcategories — and even outline how the interface might work.

✔ **Production schedule.** Include a section that outlines the production schedule, complete with client sign-off points, your team's milestones, and the client's *deliverables* (tasks that the client is responsible for). A *client sign-off point* is when the client formally accepts the recent progress (by signing a document to that effect) and knows that the company cannot ask for revisions without incurring additional costs. It's also important to determine up front who has sign-off authority for the client. Also, often, the client includes a desired due date for the project. In this case, you can work backward from that date and scale the production effort accordingly. For example, if the client wants the project done in just one month, the scope and budget of what you can accomplish is already limited.

The client's schedule is a very important element in your production timeline. Client sign-off points are necessary because they enable you to close one phase of production and move on to the next, knowing that everything up to that point has been accepted.

Outlining a client's deliverables in writing is critical because it is the only leverage you have if the schedule slips due to the client's neglect. By listing both client and team deliverables, everyone agrees to their respective responsibilities up front — and avoids surprises later.

Winning the Bid

Writing up proposals burns a lot of time — design firms and independent contractors all feel the same pain. Nonetheless, you must invest this time in order to even have a chance to win the project, so make your time count.

After spending a few years on the client side within a big company, I've seen a lot of proposals from the biggest web-design agencies in the country. The ones that won the bids all had these characteristics:

- **Demonstrated project relevance.** Proposals that discuss specific creative ideas and solutions for the project do better than generic proposals. By *generic*, I mean that some proposals only give background on the agency itself, its awards, its methodology (the same one I outline in Chapter 2), and then go into the project's timeline, schedule, and budget. Blah, blah, blah. Clients want to know how you would approach their specific project and hear some of your ideas.

- **Provided sample visuals.** Great designs that you've done for similar projects go a long way toward winning the bid. In fact, some clients even ask agencies to provide sample design directions for their particular project in the proposal. Such "work on spec" is risky, but it's often the only way to win the bid in competitive situations. For the most part, however, sharing case studies of related work and pointing out relevant features (so long as that work is live and doing its job out in the market) can create a powerful, and lasting, impression.

- **Touted solid team members.** Include a section in your proposal that provides a brief bio on each team member who would be working on the project. Clients want to know they'll have an all-star team dedicated to their project. And if you win the bid, make sure those team members are in fact on the project! I can think of one large project where the agency swapped in junior team members. The project fell apart, created a huge amount of friction, and opened the door for legal action.

Knowing What to Charge as an Independent Consultant

Knowing what to charge is always hard. You can use any one of various formulas to arrive at an hourly rate that takes into consideration your annual expenses, profit margin, and salary, but you can arrive at this number through simple common sense:

- ✓ **Ask around to find out what other designers are charging.** This information can give you a good reality check as well as a range of prices. You may find that freelance designers in your area are charging between $50 and $150 an hour.

- ✓ **Be honest about your level of skill and experience.** If you've been around for a while and you have a range of high-profile sites in your portfolio, you probably know exactly what you should charge for your freelance services, and it's probably toward the top end of the range. If you're new to web design but are an old hat at print design, your fee may be somewhere in the middle.

- ✓ **Estimate your salary and expenses.** As an independent consultant, you have to calculate what it costs you to run your business each month, how much you want to make, how much time you can honestly bill in each month, and taxes.

- ✓ **Think of all the things you need to buy in order to run your business.** Electricity, office supplies, computers, software, fonts, an Internet connection, trade magazines, memberships in industry organizations, and so on all add up. Think of a monthly budget for all these things, and then think of what you'd like to make on top of that. For example, if it costs you $4,000 a month to run your home office and you want to clear $6,000 a month, you have to figure out how to make $10,000 a month.

- ✓ **Figure out how many hours you must bill each month.** *Billable time* is all the time you actually spend doing client work. Ideally, this is at least half of your time; but more often than not, checking e-mail, writing proposals, and performing other activities cut drastically into your available time for working on specific projects.

   For example, if you assume that each year has 50 workweeks (leaving two for vacation), you have 4.1 weeks in a month. At 50 percent billable time, that leaves 83.3 hours of billable time. To make $10,000 a month, your hourly rate needs to be $120.00.

 Incidentally, I've noticed that a freelance hourly rate oddly corresponds to an annual salary. Notice that $10,000 a month is $120,000 per year, and the hourly rate is $120.00. The same phenomenon occurs in the workplace. For instance, a creative director who is paid $150,000 a year in an agency can probably charge about $150.00 an hour for consulting work. Similarly, a junior designer who makes about $50,000 a year for an agency can charge about $50.00 an hour for freelance work.

When you bid on a project, use your hourly rate to come up with an estimate of what the project will cost, but ultimately quote clients a *fixed bid* (a single flat fee). It's better to charge clients a flat per-project fee than to charge them hourly. Firstly, most clients expect a fixed bid so that they know exactly what the project will cost.

Another reason to charge a fixed bid is that if you work fast and zero in on the design quickly, you are paid for the *value* of your work, not just the few hours it took you to knock it out. Make sure that you're paid for using your brain, not your hands!

The hardest part of charging a flat rate is accurately estimating the amount of work and the time it will take you to complete the project. Spend time thinking through each step of the proposal, gauging the work, estimating how long each step will take, and putting a dollar figure next to it. Include any subcontractor's estimates, and then add up all the steps. Add 20 to 25 percent to the budget for good measure.

How Agencies Charge

Web-design agencies use formulas similar to those used by freelancers for calculating their internal hourly rates. Generally, agencies have different internal billing rates for each level of designer, from production artists on up to creative directors. The prices that web-design agencies charge clients for these designers, however, are a lot higher than what the agency pays their designers. Although such agencies may pay a junior designer $50,000 a year, they may bill that person at $100 per hour when they're calculating the costs of a project.

Although such a high price may sound heavily bloated, you must consider that agencies have a lot of overhead expenses to cover. In addition to the normal lease payments and supply expenses, agencies have a lot of non-billable, but valuable, support people, such as administrative assistants and accountants. The billable people in the organization pay for the non-billable people.

The larger the organization gets, the more expensive it becomes to keep the ship afloat. For this reason, typically each web-design firm has what is called a *minimum size of engagement*. If a client called a big design firm for a project that had a budget of only $50,000, that firm would probably refer the client to a smaller agency. Big agencies simply cannot afford to take projects unless they meet a certain budget range.

Because of an agency's minimum-engagement-budget rule, the independent consultants and the smaller design houses play an important role in taking on the multitude of smaller projects with budgets from $5,000 to $100,000.

Managing a Client's Expectations

Above all else, setting and managing a client's expectations before and during a project are among the most important tasks you have as a designer. No two people ever hear or see the same thing when they look at a project. Even when you're explaining a project to a client, the client may be thinking one thing when you mean something else. For example, if you require content from the client, make sure that the client knows when and how to deliver it to you. Also make sure that the full range of services you do *and don't* provide is clearly outlined in the proposal.

If you have nothing in writing, you'll have a difficult time describing why a certain feature was left out of the project or why the schedule slipped. Whatever goes wrong is always going to be considered your fault. When assembling the proposal, the best way to protect yourself and ward off any potential conflicts with the client is to be very clear about due dates and what content will be included in each deliverable.

Setting Client Responsibilities for the Project

In the project proposal, one of the most important elements to list is the client's responsibilities. Make sure you discuss these, specifically and seriously, with the client at the beginning of the project. Clients must understand that the project will stop in its tracks if they do not meet their deadlines for delivering content or approvals to you.

For some reason, clients tend to think that they don't have to do a thing after they sign the contract. They don't realize that you can't do your job without getting content from them. For example, when you build the product section of the website, you'll need photos and information for each of the client's products. Unless taking new photos and writing new copy are part of your proposal, the client must provide this material in a timely manner.

Just to cover yourself, pad extra time into the schedule for each client deliverable without telling them. This way, even if the client slips, you won't, and you can better schedule your team's resources and time.

Getting Clients to Sign Off on Key Milestones

In addition to feeding content and materials to you during the project, clients must also sign off on various key milestones along the way. By getting clients to sign off on key steps in the project, such as the sitemap, you protect yourself from any future arguments over the scope and quality of the project. At the beginning of the project, it's also very important to establish who has sign-off authority for the client. In some cases, a different person in the client's organization may sign off on different parts of the project.

For example, imagine that you're halfway into HTML production and your client's CEO balks, refusing to pay unless you include an interactive company-history page. If you have a signed site map with no history page on it, you can clearly state that the page was never part of the scope, and you have so-and-so's authorized signature to prove it.

Aside from protecting you from clients' tendencies to change their minds and demand new features, a sign-off policy also protects the clients. They have signed documents that assure them and their managers that they'll get what they're paying for.

While most clients are reasonable, a handful out there (think "large entertainment companies") are known for delaying feedback and noodling designs ad nauseam. Usually that's because they can't make a decision, don't want to stick their necks out, change their minds partway through, or cannot be pleased by any design that is not their own. If you suspect that you're going to be dealing with such a company, be very clear about what their fixed-bid proposal gets them and when your hourly rates kick in. For example, your proposal might include three design directions of a home page and a subpage, and two rounds of revisions on one selected design. Any noodling thereafter will incur hourly rates at X dollars an hour.

Managing the Web Project's Workflow

When you're knee-deep in a project, you have the internal challenge of managing people on your team to get the job done. For the most part, if you're working within a larger organization, project managers or producers manage the client and the team members to ensure that all the resources (content, people, and so on) are in place and to ensure that the project stays on track. This management model enables you, the designer, to focus on what you do well.

If you are on your own, managing the client and the project schedule and doing all the design and production work can keep you working around the clock.

If you're on your own, you might pick one thing that you do well and that you enjoy, and offer only that service. Doing all aspects of website design, from creative to programming, is difficult enough; *managing* the whole process by yourself is even more difficult — unless project management *is* that one service you offer. If you do only one thing (such as information design, Flash animation, or web creative direction), you need to manage only the one deliverable. When you're a specialist, marketing your services is easier than if you're a generalist. You can market directly to clients, to design agencies, and even to other freelance designers and producers who need your piece of the puzzle on their projects.

Hiring and Managing Subcontractors

As your web-design consulting business expands, you may find that you're getting more work than you can handle. If you're like me, you don't like to say no to more work! One way to handle your growing business is to find able-bodied freelancers like you — people you know you can rely on for expanded project needs — and then manage them as the project's *producer*.

For example, one client may want you to develop a series of four design directions at the very same time that another client needs other work done. In such cases, you may subcontract another designer to help you create a few of the design directions so you can get everything done on time.

When hiring subcontractors, their rates may often be close to your own rates. Plan for your subcontractors by getting a fixed-bid estimate from them that you can then roll into your overall project budget.

Marking up their services by about 15 percent is acceptable. After all, you need to be compensated for the time spent managing them.

Look at your initial client contract to see whether hiring subcontractors raises any legal issues. Often, a client simply signs the project proposal and no other legal agreement. In such cases, you are free to hire and manage subcontractors as needed. If the client, however, asks you to sign a work-for-hire agreement along with the proposal, such agreements sometimes forbid any subcontracting activity.

As for signing any agreements with your subcontractors, you too may keep your own standard work-for-hire agreement on hand for them to sign — especially for larger projects. For small projects, however, the subcontractor usually just puts a mini-proposal together that shows the work to be done, the price, and the schedule, and that's enough to go on.

At the end of the project, the subcontractor sends you an invoice. Keep these invoices in a safe place and make sure that they include the following information (you need it for tax purposes at the end of the year):

- ✔ First and last name
- ✔ Address
- ✔ Phone number
- ✔ Social Security Number or Federal ID number

It's sort of like sending out a cynical version of holiday cards: At the end of the year (in the United States) you must send out 1099 forms to every subcontractor to whom you've paid more than $600 throughout the tax year. Total up the amount you've paid them and fill out one 1099 form for each person. You can find these forms at any office supply store or at your local post office.

You must send the 1099 forms out in the mail by the end of January, or you may not be able to claim the invoices as expenses on your own taxes. Talk to your tax professional.

Use Only Five to Seven Main Categories

Five and seven are magic numbers because remembering a list of five to seven things is easy. Any more than that and our brains lose track. Maybe it's because we have five fingers on each hand. We can mentally attach one item to each digit, and if we've had enough coffee, we can remember a few more items on the next hand.

You may think I'm joking — but I've heard from psychologists-turned-interface-designers that the five-finger phenomenon actually has merit. In web design, many user interface designers suggest that keeping your list of categories down to just five to seven is best. This strategy keeps users from feeling overwhelmed in your site.

The problem with the five-to-seven rule, however, is that most modern websites have a lot more going on, and honing the site down to just five or so areas is difficult. In such cases, I've found that breaking the navigation into sets is helpful: a primary, secondary, and (if needed) tertiary set.

Each set can contain five to seven items. Take a look at the diagram in Figure 17-1. In this design, the top navigation area has five links to the main categories of the site. The side navigation area has another five links, and the bottom footer has four links. The content in the middle may have a few links too, but they are shortcuts to sections otherwise accessible in the three navigation sets.

Keep in mind that this rule applies to site global navigation and not to links that are actual content, such as a list of resource links or a list of *anchor links* (links that jump you to different parts of the same page).

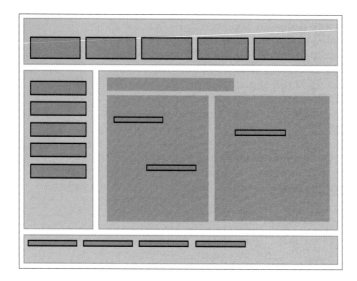

Figure 17-1: Each of the three functional areas contains five to seven links.

Develop Wireframes for Each Unique Page Layout

One of the most important steps of the web-design process — one that you should never skip — even for small-scale sites — is the development of wireframes. Like blueprints for a house, wireframes are diagram-like drawings that articulate your thoughts for laying out content on the page and figuring out the interaction required to get through the content.

You don't have to do a wireframe for each page of the site — only the unique layouts and pages with intricate interaction, such as the pages in a store-checkout process.

Wireframes are your chance to work out all the navigation nuances of the site, accommodate all the content the site will have, and get a rough idea of how everything will fit on each page before you begin developing visual designs.

In fact, I like to have the first pass of wireframes complete before I begin exploring visual design options. Without knowledge of at least the rough navigation scheme and content elements, it's difficult to develop a visual design that works for the site. Exploring designs too early in the process puts you at risk of developing something that the client loves but is just not practical and requires significant reworking. Time- and budget-wise, waiting to do the visual design is most efficient.

Always Label Your Buttons and Icons

As idiot-proof as you think your icon or illustration may be, I've found that you can never rely on pictures alone to tell users what a button does. Unless you're designing a print function or other commonly recognized task, adding a simple text label to a button or icon is a good idea. After all, no *one* picture could reliably represent the Product Catalog section of a site that offers a wide range of products.

By the time you illustrate an icon with enough detail to give users a good idea of what the section is all about, you have a picture worth framing. You may as well save some space and add a simple text label. I'm not saying you should never use icons; they can add a lot of design flavor to a site. Just be sure to supplement them with a label for clarity's sake.

Mind the Download Time

To maximize the user experience of your site, always keep in mind the connection speed of your end users and the ease with which they can access the most important areas of your site. For example, avoid long all-Flash intro sequences that must play through before users can make a navigation choice. Even if your Flash intro has a Skip Intro button, you force users to download the Flash movie to the point where they can even click the Skip button. Only then can they finally access the global navigation. Such a two-step process (that can also involve a long wait) is annoying for your repeat visitors. A better plan is to load the global navigation immediately, along with the Flash segment. That way people can bypass the Flash and get directly to the content at hand. Another strategy is to include a Cover page that allows people to launch the Flash-enabled site (which usually opens in a new window with a custom size).

Another thing to keep in mind is the fact that if a site is hosted on one side of the world, the *latency* (delay) that visitors experience when they access the site (on the other side of the world) can be significant. If you are designing a global site, you'll need to think about using a *content delivery network* (CDN) such as EdgeCast (`www.edgecast.com`) to speed up the site delivery experience and balance traffic spikes.

Provide "You Are Here" Feedback

The navigation system you design should not only provide access to all the main functional areas of the site, but also give users some sense of where they are in the website. Don't leave your visitor wandering like a mouse in a maze; being able to see the whole maze from an aerial view makes it easier to get to the payoff (the content). Your navigation system should provide the same sense of orientation and visually show people the size and scope of the site.

In Figure 17-2, a small map of the whole site immediately gives users a view of the site and a quick means to navigate through it. When a user rolls the mouse pointer over each little icon, the icon is highlighted, and a label appears, telling the user what it represents. A bread-crumb trail provides continual feedback of where the user is in the site.

Figure 17-2: This navigation system shows a miniature view of the entire site.

Make It Easy to Get Back Home

One of the functional items people forget to include most often in web design is a link back to the home page. People drill down in a site, find the info they need, and then suddenly realize that the only way to get back to the home page is by re-entering the URL.

Often, the company's logo at the top of the page is a secret passage back to the home page. Seasoned web surfers usually try to click the logo to get back home, but to a novice user (and to many international users), the logo just looks like a logo.

The best course of action is to include a dedicated link to the home page as part of your standard set of navigational buttons — usually in the secondary or tertiary navigation set. Figure 17-3 shows a small Home button in the upper-left corner that does not conflict with the primary and secondary navigation.

A home page button is included in the main navigation.

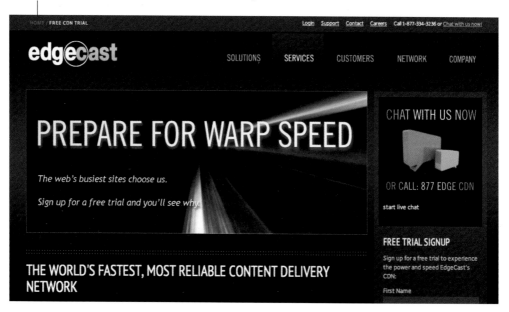

© EdgeCast Networks, Inc. www.edgecast.com

Figure 17-3: Here the tiny Home button (upper-left corner) is treated as a function like "Login" and kept separate from the main site-navigation links.

Visually Differentiate Clickable and Non-clickable Things

Although reusing graphics whenever you can to take advantage of the browser's caching ability is tempting, don't use the same graphic as a button on one page and as a decorative headline on another. For example, if you use an icon as a button that leads to the About section of the site, don't use the same icon merely as decoration for the headline on that page. Otherwise people will still think that it's a button. Give the icon a slightly different visual treatment so people know that its function has changed.

You should always treat the visual design of clickable things differently from the design of headlines, images, and other non-clickable things. Design interactive elements to look like their function. For example, linked text should always have a unique color, or be bold or underlined to separate it from normal body text. It's the same for linked headlines versus informational headlines. Buttons should also have a unique and consistent treatment throughout the site.

Develop a style guide for all design elements in your site — for links, text, a few levels of headlines, buttons, table elements, bullets, and other elements. After users figure out your system, your site becomes easier to navigate.

"One of These Buttons Is Not Like the Others"

Continuing along the same lines as "Make It Easy to Get Back Home" (Step 6 in this top-ten list) is consistency. If you've ever watched *Sesame Street,* you may remember the famous skit: "One of these things is not like the others." In this scenario, kids are taught to weed out the objects that don't fit with the rest of the group. This is an excellent analogy for user interface design.

Consistency applies not only to the visual treatment of your navigation sets but also to their placement on the page and logical grouping. Your primary, secondary, and tertiary navigation sets should always be located in the same relative location on the page. In addition, the links you include in each navigation set should be similar in function and priority. For example, if you have a few tool-like functions like "view map" and "view calendar," these should be (a) grouped together, (b) visually similar, and (c) separate from content-related navigation sets.

The best interfaces are those that remain consistent throughout a site. The user becomes comfortable with the buttons and remembers where to find them. The interface becomes almost transparent, and the user can focus on the content of the page.

If you change the design or placement of a button from one page to the next, users may not find it, or they may think that the button has an entirely different function — even if it has the same text label. They may ignore it and continue to scan the page, searching for the button they just clicked.

Tread Lightly with Real-Life Metaphors

Sometimes your client wants the interactive model for their website to be inspired by an object or a place, or modeled after an experience such as watching a movie or playing a video game. For example, a client for a children's site might want to use a 3D clubhouse for the main interface.

Although real-life metaphors provide interesting ways to think about the design of a site, they can also impose a lot of design constraints on you. For instance, as in Figure 17-4, if you want the interface to look like a digital device with chrome buttons surrounding a central screen, you suddenly have a much smaller viewing space for all your content.

Instead of taking metaphors too literally, start the creative process with a theme, concept, or story. For example, the theme "march to your own beat" may inspire interesting visuals, a customizable soundtrack for the site, and a unique twist on the copy you write throughout the site — including names for the navigation. In addition, a theme can naturally extend to other supporting media such as brochures, HTML e-mails, ads, and other creative formats.

Figure 17-4: This interface looks like a digital device and leaves little room in the interior window.

Use Color-Coding Sparingly

Another way to orient people in your website is to color-code each of the main sections. Color-coding is most useful in cases where the site has just a few main sections, but each one is deep in content. For example, a corporate site may have a branded online store that has a different color scheme from that of the main site. Or a conference website may have a few different tracks that you can color-code so prospective attendees know they're looking at the right one when thumbing through the session descriptions.

If you color-code a website, be sure to choose colors that work well together and have similar light and dark values. For instance, don't choose a set of five dark, dingy colors and one bright yellow color. If you do, you won't be able to apply the same design strategy to each color-coded section. The bright yellow one needs dark text while the dingy, dark colors need light text.

In Figure 17-5, the difference between dark and bright colors on a white background is apparent.

Figure 17-5: The first colors have similar luminance values; the fifth color is the odd man out.

A color-coded system works well only if you have a few main categories. If you have too many categories, you have difficulty choosing a set of colors that work well together and are still different enough from one another to make color-coding meaningful.

Ten Things That Can Go Wrong

*Y*ou may know how to initiate a project with a client, build a sitemap, create design directions, and make technology choices, but you must know one more thing to be a successful web designer: contingency planning. Anticipating the worst that can happen in the course of a project and planning how to deal with it are the last steps toward becoming a full-fledged web designer. In this chapter, I list the top ten things that can go wrong, why they happen, and how you can respond to keep a project on track.

"Can We Add Just One More Thing?"

When clients first come to you, they often don't know what is possible with web technologies. They don't know what you can and can't do — or how much anything really costs — so they don't ask for it in their Request For

Proposal (RFP). After a project is under way, however, and clients start to see the site take shape, their eyes tend to grow wider and wider with all the cool possibilities.

As clients become familiar with the web-development process, they may often ask you to throw in an extra Flash movie here, a personalized greeting there, and all manner of extra features to liven up the site. In web-design circles, these little additions to the project are called *scope creep.* If you give in to these little client requests, the *scope* of the project can slowly *creep* upward, getting bigger and more costly until you're basically working for free — or worse, going into debt!

Identifying *and resisting* scope creep whenever it happens is critical. Aside from losing your shirt financially, scope creep causes two other huge problems:

- **The ripple effect.** Although a change may seem small at first, you must look at how it affects production of the rest of the site and the ongoing maintenance of the site. Sometimes, just by changing one little thing, you break something elsewhere in the site because it was never planned for in the first place. Or you cause unforeseen technical or customer-support issues in the future. For example, adding customer ratings and reviews requires a live human on the client's end to moderate and respond to the incoming data.

- **Production inefficiencies.** Because scope creep can come at any time in the web-design process, you cannot implement the new feature without causing production inefficiencies. Adding a new feature midstream causes the team to stop what it's doing, redo tasks already completed, and refocus on the addition. From start to finish, midstream changes take more time to implement than they would if they were in the initial plan.

Still, scope creep happens — and because you're the customer-service type, you find it tough to say no. Here's how to manage scope creep gracefully:

- **Get everything in writing.** Before you begin work on a project, make sure that your proposal clearly states the scope of the project — what you're including, what the client must provide, and what the project does *not* include. Also make sure that your sitemap is detailed enough to show how all the proposed content works together.

  If everything is in writing, no one can question what was included in the original deal.

- **Share the budget ramifications.** When a client asks you to insert a little something in the site, say, "Sure, I'd be glad to! Let me come back to you with what that would cost and how much time it would add to the project."

Need I continue? Sharing the realities of an expanded budget and time schedule often quickly turns a client around. If your client decides to move forward with the addition, at least you and the client have clear expectations about how it impacts the project.

"We Don't Have Time for a Sitemap."

Often clients come to designers at the very last moment and ask for an entire site designed and delivered within a ridiculous timeframe. The client insists on a crazy schedule, usually to try to meet an important conference or meeting on a hard date.

In situations like these, you may be tempted to dispense with the proposal, the project plan, and the sitemap so that you can dig right into the design directions. The problem with rushing in, however, is that neither you nor the client has a road map to guide you. Without a road map, you have no idea what to include in the design directions — you plod in the dark, wasting time as the deadline slowly ticks closer.

Even worse, when you dispense with the planning phase, you set yourself up for disaster in terms of client expectations. The client may be thinking one thing, and you may be thinking another. Midway through the project, the client may not see what he expected to see, and panic follows.

Ironically, the most time-efficient way to proceed is to invest a little time up front creating a proposal that clearly outlines the content and goals of the site — and to follow that with a sitemap that shows how you plan to arrange the content. You can do both these things in just one to two days of working closely with the client. Then, with a clear plan in hand, you can knock out the design directions and produce a site that the client loves — with plenty of time to spare.

"The Clients Want THAT Design?"

When you're presenting design directions to clients, you may be tempted to shower them with a ton of options to choose from. Offering them lots of options gives them the impression that you've spent a lot of time thinking about their project, and it gives them a lot of ideas to consider.

The problem with this logic, however, is that it's difficult to come up with more than four to six directions that are distinctive *and* that you like. You always have a favorite and a least-favorite design. For some reason unknown in the cosmos, clients have a knack for falling in love with your least-favorite design. Therefore, never present a design that you can't live with.

To assemble a good group of designs to present, have a few different designers each come up with one or two designs. This way, you're sure to get an assortment of unique designs. From these, choose the top three to six designs that you feel good about presenting to the client. (Generally, three design directions are plenty!)

If you are an independent consultant and don't have a staff of designers, try finding a few like-minded independent designers to help you develop design directions for each project.

"Who Needs Usability Testing When You Have Me?"

You may laugh, but I've heard the sentiment, "Who needs to test when you have me?" expressed by more than one web designer. Often designers find that they simply don't have enough time or money to organize a formal user test for a new website — many times that's because the designers never planned for testing in the first place. All too often, testing is considered an unnecessary expense in the budget — even by the clients.

If this omission happens in a large project, a client can end up spending a lot of money on a project that simply doesn't work. Without testing, no one knows about problems until the site is live on the Web — and (oops) the negative customer feedback starts rolling in. After a user has a bad experience at a site, a second visit is not likely. Testing is crucial.

For large enterprise sites, planning and budgeting for formal user tests are imperative. For small-to-medium-size sites, you can still plan for user testing, but you don't have to go all-out with the formal, expensive, time-consuming procedures. Organizing small, informal testing intervals along the way — using friends, colleagues, and even the clients themselves — is better than nothing at all.

"But I'm Sure I Can Make This New Technology Work!"

As you wade knee-deep into production, the programming folks working around the clock can very easily lose track of the time schedule. Most programmers and HTML people that I've met love the challenge of solving problems and doing what others say can't be done.

The relentless pursuit of solving problems and adding cooler features (a.k.a. *gold plating* in the industry) can, however, quickly become a drain on the project's schedule. The project manager must keep a close eye to ensure that the technology team stays on track and doesn't spend more than the allotted time on any one technical issue.

Tinkering is not limited to just the technology team: Designers are also known to push pixels around for hours until they get the perfect design. To keep a project on schedule, the project manager must stay on top of the milestones and where the team lies in the process.

"We're Planning for an International Audience?"

Although many sites on the Web are in one language, a growing number of companies are localizing their sites to cater to the needs of the international marketplace. *Localizing* entails translating the website into new languages and, in many cases, implementing a global content distribution scheme designed to speed up international site load times.

If the Web is a global medium, why would you need a global content distribution service? If you've ever tried loading a website from across the world, you've probably noticed that the performance can be pretty bad. A site hosted on a faraway server may be lean in terms of file size, but its sheer distance from you makes it load slowly. If you look at it from the European perspective of accessing sites hosted in the United States, you realize that a lot of European customers are experiencing far slower service. Asian customers in China have it worse. All inbound sites are filtered through "the great firewall of China" to ensure only culturally appropriate content gets through.

Along with a content distribution network (CDN) — which, as discussed in Chapter 15, creates copies of your site's pages and content on servers all over the world to speed up local performance — you may also need to offer the site in multiple languages and have content segmented by region or country. I've found that up to 50 percent of a web company's business can come from overseas. The problem, however, is that this 50 percent is distributed across several languages.

The best practice is to use a *detection code* to direct users automatically to the appropriate country's website. Putting a handy navigation tool on the website that would allow users to switch to a different country or region that the business supports, however, is the next best thing. It's important to mark this switching tool clearly with a globe or flag icon so that if users don't read the language — or language characters — of the site they're directed to, they can visually recognize how to change sites.

Notice that if I were traveling in China, and checked the Air China website, the default language would be Chinese. As illustrated in Figures 18-1 and 18-2, without the little red flag in the main navigation, I would not know where to click to change the language to English.

Lastly, rather than offering every language for every region, you should tie your language offering to the country or region selected. As shown in Figure 18-2, there are just three languages associated with the China country site. The common practice is for companies to offer their "home" language (for example, American companies would offer English) as well as the official languages for that region or country.

A flag icon marks the language menu.

© Air China. www.airchina.com

Figure 18-1: The Air China website offers users a small country flag as a visual clue of where to change the site's region and language.

© Air China. www.airchina.com

Figure 18-2: Notice how language options are tied to specific country and region options.

"The Site Needs to Work on Mobile Platforms?"

When embarking on a new web-design (or redesign) project, ask if the client would like to consider also creating a mobile-friendly version of the site, or a purpose-built mobile edition of the site.

✔ "Mobile-friendly" simply means the site is viewable on mobile platforms (no Flash animations, for example) and utilizes code techniques that allow proper display of the content.

✔ A mobile edition of the site is a drastically scaled-down version of the site; as such, it requires a different approach to information architecture and visual design.

Clearly, going down either of these paths will add to your timeline and budget, but these days, mobile browsing is an indispensable consideration to address at the start of any new project. Many clients just assume that their new full-size website will just magically work on mobile devices. In fact, I've seen many stakeholders try to use their iPads or other mobile devices to check on the progress of sites during development — only to wonder why "it's not working."

Going live without any consideration to mobile browsing may get you in trouble with the client if it's not part of the up-front discussions. They are hiring you as the expert to ask these kinds of questions.

Another trend in web design is called "responsive design" — whereby a page automatically reconfigures its layout based on the viewing size of the browser window — whether desktop and mobile. A good example of this approach to design can be seen at www.anderssonwise.com. Try resizing your browser window, even making it very narrow, and watch how all the content modules re-arrange themselves.

"You Mean We Need to Maintain the Site Now?"

One thing to be very mindful of at the beginning of your discussions with a client is the ongoing maintenance plan of a website once it's live. Often, clients are unprepared to take the reins of their new site — and at least as often, agencies fail to design a site that's a practical match for a client's ability to handle it. Clients may not have the internal staff necessary, the technical support, or the know-how.

A part of your proposal should be training for the client's staff, hosting for the website, a technical-support contract, staff suggestions, or any other plan that makes sense for the client. I recently had to redesign a large global site because it was built on an uncommon platform that the client was unable to maintain or make simple changes to. Something as simple as adding or deleting a page of the site took a phone call to the original agency — which charged a $400 maintenance minimum.

"Oops, We Forgot to Add Analytics"

Generally speaking, the client's marketing executives will want to see how their new investment is doing in terms of visitors, sales conversions, and other types of metrics, all with an eye toward justifying their expenditure. Adding analytics to your site is a fairly simple process — and if you use

Google Analytics, it's free. You simply register for a Google Analytics account, and then copy and paste their code into each of your web pages.

You'll be able to see how many visitors come to each page of your site, the percentage of visitors that "bounce" away from your site (come to one page and exit), what cities and countries visitors come from, and how they found your site ("referrals"). If you have an e-commerce site, you can also use analytics to see how far users get through the checkout flow, where they "abandon" the process (giving you clues on where to focus renewed user interaction and visual design efforts), and what your "conversion rate" is (percentage of people with make it all the way through). All these metrics are invaluable for clients, whether the site is a main company site or a limited time promotional site.

"If We Build It, They Will Come."

What worked in the movie *Field of Dreams* won't work for a website. With so many websites on the Internet, getting people's attention and drawing them to your site is very difficult. You cannot launch a site anymore and expect people to just find it or even care about your offerings. That's why you and the client must build a solid marketing plan and start executing it even before the site is live on the Web.

The best marketing plan for a website is one that combines traditional offline marketing and public-relations techniques with online tactics. By *offline*, I mean every advertising medium that is not the Web: radio, trade shows, direct mail, billboards, print ads, and even TV commercials. Online techniques can be much less expensive and just as effective. Some ideas include

- ✔ **Social media marketing.** Having a Facebook site, developing custom Facebook applications, and running a Facebook ad campaign can be an effective way to reach a very targeted audience. Facebook's ad-monitoring tools help you control your marketing dollars and (through the ad-insights portion) show you how your campaign is performing for certain demographics and geographic regions.

- ✔ **E-mail marketing.** Sending HTML e-mails (the fancy ones that come in with nice graphics) on a regular basis to your customers is a dicey call. I personally delete all such marketing e-mails unless I know they will offer valuable content. Redfin.com, for example, sends daily e-mail alerts that are customized to my needs. I open these e-mails but delete the 20%-off-sale daily notices from everyone else. Bottom line: You should only send out marketing e-mails that truly have value for your customers.

- ✔ **Video and Flash ads.** Buying banner ad space through an ad-placement network or an advertising agency can be a successful strategy because you can tailor your creative approach as you see how it responds in the marketplace. Video-based ads are definitely the current trend, although many Flash banners are still out there. There is quite a science these days that goes into managing an ad campaign. Whenever you, as a consumer, see a banner — even if you don't click on it — it's counted as "an impression." Once you've "seen" the ad (whether you noticed it or not), you are logged on the ad network's backend, and the next ad they show you may be a slightly different version to up the ante. Advertisers are also looking at your web-browsing history, or searches you have made, to deduce something about your interests, and will try to serve up appropriate ads.

✔ **Co-promoting with other companies.** Another effective marketing tactic is to partner with other online companies whose customers can benefit from your offerings and vice versa. For example, if your site sells custom reading glasses, try partnering with a book-club site and running a promotion such as, "Sign up today for the book club and receive 10% off ACME custom reading glasses."

With this approach, you can have a much greater presence on the partner's website than with a banner ad, and your partner may even actively promote you in its online and offline marketing campaigns.

✔ **Search engine optimization.** *Search engine optimization*, or *SEO* as it's called, is an inexpensive way to help promote your site. When people use a search engine such as www.google.com to look for a website, they enter a series of keywords and phrases such as "horse, sale, dressage, warmblood" into a search field. To find websites that match these keywords and phrases, search engines look through not only the text of web pages but also the page's title and the <meta> tags contained in such HTML code as H1, H2, and meta tags. When you build a site, make sure that such keyword-rich text is integrated everywhere that makes sense so you can increase your chances of being listed high on the search results page. Be careful, however, not to overdo it on keywords. *Keyword stuffing,* as it's called, is something that search engines watch out for. If they suspect your site is guilty, they can lower your relevance ranking, making your site appear lower in the results list. Ouch!

Index

• E •

• *Y* •

• *Z* •